.31
2
11

31. J.

BOOK

D1621199

30109 0 06963204

# THE GERMAN RESISTANCE TO HITLER

# THE GERMAN RESISTANCE TO HITLER

*Resistance Thinking on Foreign Policy*
Hermann Graml

*Social Views and Constitutional Plans of
the Resistance*   Hans Mommsen

*Resistance in the Labour Movement*
Hans-Joachim Reichhardt

*Political and Moral Motives behind
the Resistance*   Ernst Wolf

*With an Introduction
by* Professor F. L. Carsten

B. T. BATSFORD LTD   LONDON

Published originally under the title *Der deutsche Widerstand gegen Hitler: vier historisch-kritische Studien von Hermann Graml, Hans Mommsen, Hans-Joachim Reichhardt und Ernst Wolf.*
Edited by Walter Schmitthenner and Hans Buchheim.
Copyright © 1966 by Kiepenheuer & Witsch, Köln-Berlin

English translation copyright © 1970 by B. T. Batsford Ltd

Translated from the German by Peter and Betty Ross
Dr J. C. G. Röhl, of the University of Sussex, helped in the preparation of this edition


Printed in Great Britain
by Bristol Typesetting Co Ltd, Bristol, for the publishers
B. T. Batsford Ltd, 4 Fitzhardinge Street, London W1

7134 1112 0

# Contents

# Introduction

Twenty-five years after Colonel Claus Count Schenk von Stauffenberg planted the bomb that failed to kill Hitler, the German
Resistance to Hitler and National Socialism is still a highly controversial subject, in Germany as well as in this country. In Germany the topic has been marred by political controversy between
the two Germanies which have emerged from the war, by the
concentration of West German historians on the rôle of the military, the July plot and the attempts on Hitler's life, and the
corresponding concentration of the historians of East Germany on
Communist activity. There, all other forms of resistance and
opposition are rated as unimportant and somewhat suspect, while
some prominent West German historians have condemned Communist work on behalf of Soviet Russia as treason.

Several very prominent British historians, too, consider the
whole German opposition to Hitler highly overrated and its
motives dubious and suspect: partly because its members and
sympathisers were so few in number, partly because all its attempts
met with so little success, partly because the efforts of West German historians to stress the importance of the July plot and the
idealism and nobility of purpose of the participants have caused
a natural reaction. After all, the leading plotters belonged to the
establishment and to highly conservative circles; their ideas were
often not only conservative but strongly nationalist, and their
activities matured at a time when it had become obvious that
Germany had lost the war. Were these 'good Germans' not trying to save something from the wreck, to preserve a powerful
Germany with its dominant position in central Europe, to replace
National Socialism by a German nationalism no less dangerous
in the long run? Naturally, such opinions were most loudly
voiced by British historians with a pronounced anti-German bias,

but up to a point they have gained credence in much wider circles. National prejudice, anti-German sentiment and political misconceptions have contributed to distort the picture.

In assessing the importance of the German Resistance we have to remember that – in contrast to the resistance in the German-occupied countries – it never reached mass proportions. The large majority of Germans, until the bitter end, remained loyal to Hitler and willing to cooperate with the state and its organs. Even those critical of one or the other aspect of Hitler's policies, e.g., his religious policy or the killing-off of the mentally sick, would loudly proclaim their loyalty to National Socialism; or they would sincerely believe that, if the *Führer* only knew, such things simply could not happen. For an opposition to have to work in an environment utterly hostile and ready to denounce any oppositionists to the mercy of the Gestapo had far-reaching consequences. It created not only constant fear, but a feeling of isolation, of swimming against the current, of helplessness and futility, almost of hopelessness. While members of the French or Norwegian resistance always knew that they could find shelter and succour almost anywhere among their compatriots, the exact opposite applied to the German Opposition. Its members were increasingly thrown back upon their own resources, confined to minute circles of conspirators, reduced to draft ever-longer memoranda on the future of Germany, to compile ever-new lists of future ministers and civil servants. The introspective and speculative character of so many of its political activities can largely be explained by the environment within which the German Opposition was forced to work. One might add that these traits also corresponded to certain German characteristics which were far older than Hitler.

Recently a more sober spirit of reassessment has begun to influence West German historians, replacing the earlier enthusiasm about the resistance. It is the merit of the four essays collected in this volume that they shed new light on the subject, and above all that they make no attempt to conceal or to whitewash. The essays are rightly critical, if not of the German Opposition as a whole, then of certain of its characteristics and plans. The first two essays discuss the ideas and projects of the small conservative circles whose activities culminated in the bomb plot of 20 July

1944. The third is devoted to the much-neglected subject of Socialist and Communist resistance; and the fourth deals with the opposition of the Churches, especially of the ' Confessing Church' which came to oppose National Socialist religious policy.

Dr Graml, the author of the essay on the conceptions of the German Opposition in the field of foreign policy, demonstrates that its conservative leaders – men such as Carl Goerdeler, General Beck and Ulrich von Hassell – never changed their basic ideas. What they aimed at preserving was not only the German frontiers of 1919, but a Germany enlarged by Alsace and Lorraine, by the ' Polish Corridor ', and by the German-speaking parts of the old Habsburg monarchy: frontiers that would have guaranteed such a Germany a dominating position in central Europe and far beyond, in the Balkans and in Scandinavia. The ideas of this leading group were those of the pre-1914 world. Its members considered Europe the heart and core of the world, the white race predestined to dominate the other continents and Germany entitled to regain her colonies. Basically, they wanted to restore Bismarck's *Reich* in which they had grown up, but it was the *Reich* with the additions made by the Austrian lance-corporal. It should be added, however, that the ideas of other German opposition groups were very different from these Great German dreams, which took no account of the changed reality, of the rise of the United States and Soviet Russia, and of the movements for independence in Asia and Africa.

In a similar way Professor Mommsen emphasises how strongly conservative were the constitutional and political ideas and plans of these opposition leaders. They belonged to the upper stratum of society, had been hostile to, or at least critical of, the Weimar Republic, and were completely isolated from the lower-middle and the working classes (the former being the social group most loyal to National Socialism). The conservatives in the Resistance were opposed to the egalitarian and democratic tendencies of modern society; their ideas were often anti-rational and anti-modern; they disliked the modern mass parties, which allegedly threatened the unity of state and society; they believed National Socialism to be another form of Bolshevism; and they desired the reestablishment of a paternal, strong central authority. In economic and social matters their thinking was equally traditional, and they approved of certain institutions established by Hitler's dictatorship. Significantly, the German writer and statesman who exercised the greatest influence on their thinking was the Freiherr vom Stein, the great reformer of Prussia at the beginning of the nineteenth century, who had dreamt of a return to medieval glory and medieval Estates, and whose ideas had been a mixture of the enlightenment and romanticism. But Stein had been active in the early nineteenth, not in the middle of the twentieth century. On these issues, the members of the Kreisau Circle (named after the estate of Count Helmuth James von Moltke) thought in a fashion very similar to that of the older conservative leaders. In many ways they still adhered to the ideology of the right-wing opposition to the Weimar Republic, of the university professors and writers who in the 1920s proclaimed the cause of the ' conservative revolution '. They failed to see that the world had changed, that the old Prussia of the ' Iron Chancellor ' could not be revived. Their social and constitutional plans were hopelessly out-of-date. They could never have become the blueprint for a post-Hitler Germany, or for a modern industrial society.

If it is important to say these things clearly and unequivocally, it is even more important to do justice to the resistance of German Socialists and Communists about which much less has been written by Western historians. As Dr Reichhardt points out, this is partly due to the lack of documentary evidence : most of the persecuted understandably refrained from committing their ideas to paper – in contrast with the conservatives, who were extremely prolific in this respect, to their own detriment. What evidence there is on the German Left often comes from the files of the Gestapo and the ' People's Court ' and thus has to be used with great caution. Hence the author only discusses Opposition activities in Berlin, for which he has collected a good deal of new material. Indeed in Berlin, as this writer can confirm from his own experience, there was intense oppositional working-class activity in the years after 1933. By sheer necessity, but also on account of a deep distrust of the established party leaders, what remained of the working-class movement broke up into numerous local groups and organisations. Only those Communists loyal to the party line tried to maintain a centralised organisation. Most other groups were strongly left-wing but suspicious of the Communists because of their political orthodoxy and their refusal to adapt their tactics to the conditions of the totalitarian dictatorship.

After more than 30 years it is virtually impossible to give even an approximately correct picture of the welter of left-wing groups of the years 1933-36. As soon as they expanded beyond a certain limit or tried to start activities on any larger scale they became the victims of the Gestapo. But during the early years of the Third Reich soon new groups arose to take their place. After about 1936 it was more generally realised that only very small groups had a chance of survival and that the range of their activities had to remain extremely limited if they did not want to share the fate of their predecessors. Only the Communists continued to sacrifice themselves by methods of 'mass' propaganda and by following precepts of underground work emanating from headquarters in Moscow, but utterly unsuited to the conditions of the Third Reich. There is no doubt that, partly for this reason, the number of Communist victims of the Gestapo and ss terror is much larger than that of any other group or party, probably larger than that of all other groups taken together.

Yet the honours of the day must go to small groups such as the *Roter Stosstrupp*,[1] *Neu Beginnen*,[2] the *Sozialistische Arbeiterpartei*,[3] and the *Internationaler Sozialistischer Kampfbund*,[4] which attempted to learn from past failures, to adapt their policy to changed conditions, and to think of the future along less doctrinal lines. At first they enjoyed the advantage that the Gestapo knew virtually nothing about them, but later they too suffered heavy

1 This group was formed largely by former members of the *Reichsbanner Schwarz-Rot-Gold*. The change of name from Black-Red-Gold to Red indicates the strong shift to the Left among its members

2 *Neu Beginnen* took its name from a pamphlet published in 1933. The group consisted of critical former Social Democrats and Communists and was formed some years before Hitler

losses. They were active at a time when there was no sign of any opposition on the side of conservatives and liberals, when even oppositional members of the middle classes were quite unwilling to render any help. Among the socialist workers of Berlin, on the other hand – and not only of Berlin – strong anti-Nazi feelings remained alive for a long time. Their unswerving loyalty to the cause of Socialism or Communism is indeed one of ' the few positive features in German history during the years 1933 to 1945 '. Even during the war this activity continued on a minor scale, and many hundreds more had to pay with their lives for their convictions.

The resistance of the Churches to National Socialism is a much more controversial subject. On the Catholic side, the conclusion of the Concordat with the Holy See in the spring of 1933 proved an effective barrier to any opposition. Within the Protestant Church, there was a strong tradition of obedience to established authority, of clerical nationalism, of opposition to the Weimar Republic, and of anti-Semitism. These factors led the Protestant Church to its fatal, and in many cases enthusiastic, welcome of the ' national revolution '. The ' Confessing Church ' came into being as an opposition movement to the so-called ' German Christians ', but it never objected to National Socialism as such. Even Pastor Niemöller called himself a convinced National Socialist. Hitler's anti-Semitic measures were opposed only in so far as

---

came to power. Its manifesto was published in English translation with a preface by no less a person that H. N. Brailsford : Miles, *Socialism's New Start*, London, 1934

3 The SAP was a left-wing splinter party founded in the early 1930s by radical Social Democrats who then combined with a right-wing split-off from the Communists. It was active in many parts of Germany, especially in Saxony and Silesia

4 The ISK was founded by the neo-Kantian philosopher Leonhard Nelson, who rejected Marxism and adhered to an idealist socialist philosophy. At first working within the Social Democratic Party as a radical ginger group, the ISK in the later 1920s formed its own independent organisation

they were directed against Christians of Jewish or partly Jewish origin, aimed at separating them from their Church. In the end the ' Confessing Church ' became a kind of resistance movement ' against its own will ', as Dr Wolf puts it. Indeed, the conciliatory and equivocal attitude adopted by the Churches – not of course by all individual churchmen – is one of the darkest chapters of the history of the Third Reich. The Churches had their martyrs, priests who refused to compromise and who helped the victims of the régime, but they were only too few.

The untarnished picture presented in these essays will, it is hoped, help to redress the balance, to provide the English-speaking world with a clearer picture of human aspirations and human plans, conceived under conditions which are almost impossible to describe to those who have never known a régime of naked terror upheld by mass enthusiasm. In spite of all reservations, these ideas bear witness to great idealism, to a readiness to suffer, if need be to die, for convictions honestly held, and to ordinary decency in the face of evil. As a leaflet of the Munich students, who belonged to the group of the ' White Rose ', proclaimed in the midst of the war : ' Is it not a fact that today every decent German is ashamed of his government?' Although the German Resistance did not succeed in its endeavours and the various attempts on the life of Hitler all ended in failure, it has left an important legacy which has continued to influence German life and politics. It has played an important part in the political education of the younger generation. It has enabled the Germany of the 1950s and 1960s to take its place among the nations of Europe, on the basis of moral principles which only a small minority of the Germans upheld during the years of tyranny. Shortly before his execution in 1944 the Social Democratic leader Julius Leber sent a message to his friends : ' To pay with one's life in the service of so good and just a cause is an appropriate price. We have done what has been in our power to do.'

F. L. Carsten

# Chronology

**1933**

*30 January:* Adolf Hitler becomes Chancellor of a so-called
' national government ' consisting of National Socialists and
German Nationalists. Step by step, the totalitarian National
Socialist system is established

*23 March:* Speech by the Social Democratic party leader O. Wels
in the *Reichstag* against the Enabling Law

*September:* M. Niemöller founds the Emergency League of Pastors (nucleus of the ' Confessing Church ') in Berlin-Dahlem.
By Christmas, some 6,000 pastors (one-third of all Protestant
clergymen) have joined

**1934**

*7 February:* Rosenberg's *Der Mythus des 20. Jahrhunderts* is
placed on the Index by the Catholic Church

*22 April:* First general meeting of the ' Confessing Church ' in
Ulm

*7 June:* First joint pastoral epistle of the German Episcopate,
' Exposition and Defence of the True Faith against the
Errors of the Time '

*17 June:* Papen's speech in Marburg (drafted by Edgar Jung)

*19/20 April:* The Protestant Church appeals to the ' emergency
rights of the church ' (second confessing synod)
 ' Underground' activity (in units of industry and elsewhere) starts in Socialist and trade-union circles

**1935**

*4/5 March:* Rejection of the National Socialist ideology at the
' confessing ' synod of the Protestant Church of the Old
Prussian Union (' We see our people threatened by a mortal
danger. The danger consists of a new religion ')

Further Nazi measures against Catholic schools

*August:* Memorandum by the German Catholic bishops to Hitler, on the state of religion and the churches

## 1936

*May:* Memorandum (intended for Hitler) of the radical wing of the militant Protestant Church against the ' de-Christianising' of German life, and against the ' abolition of the constitutional state'

*10 September:* Joint pastoral epistle of the German Episcopate on the protection of denominational schools

## 1937

*4 March:* Circular of Pope Pius XI ' with burning concern' over the ' new national heathenism'

Climax of the battle of the churches : about 800 members of the ' Confessing Church' and numerous Catholic clergymen are arrested and sent to concentration camps

## 1938

*5 May:* First memorandum by the chief of the general staff of the army, General L. Beck, against Hitler's policy of aggression

*3 June:* Beck's second memorandum

*16 July:* Beck's third and major memorandum (warning of catastrophe)

*29 July:* Beck's report to the Commander-in-Chief of the Army, General von Brauchitsch (first move in the planning for a *coup d'état*)

*19 August:* Churchill's talk with Ewald von Kleist

*19 August:* Joint pastoral epistle of the German Episcopate on the fight against church and Christianity in Germany

*31 August:* Beck's dismissal (made public only at the end of October)

*7 September:* E. Kordt submits to the British Foreign Minister, Lord Halifax, a declaration of Undersecretary von Weizsäcker (request for the British Government to take an unequivocal stand against Hitler's policy of war)

*28 September:* Hitler's arrest planned for the first time (Halder-Witzleben-Oster action); impracticable because of the Munich Agreement

*12 December:* Formal stand on 'The Great Lie of Political Catholicism' submitted by Dr Konrad Graf von Preysing, Bishop of Berlin, to the members of the Reich government and the German bishops

## 1939

*Summer:* The following report abroad on Hitler's policy of war: Goerdeler in England and France; Pechel in England; Trott zu Solz and the Kordt brothers in the United States and England; Schlabrendorff in England

*3 September:* General von Hammerstein (Commander-in-Chief of an army group in the west) plans to arrest Hitler during a visit to the front. (Hitler's visit is called off)

*October:* First attempt by J. Müller to establish contact with the British Government via the Vatican

*11, 31 October:* Memoranda of General W. Ritter von Leeb (Commander-in-Chief, Army Group c) against Hitler's planned western offensive

*November (beginning):* First plan for assassination of Hitler (Halder-Oster-Kordt) not carried out, because of the Bürgerbräu plot (Elser) on 8 November and the hesitation of the generals

*27 November:* Closer contact established between Leuschner (SPD) and Kaiser (Christian trade unions), and Beck and Goerdeler

*November-February 1940:* Trott zu Solz sounds out opinion in the United States

## 1940

*January-February:* First constitutional programme worked out in the event of Hitler's overthrow (Goerdeler-Hassell); the primary demand, to restore 'the dignity of the law'

*22 February:* Consultation of Hassell with J. Lonsdale Bryans in Arosa

*14/15 April:* Second consultation

B

1941

30 *May:* Goerdeler's peace plan, intended for the British Government

20 *June:* Joint pastoral epistle of the German Episcopate on the oppression of the church in Germany

16 *July:* Cardinal Bertram's memorandum to the Reich Ministry of Justice on the killing of insane persons

28 *July:* Bishop Clemens Graf von Galen files a complaint of murder with the police president of Münster, concerning the killing of so-called ' unproductive citizens ' in medical establishments

4 *August:* Plan to assassinate Hitler during a briefing session in the headquarters of the Middle Army Group (von Bock); abandoned because security measures are too strong

*November (end):* Renewed attempt by the Beck-Goerdeler resistance group to establish contact with the American Government (via P. L. Lochner)

*December (end):* Field Marshal von Witzleben is prepared to stage a revolt on the Western front, with Beck and Goerdeler (abandoned in March 1942 when Witzleben undergoes an operation)

1942

*April:* Goerdeler meets the banker Wallenberg in Stockholm to sound out Allied readiness to negotiate peace. (In November, the two meet in Berlin. Contact continues until 1944)

*Whitsun:* Sessions of the Kreisau Circle on the Silesian estate of Graf von Moltke (near Schweidnitz). (Similarly in October 1942, and at Whitsun 1943)

*July:* Goerdeler, in Smolensk, tries to win Field Marshal von Kluge over to the Opposition

26-31 *May:* Schoenfelder and Bonhoeffer make contact with the Bishop of Chichester in Sweden

1943

*February:* Student's rebellion in Munich (Hans Scholl and his sister Sophie, *Restoration of Honour*)

22 *February:* Execution of Hans and Sophie Scholl

*13 March:* Time bomb in Hitler's plane (Schlabrendorff-Tresckow) fails to explode

*21 March:* The plot in the arsenal cannot be carried out (Gersdorff)

*26 March:* Secret memorandum of Goerdeler to the generals urging a *coup d'état*

*5 April:* Dohnanyi and Bonhoeffer arrested

*17 May:* Letter from Goerdeler to General Olbricht on creating the right conditions for the *coup d'état*

*July (beginning):* Lt-Col Graf von Stauffenberg initiated into the conspiracy

*25 July:* Letter from Goerdeler to Field Marshal von Kluge

*9 August:* Final draft by Kreisau Circle of a reform proposal (instruction of officials and principles for the reorganisation, with demand for ' punishment for violators of justice ')

*26 August:* Discussion, Popitz with Himmler

*September:* Discussion, Beck with Goerdeler and von Kluge in General Olbricht's home (birth of 20 July plot)

*October (beginning):* Graf Stauffenberg appointed Chief of Staff of the General Army Office

*November (end):* Building on Tresckow's preparatory work, Stauffenberg has completed technical preparations for the assassination

1944

*January:* Members of the Solf Circle are arrested. The Kreisau Circle is broken up by Moltke's arrest

The German Intelligence organisation comes under Kaltenbrunner's control

*11 February:* Bomb plot against Hitler prepared. (Not carried out because Himmler absent from the session)

*9 March:* Plan to shoot Hitler during a briefing session

*15 May:* Field Marshal Rommel and General von Stülpnagel (Paris) plan Hitler's arrest and trial by a German court

*4/5 June:* Arrest of the Social Democrats Leber and Reichwein

*1 July:* von Stauffenberg, colonel in the general staff, appointed chief of staff of the commander of the replacement army; on

*11 July:* he tries for the first time (Obersalzberg) and on

*15 July:* for the second time (*Wolfsschanze*) to carry out a plot against Hitler

*17 July:* Field Marshal Rommel seriously wounded in an attack by low-flying planes

*20 July:* Stauffenberg's bomb demolishes Hitler's briefing barracks at Rastenburg, East Prussia, but Hitler escapes unhurt. Believing Hitler to be dead, Stauffenberg orders ' Operation Valkyrie' to begin. That night, General Beck commits suicide. Stauffenberg and the other anti-Hitler officers in the Bendlerstrasse executed by firing squad

*21 July:* General Henning von Tresckow commits suicide at the front

*8 August:* Peter Graf Yorck von Wartenburg executed

*26 August:* Adam von Trott zu Solz executed

*8 September:* Ulrich von Hassell executed in Plötzensee prison, Berlin

*29 September:* Wilhelm Leuschner, trade unionist and Social Democrat, executed

*30 November:* Professor Jens Jessen executed in Plötzensee

1945

*5 January:* Social Democrat Dr Julius Leber executed in Plötzensee

*23 January:* Helmuth Graf von Moltke and the Social Democrat Dr Theodor Haubach executed

*2 February:* Dr Carl Goerdeler, Professor Johannes Popitz and Father Alfred Delp, s J, executed

*9 April:* Admiral Wilhelm Canaris, General Hans Oster and Pastor Dietrich Bonhoeffer murdered in Flossenbürg concentration camp

# Resistance Thinking on Foreign Policy

HERMANN GRAML

Early in 1939 Carl Goerdeler wrote a memorandum, *Die nächsten praktischen Schritte* ('Next Practical Steps'), the essence of which he summed up as follows : 'To free the world from its present cataleptic condition stronger forces must, by their momentum, break the spell of Hitlerian ideas.'[1] By 'stronger forces', he did not mean a concept of social and domestic policy superior to National Socialism, but 'an international order of peace' equally acceptable to Germany and Europe; an order so rational and convincing that if Hitler, predictably, refused to conform to it, he would be branded a 'national bandit' and effectually swept away by the wrath of the German people. A few years later, in the middle of the war, Graf Moltke expressed his belief that 'the end of the war poses an opportunity for the favourable reconstruction of the world such as has not presented itself to mankind since the decline of the medieval church.'[2] He also assured an English acquaintance that he and his friends were prepared to help the victors 'win the peace' as well.[3] Common to all three statements is the notion that opposition to Hitler and the National Socialist régime should not aim solely at liquidating the Third Reich; it should also combine the duty of reorganising German internal affairs with an attempt to reform and revolutionise international relations. For the state of international relations had both facilitated Hitler's rise to power and failed to prevent a new form of imperialist policy from precipitating Europe and the world into a catastrophe of unprecedented dimensions.

On the other hand, Goerdeler himself advocated a foreign policy which, although less expansionist than Hitler's, hardly seemed compatible with the proposed reconciliation between Germany and Europe. At the end of 1944, when under Gestapo arrest, he still insisted that Germany must retain her 1914 eastern frontier as well as Austria and the Sudeten areas, gain the South Tyrol and have her share of European colonial possessions overseas.[4] At the beginning of 1940, after the German Army's triumph in Poland, other undoubted opponents of Hitler in Germany treated the 'Greater German solution' as irrefragable and even spoke of German leadership in Europe.[5] Later, when the course of the war had put an end to all dreams of German hegemony, Ulrich von Hassell noted that the overthrow of Hitler was becoming daily more urgent: but the reason for this was ' so that at least a rudiment of the Bismarckian Empire might be saved '.[6]

Students of the German Resistance, and in particular of those groups connected with the 20 July plot (unfortunately we cannot here discuss the significance of the foreign policy views of organisations such as the *Rote Kapelle* or the *Nationalkomitee Freies Deutschland*) have found it difficult to reconcile the Opposition's apparently universal, or at least supranational, outlook on the one hand, and their advocacy of a policy of strength and national interests on the other; generally the contradiction remains unresolved. In his commentary on some of Goerdeler's and Beck's memoranda, Wilhelm von Schramm writes: ' The main object of the German revival, as seen by Beck, Goerdeler and their political friends, was the federation of the countries of Europe. This had remained their aim since the years when they had gone on their political travels – Beck to France to wait on Pétain and Gamelin, and Goerdeler mainly to England and America in order to set up lasting contacts there.'[7] By contrast, George K. Romoser roundly contests the political viability and the seriousness of the Opposition's proposed foreign policy:

. . . the political hopes of the conspirators in regard to foreign policy were to a considerable extent unreal fantasies. This term can be applied, above all, to their territorial aims. Many of the conspirators were preoccupied with questions of national interest. One need only read the memoranda of Carl Goerdeler, Ulrich von Hassell, or even of Adam von Trott zu Solz to discover the existence of vague, unrealistic foreign policy views . . . in their thought there was often an identification made between certain German national interests, and defence of the Western world and the Western tradition.[8]

Romoser's second accusation is justified, yet it means little. The claim that national and general interests in some measure coincide is common to most foreign policies; and an antithesis between German and Western interests cannot simply be assumed. As for Schramm, we shall presently show that his premise is false. Assessments like these, in fact, each erring in one direction or the other, are typical of the black-and-white approach of many historians. On the one hand there are those who appear simply to regard any expression of national thinking as final and, in the manner of Bismarck, any manifestation of European thinking as a mere disguise, then proceeding to class the exposed hypocrites with Hitler. Thus Romoser crassly misinterprets Hans Rothfels, accusing him of having suggested that the Opposition fought ' as European shock troops ', while failing to mention that the Nazis claimed to be doing the same.[9] This necessarily overlooks the fact that the ideas of the German Resistance evolved; from its internal tensions and disagreements there eventually emerged a movement towards a changed Europe. On the other hand there are commentators who, in their efforts to dissociate the Resistance groups completely from Hitler, wholly deny the Opposition's affinity with the traditional trends in foreign policy then predominant in Germany. The claims of the Opposition, both in territorial matters and in the field of power politics, are dismissed in a brief reference to natural patriotism, and the Opposition itself is firmly classified with the world of the EEC and NATO. This is to ignore the environment of the Resistance, a Germany which still failed to accept the inevitability of defeat and to adapt its foreign policies accordingly. Instead of treating the Opposition as a monolithic and static entity, and its views on foreign policy as proof of either rabid nationalism or devotion to the European ideal, we shall here try to see them as they really were. We shall attempt to find out what conceptions the German Opposition evolved in the twofold struggle, on the one hand with Hitler, and on the other with a revolution in European thinking that was brought about not only by internal events but, to an almost greater degree, by the rise of the two world powers and the beginning of decolonisation. We shall also try to relate these conceptions, not merely to Hitler, but to the realities in Europe at that time.

## *The Conservatives*

The nucleus of the group of National Conservative ' notables '[10] which, between 1938 and 1942, was to determine the typical form of the Opposition's potentially activist section, consisted in Colonel-General Beck, Carl Goerdeler, Ulrich von Hassell, Johannes Popitz, and the *Abwehr* circle round Major-General Oster. At the outset, however, this group's views on foreign policy were still completely dominated by the outlook of a Europe which had once regarded herself as the centre of the universe. The concepts of inter-European power politics and the claim to have power of disposal over the Afro-Asian world were the natural inheritance of the members of this group. In so far as they had developed a feeling of pan-European solidarity, it was based upon a sense of the supremacy of the ' white race ' that was shared by all the other nations of Europe. Not only was this expression constantly on Goerdeler's lips, but he used it to demonstrate the necessity for European pacts in the same way that the monarchical principle was used in the nineteenth century to help cement foreign alliances.[11] They all belonged to a generation and a class which had experienced and favoured Germany's entry into world politics. Hassell, for instance, son-in-law of the creator of the German Navy, Grand Admiral of the Fleet von Tirpitz, spoke quite naturally of ' the dynamic development ' of Germany's ' economic position and world standing, which she effected as an equal, and moreover independently of, other world powers '; and Hassell's father before him, from being a simple Hanoverian second lieutenant, had finally become a Prusso-German officer of the General Staff, and a zealous advocate of Wilhelmian Germany's imperialist, colonial and international policies.[12]

During the First World War these men probably remained untouched by pan-German fantasies and crude dreams of hegemony; the idea of widespread German expansion and conquest within the continent – either eastwards or westwards – was quite foreign to them both then and later, and so too were the *völkisch* or racialist plans for national ' evacuations ' and resettlements. Yet the conception of a Central Europe that would be politically and economically independent, as propounded during the first three decades of the twentieth century by Friedrich Naumann, Franz von Liszt, Wilhelm Schüssler, Hermann Oncken and Heinrich von Srbik, carried considerable weight. In other words, Europe as a whole did not initially hold the leading place in the foreign-policy ideas of this group. On the contrary, their thoughts centred upon Bismarck's German Reich, which would be complemented by additions along Greater German lines from the inheritance of the dying Habsburg Empire[13] and become the heart of a stable Central European structure; at the same time colonial policy would provide a basis and manifestation of Germany's world standing. In essence their outlook combined the idea of a nation state with a 'reasonable' imperialism by which Germany's smaller neighbours would in some measure stand to gain.

Now these men had, in fact, seen Germany's entry into world politics culminate in ignominious political and military defeat and, unlike Hitler, they had realised that the bid for world power must not be repeated, at least not in the same guise as between 1914 and 1918. In 1939 Hassell wrote that Germany would have to renounce ideas of a position as a 'world and sea-power of the first order'; and in a letter to his father-in-law, Tirpitz, he expressed especial admiration for the 'breadth and elasticity of mind' which had permitted the admiral after the war to draw the logical conclusions from defeat and 'for the time being to close the book of German world politics'.[14] Yet the crucial events of 1918 did not bring about any fundamental change in their ideas. For were not the absurd excesses of German political ambitions responsible for the defeat? And as these men had not been party to those excesses, the result of the war seemed to them in no way to compromise the basic rightness and practicability of their more moderate conception of foreign policy. By applying a cautious and patient policy, it would still be possible to achieve the 'Greater German solution' and to create in Central Europe the requisite preconditions for the Greater German Reich. On no occasion did the Hassell, Beck and Goerdeler group cease to feel that Germany's real place, by reason of her economic, political and military strength and potential was among the major powers and that she must, at least on the Continent, win back her old

position. Thus Hassell remarked that Germany's task first and fore-
most, was ' the reconstruction of her position as the heartland
[*Herzland*] of the European continent ';[15] over and beyond that he
left no room for doubt that, wholly in the spirit of Schüssler and
Srbik,[16] he regarded Germany's Baltic and Balkan neighbours as
obvious complements to her Central European sphere of influence.
He insisted, however, that German influence should be exerted
only with the greatest subtlety.[17] Beck expressed Central European
expansionist ideas – which here again should not be mistaken for
crude claims to supremacy – and these not only in his memoranda
written for Hitler; in discussions with General Gamelin in 1937
he actually intimated the same thing.[18]

It is, however, characteristic of this aspect of the Opposition's
expansionist theories that no restriction on Germany's sovereignty
as the central power was ever envisaged, but rather, an extension
of German sovereignty among her immediate neighbours and,
further afield, the construction of less obvious forms of hegemonic
leadership. That the First World War did not bring about any
change in their basic national attitude is clearly apparent from
their reaction to Versailles. They rejected the Paris treaties, not
on the grounds that these expressed an outdated nationalism
which could have no further place in a Europe where war had
wrought such fundamental changes, but because Versailles
wounded their patriotism and curtailed Germany's national and
political opportunities. It is significant that even during the
Second World War Goerdeler, recalling the days of the Weimar
Republic and still thinking in terms of the old European power
parallelogram, characterised Locarno not so much as the beginning of Franco-German understanding, but as a shift of power
useful to Germany and the first step towards her return to the
concert of powers.[19] Between the two World Wars, in short, this
group's thinking in regard to foreign policy was concerned solely
with healing the wounds inflicted upon the German national consciousness and with restoring, strengthening and expanding Germany's position in Central Europe. Hence their proposed foreign
policy may be summed up simply as the revision of Versailles,
extended to include the German claim to portions of the defunct
Habsburg Empire. Goerdeler drew up a list of ' vital German

questions' (*deutsche Lebensfragen*) which formulated the concrete demands of this programme, and which no doubt represented the national sentiments of a clear majority of the German
people, as well as to some extent the national interests of his
country. These were : union with Austria and the Sudeten areas;
the elimination of the ' Polish Corridor '; and, as a tangible proof
of Germany's equality with the rest of the world, the acquisition
of colonies.[20] Hence in England, Belgium, France and America, in
1937 and 1938, Goerdeler put forward, not European ideas, but
his inventory of ' vital German questions ' – the aims, that is,
of a non-National Socialist government.[21] He presented himself
to the world frankly and openly as a prime example of a figure
common in German, and indeed European, diplomatic circles at
the time – the revisionist politician. Hence Trevor-Roper is not
wholly wrong in saying :

> These men . . . also had war aims, or perhaps one should say,
> political aims which might only be attainable through war,
> although they hoped to find peaceful means . . . They wanted
> to regain lost Reich territory. Yet their territorial claims were
> limited . . . For this reason 1940/41 saw a parting of the ways
> in Germany also.[22]

Two of these statements, however, would seem to be somewhat
inexact. First, it should be said that a policy of attaining aims
by force of arms had been renounced by men like Goerdeler and
Hassell, for in no circumstances did they desire war. As early as
1938 Beck had reached the conclusion that war in Europe had
become an anachronism and virtually impossible on military
grounds;[23] in the course of the following year his rejection of
war became so intense that it seemed deceptively like sceptical
pacifism.[24] The circle round Goerdeler and Hassell was unanimous with Beck in condemning war as an instrument of revisionist
policy – although later Goerdeler was sometimes to express a
different view.[25] They feared, moreover, that war would give rise
to or accelerate undesirable economic or social processes.[26] Above
all, they were never for a moment in doubt that a war instigated
by Germany would end in defeat. Beck had demonstrated in
1938 that since no one was threatening Germany, she need no

longer fear attack by her neighbours; yet were she herself to attack, she would undoubtedly be confronted by a coalition too powerful for her to withstand.[27] Furthermore, both Goerdeler and Hassell were convinced that a lost war would not only entail a peace far harsher than that of Versailles, but would also mean a socialist revolution of the kind that had narrowly been prevented at the end of the First World War – this aspect of their thinking was determined by the events of 1918.

For these reasons, Trevor-Roper is also wrong in suggesting that the parting of the ways between the National Conservatives and Hitler came after Hitler had completed the revisionist phase of his foreign policy. In fact it came as early as 1938 during the Sudeten crisis with Hitler's decision to back up his revisionist policy by force of arms, and hence must be seen as due to that revisionist policy itself. The motives are obscured by a number of factors : firstly, opposition to Hitler on ethical grounds and in regard to internal affairs was now strong and, with the imminent threat of war, only needed some impulse to actuate it; secondly, there was the fear of the economic, social and political consequences of a war. If these factors are disregarded, and the situation is considered only in relation to foreign affairs, it immediately becomes evident that this is the key to a further crucial motive, if not indeed *the* crucial motive for the planning of the *coup d'état* in 1938. At that time Hassell and Goerdeler often spoke of Hitler's ' criminal war policy '; by this they meant not only the iniquity of war, but the fact that Hitler, as compared with 1914, was playing for much lower winnings with a much higher stake, and was in danger not only of losing his stake but eventually of gambling away what he had won. It is not just a quirk of Opposition history that Goerdeler's first criticism of Hitler's foreign policy, towards the end of 1934, was directed against the Non-Aggression Pact with Poland which Goerdeler, who always laid his cards on the table, assumed to be almost tantamount to a renunciation of Germany's 1914 eastern frontier.[28] Indeed the fact that Goerdeler advocated a revisionist foreign policy in opposition to Hitler typifies a basic position of the Resistance : in changing circumstances and in the face of changing perils, men like Beck, Hassell and Goerdeler felt themselves to be the guardians of the ' true national interests ' of Germany, which were being sacrificed by an unscrupulous gambler and his megalomania.

When Hassell wrote in his diary that ' the point has now been reached beyond which Talleyrand left Napoleon '[29] his comparison was wholly appropriate: so far as foreign policy was concerned, the decision was for him, as it had been for Talleyrand, simply between a man and the state. During his travels abroad Goerdeler had discovered an increasing inclination, notably in Britain, to scrap the Versailles system and to satisfy German claims – there might even be a chance for Germany to regain her former colonies. In Belgium he had discussed the possibility of German participation in developing the Congo.[30] He had gained the impression that there were no longer any insuperable obstacles to the revision of Versailles, although this would require patient negotiation. Hence he was utterly appalled to realise during the course of 1938 that Hitler, who was also aware of the British attitude but had drawn different conclusions from that knowledge, was determined to attack Czechoslovakia and to conquer by force of arms the Sudeten areas, if not the whole of the republic. Whether at this time Goerdeler took seriously the information imparted to him by the Führer's aide, Wiedemann, concerning much more comprehensive plans for aggression, is doubtful and of no particular relevance in this context. Since the use of force, in Goerdeler's opinion, would mean war with England and France – a war which Germany could not win – it was obvious that Hitler's policy would definitively preclude union with the Sudeten areas, the elimination of the Polish Corridor and the solution of the colonial question. Indeed, as Goerdeler with remarkable frankness told an English friend who had come to see him at the instance of Sir Robert Vansittart, a short war would be enough to turn world opinion against Germany, so that even a ' liberal and reasonable ' government would no longer be able to solve ' Germany's vital questions '.[31] Therefore, he went on, war must be prevented under all circumstances and at all costs, and to this end he developed a plan for a *putsch* which postulated British support. In other words, the *coup d'état* planned to take place during the Sudeten crisis would have been not least an attempt to salvage German revisionist policy.

Goerdeler's criticism of Britain's appeasement policy was not directed at its underlying concept, but at the fact that London was negotiating with the wrong partner; and the alternative he transmitted to the British government was not a different policy, but a different partner – one who, unlike Hitler, would be trustworthy and would employ acceptable methods. In his discussions with British emissaries he implored London to take a firm stand against Hitler, criticised Lord Runciman's mission to Czechoslovakia, and requested British diplomatic support for a generals' *putsch* in Germany;[32] at the same time he informed them that, so as to have a pretext for intervention in Czechoslovakia, Hitler was planning to have Konrad Henlein or Lord Runciman assassinated. Hence the solution to the Sudeten question advocated by Goerdeler in these discussions was a plebiscite – in other words an *Anschluss* – following which, in cooperation with a liberal German government, it would be possible to solve the problems of the Corridor and the colonies. Thus, he was actually putting forward demands which Hitler had either not yet made or had ceased to make.[33] Goerdeler's programme did not, of course, consist exclusively in territorial claims. He further proposed a close alliance between Great Britain, France and Germany – after the latter's wishes had been satisfied – and in addition Germany's return into a reformed League of Nations.

On 4 December 1938, after the Sudeten crisis, he again summed up the aims and objects of a ' reasonable ' Germany in a memorandum for Ashton-Gwatkin at the Foreign Office, reiterating his demand for the return of the colonies and the elimination of the Corridor. Once Germany, who was not, he alleged, seeking hegemony in Eastern Europe, had been satisfied in these respects, she would make no more demands, would stop sending aid to Franco and would, in addition, support the Western powers against Italy in the Mediterranean and against Japan in the Far East. At the same time, he wrote, England, France and Germany must together create a new League of Nations on a totally new basis since the existing organisation had become discredited.[34]

In March 1939, after the occupation of Prague, Goerdeler put forward the same programme in a further memorandum with an addendum to the effect that a neutralised Czechoslovakia should be restored under international supervision within the frontiers agreed at Munich. The memorandum further contains a sentence : ' The independence of European states is guaranteed, in so far as they do not see fit to enter into mutual alliances which restrict their sovereignty.' Free trade is proposed, though with the qualifying remark that mutual trade agreements between individual states and groups of states could not, of course, be excluded. The memorandum concludes by stating that ' within the framework of a reasonable balance of power ' Germany must be allowed to give to events along her eastern borders that special attention which past experience had shown to be justified.[35]

Gerhard Ritter's statement, in his commentary on these ideas, that Goerdeler ' envisaged the Reich of the future . . . as a genuinely peaceful power, forming part of a stable European community of nations with a character wholly that of a partnership ',[36] is one that requires modification. What Goerdeler imagined was no doubt a pacified Europe, resulting from the satisfaction of German claims, but it was not a united Europe. The idea of a federation of European states as a ' distant objective ' is, indeed, mentioned once in Goerdeler's record of his travels at this time, but what he in fact proposed to his English counterparts was a reversion by a government liberated from Hitler to the policy of Locarno, provided that the still unsatisfied German demands in the east had been complied with, and that the Western powers were prepared to share their influence in the League of Nations with Germany. This policy was a logical continuation of that pursued by Stresemann. But Goerdeler, as a direct consequence of Hitler's *coup* and of Germany's growth of power, was gradually beginning to think in terms of horizons which had lain far beyond Stresemann's field of vision. His allusion to the tolerable limitations of the sovereignty of European states cannot, in view of the situation at that time, possibly be interpreted as an attempt to keep the door open for any larger pan-European federations. A remark of this nature, coming from a German at the end of March 1939, could only be understood as a demand for the recognition of Germany's protectorate over Prague and

C

Bratislava and as such no doubt it was meant. The same thing applies to Goerdeler's remark that 'mutual trade agreements' could not be excluded. At the end of March 1939 this phrase could have been coined only as a result of the recently concluded German-Rumanian trade agreement which had so shocked Europe, and which had been intended to pave the way for German economic supremacy in the Balkans. Although alarmed by the reaction of the Western powers, Hassell described the agreement as 'a nice framework'.[37] Goerdeler's revisionist policy gradually turned into power politics; this was substantially watered down by a view of Central Europe which envisaged imperialism of the benevolent despot variety – in its style and scope, it again showed a significant blend of the National-Liberal, pan-German and Prussian *étatiste* spirit.

It need hardly be said that such ideas, had they been able to be put to the test of reality, would not have been in keeping with the outlook of Europe between 1937 and 1939. For after the First World War, the continental European countries, in spite of their half-hearted professions of European solidarity, of a desire for collective security and of support for the League of Nations, had never fundamentally departed from the ways of traditional power politics. French foreign policy must be held responsible for the fact that the 'system of Versailles' was never able to develop into a true international order. Driven by the necessity, which the war had immeasurably intensified, for security abroad, the Quai d'Orsay saw to it that behind the façade of the League of Nations the old game of continental European alliances continued, although its pattern may have changed: nor did the French permit any fundamental revision of the concepts or procedure of international affairs. However suitable or useful in the existing circumstances the steps taken at Locarno may have been, they failed to introduce anything intrinsically new: it was only one move in the game, and fundamentally all it meant was that henceforth Germany, with certain reservations, might also play a part. Because of the imperialism of Italy and Japan, both of which utterly ignored the League of Nations, and later because of Hitler's foreign policy, Great Britain, hitherto an advocate of collective security (though more out of *laissez-faire* than anything else), was eventually compelled to take the initiative in the restoration at least of the concert of powers – a policy that culminated in the meeting at Munich. At the beginning of 1939 Europe was again where she had been in 1914.

Thus the basic principles of Goerdeler's foreign policy were not inherently different from the concepts that obtained elsewhere in Europe. The real question was whether the extent of the German claims as represented by Goerdeler was tolerable to Europe. From the impressions he had derived in England and France, Goerdeler rightly concluded that the answer to this question might very well be in the affirmative; even German hegemony in Central Europe and the country's economic expansion in the south-east were accepted by London, not merely as provisional but as irreversible : this is quite clear from the notes of the British foreign minister, Lord Halifax. Had Goerdeler become Chancellor at this time, as a result of a *coup d'état* effected without foreign support, the realisation of his proposed foreign policy as well as the consolidation of Hitler's gains would have been altogether feasible, especially since Goerdeler was sincere in stating that Germany would be satisfied by the solution of the ' vital German questions '; his undertaking was equally genuine when he promised to keep, by way of international guarantees, a satisfied Germany within the frontiers thus attained and to participate in an ' international peace front '.

Nevertheless such ideas could not serve as a basis either for an alternative to Hitler that would be enduring and progressive, or for an alliance aimed at his overthrow between the Opposition group, represented by Goerdeler, and the British government. Certainly, Goerdeler was not misleading Vansittart in September 1938 in telling him that Europe had ' reached a turning-point in her history '; the choice was now between renewed aggression, resulting in victory for Hitler, on the one hand, and the success of the German Opposition, followed by cooperation with the European powers, on the other.[38] But quite aside from the question of whether success for the Opposition was possible, Goerdeler's programme showed far too great a preoccupation with German interests and failed to take account of the political and diplomatic problems, not to mention the interests, of other powers.

Indeed, there seemed little difference between Nazi and Opposition policy: on occasion, Goerdeler made demands upon the British – for instance in regard to Poland – which Hitler himself had not yet made. Goerdeler's concept was conditioned largely by the psychological requirements of the internal situation in Germany, for the only antidote to Hitler's political successes at home and abroad seemed to lie in the Opposition assuming the credit for those successes. This would have proved no argument in the international sphere, however, since for Britain to throw in her lot with the Opposition, which she in fact never seriously contemplated doing, would have meant in effect conceding to the latter, on the grounds that they were more easily satisfied, what was being conceded to Hitler. Thus the choice was not a genuine one. A policy of concessions could be equally well conducted with Hitler, so long as the necessity to fight the Germany he led had not been proved beyond doubt. In any case, the realisation of Goerdeler's ideas would not have meant progress for Europe, for while there might have been some lessening of tension, the heart of Europe would have contained a National Conservative bloc forming an obstacle to any closer federation within the continent.

## The Reich as a Power for Order in Europe

A new element was introduced into this situation, not by Hitler's attack on Poland, but by his pact with the Soviet Union. It would be difficult to exaggerate the significance of the transitory Russo-German agreement in the thinking and planning of the National Conservative opposition. The alliance had a truly galvanising effect on the group round Hassell, Goerdeler and Beck. The fact that in the autumn of 1939 they once more began to concentrate their energies on preparing for a *putsch*, and busied themselves with establishing contacts with England, is attributable not so much to Hitler's intention to attack in the west after the conquest of Poland, as to Moscow's reentry into European politics. For the manner of that reentry was regarded as a threat, and not as the return to normal Soviet-German relations which would have been in every way acceptable to the Opposition. Several of Beck's memoranda at this time stress the consequences of this ' crucial turning-point '. ' Russia now stands exactly where she did in 1914. Having settled the Far East question, for the time being, at least, she is now free to concentrate her whole attention on Europe.'[39] The Polish buffer state, which ' had undoubtedly rendered good services to Germany ', had been wantonly destroyed, and this in turn had already led

> to the appearance in South-Eastern Europe of reactions un-favourable to Germany, both as regards the present war and the more distant future. The Balkan states are lost to Germany . . . At the very least, Germany has lost her moral sway over Finland and has antagonised the Scandinavian countries. But developments yet more unfavourable to Germany may be anticipated in the Baltic region.[40]

Beck held that Germany's strategic mobility had been curtailed in the east, and the possibility could not be excluded that ' in the later stages of the war in Russia, Germany would be exposed to serious, and under certain circumstances, mortal danger '.[41] Hassell, too, noted angrily that

> in foreign policy, all the most important positions have been sacrificed in a last-minute attempt to extricate the country from a dire emergency, culpably incurred. . . . The Baltic and the eastern frontier are forfeit. Aside from the fact that it is politically immoral to abandon the Baltic countries, the *dominium maris baltici* has been seriously imperilled. [42]

But from his personal knowledge of Hitler Hassell added : ' It is very possible . . . that Hitler is secretly considering an attack on Soviet Russia. This could but aggravate the outrageous nature of his policy.' Goerdeler, who had already warned against Russian intervention in the spring of 1939, was of the same opinion.[43] In a memorandum deriving from Oster's circle it was further pointed out that ' in the south the German sphere of influence would be gravely impaired by . . . a Russian advance into Rumania; indeed such an advance might ultimately destroy a German Balkan policy that has held great promise for the future '.[44] What was regarded as even more important by Commander Liedig, the writer of this memorandum, however, was the fact that Germany, through allying herself with Russia, 'had now irrevocably become England's mortal foe', and was moving towards 'separation from Europe'. In the same spirit Beck pointed out that 'Germany more than ever before, now stands alone' and that 'the danger of a coalition against Germany has grown'.[45] When it is remembered that at this time Germany was at war with France and England, and that neither the campaign in France, nor Hitler's *volte-face* in regard to Russia, were yet assured of success, it will be seen that these assessments of the situation both at home and abroad were far from inaccurate.

But in the view of the Conservative Opposition, Germany's isolation rendered her dependent on the Soviet Union to an extent which could hardly fail to have internal repercussions: for they felt that the National Socialist régime, already in their opinion half Bolshevist, would now become progressively more so. It was at this time that Lieutenant-Colonel Grosscurth, Oster's confidential agent in the OKH (High Command), noticed the first symptoms of this process, an instance being the proposal to attach 'political commissars' to the army.[46] The National Socialists had 'burned their idols and made idols of what they had burned', remarked Hassell, and he agreed with Goerdeler that in this sense too Hitler's Russian policy represented 'a tremendous danger', the more so since the Nazi *Weltanschauung* was a structure without substance and might easily collapse. Both arrived at the same conclusion: 'The advance of Bolshevism along the whole front close to our frontier, together with the socialism which a war economy inevitably produces, must have the gravest possible consequences for Germany.'[47] Already Liedig saw Hitler as 'Stalin's satrap' – and even Quartermaster-General Wagner concurred. Wagner's intellect resembled a Verey light: every now and again it would soar up like a flare so that the political landscape was revealed in its true light; no sooner had the flare burned out, however, than the Quartermaster-General would find himself stumbling anxiously in the dark in a helpless game of follow-my-Führer. Yet even he wrote in September 1939 that 'it can only be hoped that the two ideologies do not converge too rapidly. That would be fatal.'[48]

The situation also seemed to present positive possibilities, however. Hassell immediately noted that the German-Soviet pact might strengthen the desire of the Western powers ' to maintain a strong and a healthy Germany, though not under a leadership that was half or more than half Bolshevist '.[49] Now that Hitler had lightly cast aside that tool of German foreign policy which had already proved so valuable at Munich – the British fear of Bolshevism – the Opposition was free to turn the fear to its own account. Between the time of the Sudeten crisis and the outbreak of war there had been virtually no lever by which the Opposition could have shifted the British or the French governments on to their own lines of thought; it was now felt that such a lever had been found. The ' politicians of the Entente ', according to Etscheid's memorandum of January 1940, written for the OKH,

> had become strongly convinced of the danger of Bolshevism by what had happened in Spain, France, Poland and Finland. The need to hold back, or better still to repulse, the Soviet advance into Europe, the possibility of basing the understanding with Germany upon such a mandate, and the prospect that at the same time Japanese claims to hegemony in the Far East might be silenced, are all factors that hold excellent prospects of agreement.[50]

Above all, Liedig's memorandum concluded that Great Britain – and also France, according to Etscheid – would, in the event of a revision of Russo-German policy, ' pay a good price for Germany's reversion to Europe and to the European community of nations '.[51] Were Germany to ' make a clean break with Bolshevism ' and put her ' mobile armed power at the disposal of threatened Finland ', thereby shielding the whole of Europe, she would then naturally be in a position to demand something in return from England, namely the ' position which is her due – that of supreme Continental power ', and confirmation ' in her territory, German by heritage and by language, in the whole of its present extent '. In October 1939 Hasso von Etzdorf and Erich Kordt stressed the obvious need to restore a residual Czechoslovakia and a residual Poland, if Germany was not to be ' encumbered with alien peoples ', but for both geographical and economic reasons, a decisive influence must be maintained in those countries.[52] Now, for the first time we find phrases such as ' the mission before the Reich is to bring order and peace to the peoples of Europe '.[53]

Undoubtedly many of the formulations and demands contained in these memoranda can be ascribed to tactical requirements – the need to win the support of the generals, essential to a *coup d'état*. They had to be persuaded that a *putsch* against Hitler was not only necessary but would also cost nothing in terms of foreign policy, and might even be profitable; a reference to ' compensation . . . for the sacrifices and laurels of the Polish campaign '[54] is clearly intended for the benefit of those generals, who were always suspicious of politicians and diplomats gambling away the gains of the military. But the pattern of ideas behind these calculated arguments is not difficult to discover. And in a statement of 23 February 1940 for transmission to an English correspondent and intended as a serious memorandum from the German Opposition, even the more temperate Hassell named conditions that were almost identical to the aims of people like Liedig, Etzdorf and Etscheid.[55] He too spoke of ' a healthy, vigorous Germany as an indispensable factor . . . in face of Bolshevist Russia ', and while he renounced the revision of western frontiers, he declared that the union of Austria and the Sudetenland with the Reich must remain outside the field of discussion, since otherwise there was a danger that ' armed dispute would very soon flare up once more '. He further demanded from Poland the frontier of 1914, going on to say that the future peace should be based on the ' principle of nationality ', but with ' certain provisos of historical provenance '. Since his ensuing remarks concern ' the restoration of a Czech republic ', and since it can be assumed that an experienced diplomat like Hassell did not use a phrase of this kind unwittingly, we can only conclude that the Opposition intended to convey to London that Bohemia, Moravia and Slovakia would have to be separated, the territories retaining their formal sovereignty but without prejudice to Germany's claim to leadership. London and Paris, Etscheid maintained, had finally realised that ' to load immature peoples and artificially created states with all kinds of tasks would not make for stable conditions in Europe '.[56] This no longer represented a return to Munich, as implied in Etzdorf's memorandum. Indeed, the consolidation of all Hitler's conquests – excluding the General Government in occupied Poland and the open 'protectorate' in Bohemia – as also of Germany's position of unchallenged hegemony in Central Europe was now regarded by the group round Hassell and Goerdeler as both desirable and feasible – provided Hitler was overthrown.

The situation was now menacing, and action seemed imperative. The knowledge in the autumn of 1939 that Hitler was proposing to attack France intensified the urgency of the Opposition's activities. For if, as was anticipated, the offensive was halted this would only increase the dangers and diminish the opportunities. It was not because he had learned of Hitler's plans for an offensive, but as a result of a conversation with Goerdeler about the hazards and possibilities of the Führer's Russian policy, that Hassell wrote: 'The whole situation points to the conclusion that it is high time the brakes were applied to a vehicle that is now barely under control.' In the case of Halder there can be no doubt that military considerations predominated, while Oster's motives were rather more complex.[57] But supposing the brakes could still be applied, would it be possible to remain in the vehicle? It is true that the Opposition's plans could not compare either quantitatively or qualitatively with those of Hitler; while the claims of the 'representatives of the true national interest' had grown, their path was steadily diverging from Hitler's. Yet this divergence did not bring the Opposition any closer to Europe. Their speculation on anxiety in Britain and France, as also in Scandinavia and South-Eastern Europe, about Soviet penetration was certainly not wholly unfounded, for those entrusted by the British government to make contact with the Beck and Goerdeler circle had, in fact, evinced a marked interest in a return to the political situation before Munich.[58] Yet in two respects the Opposition had perhaps assumed too much, overestimating not only Britain's fear of Bolshevism and the Soviet Union, but also her consequent readiness to recognise the position attained by Germany.

The hegemony tacitly conceded to the Reich by the Munich agreement might still have been acceptable, but the extent of the *imperium*, which the Hassell and Goerdeler group wished to retain, even in modified form, was another question. It is true that the West looked upon Moscow with foreboding – a foreboding aggravated by Russia's action against Finland – but for the time being Germany's crushing superiority on the Continent constituted the greater threat to England and more especially to France : it is significant that those in opposition were always conscious of potential reactions in Paris.[59] Even a ' sane and liberal ' German government would probably have had to offer a return to the pre-Munich territorial as well as political *status quo*. For over and above the exclusion of Russia from Europe implicit in such a plan, this would involve what, in view of the changed situation, would doubtless be a welcome diplomatic as distinct from a military align-ment against the East. It is altogether typical of the situation that Theo Kordt at once fell foul of Vansittart's emissary, Conwell Evans, by his refusal to agree, in the event of a successful *coup d'état*, to an immediate evacuation of Poland in the face of the Russian threat;[60] moreover, the partition of Poland between Ger-many and Russia was now an obstacle and not to Hitler's peace-feelers alone. For what could the Opposition mean when in one and the same breath they spoke of the restoration of Poland and demanded the eastern frontiers of 1914, without any indication as to how they proposed to shift the new Soviet western frontier back to the east? Of course, some arrangement would have been reached had peace negotiations really taken place; a Goerdeler administra-tion would certainly not have sought to impose by force many of the German claims which it put forward in principle. Taken as a whole, however, the basic propositions advanced by the National Conservative Opposition, more especially after the German show of force in Poland, could not be seen by the Western powers or by Europe in general as a lasting solution to European problems. Had London and Paris nonetheless accepted Hassell's and Goer-deler's proposals – for to continue to fight a Germany that had returned to sanity and forsworn aggression would have been more than ever distasteful – the hegemony resulting from the peace would have been no more conducive to liberal and demo-cratic federation in Europe than was the hegemony of Sparta to federation in Greece.

Rapid victory in France put an abrupt end to such reflections. It is remarkable that the nucleus of the National Conservative group still refused to align itself with Hitler. As Hassell's writings of the summer of 1940 and Goerdeler's memoranda of the same period testify, their opposition to the Führer and his régime, based as it was on ethics, religion and questions of internal politics, never for a moment wavered.[61] And Nazi supremacy in Europe, as Goerdeler wrote on 1 July, formed an excellent hotbed for the propagation of Bolshevist ideas, although these were already prevalent enough in Germany as a result of ' financial madness, economic duress, political terror, lawlessness and immorality '.[62]

Speaking before the war Hassell had once said that in politically active people ' the individual personality cannot but be invaded by those contemporary ideas which have erupted with primeval force '. For the military victory in France had not simply been a victory for Hitler, but also for Germany, and there can hardly have been a German who remained wholly unmoved by the situation thus created, even though his feeling might not, as Hassell remarked, be one of joy.[63] It was clear to the Opposition that Hitler had gained little by his victory politically, although it had largely eliminated the Russian threat, because although Germany could not beat Great Britain, neither, on the other hand, could the Führer make peace. Yet would this also be true of a Reich freed from Hitler? Influenced by what they now deemed to be Germany's established and expanded Imperial position, Goerdeler, Hassell and Popitz developed their idea of German leadership in Central Europe to an idea of German leadership of the whole of Europe; there floated before them the seductive vision of a German Reich of medieval proportions and Prussian and Conservative in character.

In the memorandum of 1 July 1940 already mentioned, Goerdeler had written for the first time of ' German leadership ' in Europe,[64] and even before the attack on Russia, the rebirth of the imperial concept had been unequivocally expressed in a lecture given by Popitz upon this very subject on 11 December 1940 before the Wednesday Club.[65] After dismissing as a ' romantic daydream ' the universalism of the medieval Reich concept, whose too evident claim to supremacy had aroused the antagonism of all other countries, and as ' the reality of a weak Germany ' a federation disrupted by ' pluralistic and polycratic elements ', he went on to say that a modern and viable Reich concept would envisage a politically united country which would exert a ' determining influence ' upon other areas and states beyond its own frontiers, ultimately enjoying ' special rights ' in those areas. From the standpoint of international law, this would represent a ' *Grossraum* ' (greater area) and politically speaking, a ' Reich '. However, Popitz rejected ' phrase-making about the extent of the necessary curtailment of self-determination '. The formation of a sphere of influence extending beyond the frontiers of Germany and the consolidation of that influence might better be left to the ' historical course of events '; agreements of an economic nature which would become ' progressively more comprehensive ' were the ' appropriate means '. Yet ' premature constitutions ' through which ' the extent of the surrender of political power ' would become manifest to the states to be annexed would be less likely to woo the latter than to frighten them off.

Hassell, who described Popitz's lecture as ' brilliant ',[66] was himself a good deal more reserved about the political forms of German leadership, and the hypocrisy advocated by Popitz was entirely foreign to him. Nor was this simply an expression of the difference between the administrator and the diplomat; the two men differed both in character and outlook. At this time Hassell, too, was talking of ' the West under German leadership '[67] and of ' ordered cooperation '.[68] His ' *Grossraum* ' extended far across Central Europe and included within the German magnetic field the Balkans as well as, after 22 June 1941, the Baltic states, Finland, Scandinavia, Belgium and Holland. But, unlike Popitz, Hassell had no wish to impose upon these states, ' a curtailment of self-determination '. On the contrary, he constantly reiterated in articles published during those years that such a *Grossraum* could only survive if leadership by the central state did not involve the others in ' servitude ',[69] if the peoples ' within the new order were given their full dues ', and if ' their political independence and their cultural identity remained unimpaired '.[70] Any formulas involving a closer confederation he regarded as ' primitive '. He further strongly emphasised that, as regards the Balkans, ' the only form of relationship between the South-Eastern, the Greater Ger-

man " ethnic area " [*Stammraum*], and the partner beyond the
Adriatic which can in the long run prove beneficial to all concerned is one that does not adopt as its yardstick the immediate
interests of Germany and Italy alone but equally those of all the
participant nations of the south-east '; these ' sorely tried countries ' must feel secure in the ' total Western confederation ' and
convinced ' that their economic and social welfare is best protected within this system, where their own existence would be
safeguarded '.[71] Clearly his view of a Europe under German
leadership resembled a kind of trust in which Germany would
hold most of the shares. Goerdeler's ideas ranged along similar
lines, yet the gaze of this old National Liberal now turned to the
' national ' complements to the German nucleus which had been
unattainable before 1940; that is to say to Alsace-Lorraine and, by
degrees, to the South Tyrol as a consequence of the defeat
of France and the increasing evidence of Italy's military impotence.[72]

The spirit governing these conceptions, even in the case of
Popitz, was certainly not identical either with the theory and
practice of Hitlerian supremacy, or with the ideas then being
evolved by the more extreme official National Socialist Reich
theorists. Thus at the beginning of 1942, Gerhard Krüger wrote
an article in which he energetically refuted Srbik's thesis that the
new ' German imperial concept ' represented a ' new form of universalism ' related to the ' principle of the national state '; indeed,
the essence of the National Socialist Reich consisted precisely in
the unmistakable emphasis put upon German supremacy and the
subordination of non-German sections of the Reich.[73] Helmut
Rumpf also pointed out the significant distinction between the
terms ' leadership ' and ' supremacy ', the latter being peculiar to
National Socialism.[74] Yet there is an undeniable similarity to ideas
such as those put forward by Karl Richard Ganzer in 1941 in his
book *Das Reich als europäische Ordnungsmacht* (' The Reich as
a Power for Order in Europe ') – a book which had appeared
under the auspices of the Reichsinstitut für Geschichte des neuen
Deutschlands; Ganzer, too, had said that readiness to take over
the leadership of Europe would involve an obligation of the
highest order and that power could only mean readiness to pro-

tect. The National Conservative Opposition was as ready to protect and to lead Europe as it was to combine the principle of the
national state with a new universalism. But what should be the
substance of that universalism? Goerdeler, Hassell and Beck returned again and again to technical and economic development
necessitating larger coalitions. While this was right, the integration of Europe on the basis of economic interests postulated Germany's renunciation of a leading rôle in her understanding of the
word. Yet the very nature of their fundamental views on politics in general meant that these men of the Opposition had nothing to offer but the national principle and a conservative outlook – in other words, German leadership and an illiberal order
under a German aegis.

A characteristic feature of the writings of Goerdeler and Hassell is the recurrence of the words ' moral virtue ', ' moral
strength ', ' order ', ' conformity ' and ' orderly ' in discussions of
a Europe determined by Germany. Equally characteristic is the
rôle which Bismarck now began to assume in their thoughts.
Popitz, too, had asserted that the ' pure power-principle ' and
brute force were not enough;[75] a few weeks earlier, Albrecht
Haushofer had made similar observations to Rudolf Hess.[76] Nothing could be more natural, especially for men confronted with the
Führer, than to long for a man like Bismarck, admirably versed
in the art of diplomacy, a man of moderation in whom they could
place their trust. The fact that the thoughts of the Opposition
now turned to this statesman is also symptomatic of something
else. Fundamentally, they were incapable of envisaging the unification of Europe in any form other than that taken by the unification of the Reich under Prussia. This is evident from a remark
of Goerdeler's : ' Because Prussia did not abuse her position, but
invariably followed up the imposition of force with the cultiva-
tion of spiritual, moral and ideal values, she finally became the
magnet which, in an age when development was dictated by the
steam engine, drew into her field all other German territories.'[77]
And if they thought of Europe as a trust in which Germany held
the majority of the shares, they further imagined a German, at
once chairman and managing director, who would handle the
other shareholders and directors with as much skill and tact, yet

without abrogating any part of his sovereignty, as did Bismarck the Federal princes. Bismarck's policy, however, rested upon a firm basis, the concept of the German nation state. In the situation obtaining in the 1940s however, although the temporary basis of power, namely the German Army, existed, the claims to European leadership then being advanced lacked all idealistic and political foundation. The Goerdeler and Hassell group did not want to lead by force, yet their leadership must necessarily have been based upon the constant threat of force. The revival of the imperial concept would have been intolerable to Europe; its individual defects, such as the undefined position of France in the new Europe – she could not, it was vaguely suggested, ' remain subjugated for ever '[78] but must again become a ' factor '[79] – were of as little significance, in view of the concept's basic unreality, as the fact that there was never the remotest chance of making peace with the Western powers on such a basis.[80] Never was the National Conservative Opposition so remote from the rest of Europe as when it began to think in European terms.

Hitler's attack on Russia, while failing to provide the foundation which the German claim to leadership lacked, might conceivably have induced a change favourable to that claim, in the political climate of Europe. The events of 22 June 1941 put new life into the National Conservative Opposition, however much they deplored Hitler's action on military and ethical grounds. Hitler would never win the campaign, they argued, because Russia was invincible militarily, and Hitler himself was incapable of combining the conduct of a war with the right kind of policy. If, however, he could be overthrown in time and the campaign, no longer his responsibility, could be turned into a real war of liberation, things would appear in a different light. Hassell had, indeed, enthusiastically participated in the formulation of the conservative Reich ideology, which at the time represented his political convictions, but he had never really believed in its realisation. He was too keenly aware of the British government's sharp change of mood during the course of the war to nourish any illusions about the conditions they would be prepared to meet; even favourable news had not been able to shake his scepticism.[81] But in August 1941 he wrote, in an article combating the thesis of the

' Decline of the West ', that for the first time in modern German history there might be ' a possibility for Germany to adopt a leading rôle in Europe, instead of maintaining a balance between dependence on East or West '; but this, only if Germany avoided Napoleon's mistake in ' so distorting and emasculating ' the idea of the European mission, of which he undoubtedly dreamed, ' that he brought to those nations whom he had undertaken to liberate from British tutelage, not equality within a free federation, but servitude to France '.[82] Apart from the courageous allusion to Hitler's policy in the east, Hassell expressed in this and similar passages the feeling that it might now be possible to rally the peoples of Europe behind Germany under the anti-Bolshevist flag, to turn Russia into a weaker partner having drastically curtailed her pretensions in the Balkans, the Baltic and in Poland and, on the strength of these two factors, to begin the reordering of Europe unhampered by considerations of a Britain now rendered impotent. This presupposed that the campaign in Russia would be quickly over; to achieve this Russia would have to be restrained before she took military counter-measures, which would not involve ' exploiting ' her or eliminating her as a political power but rather tearing down ' the spiritual barriers between Russia and Europe ' by destroying Bolshevism.[83] This in turn postulated the early fall of Hitler. Hassell's bitterness over the ' hopeless sergeants ', those generals incapable of a *coup d'état* against Hitler, has to be seen in this context.

Goerdeler also perceived the supposed opportunity. It is true that his preference had always been for the acquisition of ' national ' complements to the German nucleus, but again because his ideas were rooted in National Liberal views, he always showed far greater aversion than any other members of this group to any extension of methods of direct rule or protection beyond those areas he regarded as German. To him, the national state was a firm basic concept in politics and he had therefore always been particularly sensitive to the conflict, in his eyes almost insoluble, between the theory of a *Grossraum* under German leadership and the reality of a Europe consisting in national states – a conflict which the *étatiste* spirit of the Prussian Conservatives tended to ignore. He was further very much aware of certain additional problems which presented obstacles to the realisation of his programme. Europe, he maintained, had already been ripe for federation before the war, but had been alienated from these aims by the Nazi coordination of the continent, since ' the minds and spirits of other peoples . . . are today much more hostile to us ' than during the First World War.[84] But now, sustained by the spirit of what seemed to him the possibility of a European crusade against Bolshevism, he believed that the hour had come for reconciliation between the ' concept of national states and the need for a *Grossraum* '. This conviction was responsible for his long memorandum, *Das Ziel* (' The Goal ') which must have been written during the latter half of 1941 and the early months of the following year, and which marks the climax of the desires and hopes of the National Conservative Opposition.[85] In spite of all that had happened, Goerdeler believed, it would still be possible to embark upon European federation if ' Germany were to make a voluntary and timely renunciation of undesirable political methods '. While maintaining complete freedom of ' internal conditions ' in the national states by the elimination of customs barriers and travel restrictions, it should be possible to implement ' customs agreements, coalitions, currency regulations etc.' and thence ' to develop a federation of states with military treaties '. It would ' be no exaggeration to say that, with timely action, i.e. the cessation of the war in favour of a sensible political system, there could be a European federation of states under German leadership within ten or twenty years'. But if the favourable moment was allowed to pass ' it would be a long time before even the idea of German leadership could be envisaged '.

The change that began to take place in the views of the National Conservative Opposition after the end of 1941, leading to the gradual elimination of the demand for German leadership in Europe, though not of the idea of European federation based upon independent and equal member states, cannot be attributed solely or even mainly to developments in the military situation. It is clear that Communist Russia's entry into the war and more still America's intervention, and the consequent definitive realisation of the change in world politics presaged in 1917, deeply influenced political thought. The recurrence of 1917, which this

D

time was to have lasting effects, patently inaugurated ideological, political and military conflicts of global proportions, and Europe became aware that she was only one continent among several. The Opposition, too, sensed the change. There was an intensification of the feeling of European solidarity, and at the same time the squabbles over the leadership of Europe suddenly dwindled into comparative insignificance. Hassell recognised that ' the enlarged global aspect of space has reduced European continental conflicts to a secondary rôle compared with the major problems which confront us in the world today, and which call for a united front in Europe '.[86]

With remarkable perspicacity, he in fact diagnosed a process to which many Europeans continued to turn a blind eye even after the war, and which they were later bitterly to resist. The age of colonialism, he said, was approaching its end; ' the European's intellectual and economic supremacy throughout the world ', which had seemed as enduring as a ' *rocher de bronze* ', had disintegrated. Not only in Asia and America but also in Africa, especially North Africa, ' national and social independence movements ' were on foot which, for example in Egypt, Algeria and Tunis, ' whatever the outcome of the war ', could not and should not be restrained. Europe must seek a new relationship with these emergent peoples and make them feel ' that the European is not opposed to natural development ': they must be shown that ' their economic prosperity will be strongly encouraged, in close relationship with that of the continent of Europe '.[87] An insight of this kind necessarily induced a lasting change of attitude to internal European problems. Aside from this, however, the Opposition found itself increasingly faced with the realisation that the imperial concept was slowly being dismembered, corroded and destroyed by its own parasitic hypertrophy, for as such they saw National Socialist supremacy in Europe. If, within the German sphere of influence, unimaginable crimes were daily being perpetrated in the name of that Reich which the Opposition desired to present to Europe as pacific and benevolent, how could these men advance their own claim to German leadership with a clear conscience? Nor could it now be expected that the nations of Europe would show anything but passionate resistance in the face of that claim, having regard to the 'sea of hatred' which, Hassell remarked, the National Socialists had created. One of the dominant political sentiments in Hassell's diary is sorrow over the destructive work of the parasites – and anger at the soldiers who failed to stop it. But the end of 1941 and the beginning of 1942 marked not least the beginning of the serious dialogue with a wholly different resistance group, the Kreisau Circle, and this dialectic, combined with the general change in the political climate, reorientated in certain important respects the political thinking of the National Conservative Opposition.

## The European Internationalism of Kreisau

In August 1938, Adam von Trott zu Solz, who was subsequently what might be called the 'Foreign Minister' of the Kreisau Circle, received the following letter from an English friend: 'To us, nationalism is an illusion for the masses, a tragic and terrible force; one day it must become internationalism as we ourselves feel it and live it.'[88] Indeed this fascinating group of highly unorthodox Christian Socialists, Socialist Christians and Christian-Socialist aristocrats of which Graf Moltke was the centre during the early years of the war, was distinguishable from the National Conservative notables, especially in foreign policy, by the fact that nationalism was for them no longer the determining motive of political action. It is true that men such as Leber, Haubach and Mierendorff, or Husen, Yorck and Steltzer, derived from a Europe of major powers, national states and countries founded on national claims to self-determination; a Europe of defensive hegemonies, treaty systems and contested frontiers. All this could not fail to influence their political ideas and more especially their political activity. But to these men a Europe thus disrupted could not be the final word in European politics. Instead of accepting its political values and concepts, let alone regarding them as absolute, they looked for some way of replacing this superannuated system of a dying society with a better order: 'Europe is sickening, of a condition which no longer has any place in this world – nationalism . . . it is high time that politicians too began to draw the logical conclusions and throw overboard what is known as nationalism ', wrote Julius Leber in 1928.[89]

To these men, too, Versailles was a stumbling block, not least because the treaties had wounded their patriotism and injured their country. In 1925 Leber expressed very similar opinions to those often put forward by Goerdeler when he declared that ' there will never be a German government capable of recognising the Polish Corridor, voluntarily and solemnly, as a permanent right. It is too painful a thorn in the flesh of the German republic. It is too senseless a partition of German soil.'[90] Yet they criticised Versailles even more harshly for being simply a product of nationalism, regardless of whose nationalism benefited and whose suffered. The spirit of Versailles could not cure Europe's condition and was far more likely to turn the European sickness of nationalism into a chronic condition. Thus the core of their thinking was not the revision but the overcoming of Versailles. Nor did they counter French hegemony with an explicit or implicit determination to restore German hegemony, the encroachment of Poland with the decision to reconquer actual or alleged German territories; what they sought instead was Franco-German or German-Polish understanding. It was a demand put forward continuously during the twenties by Reichwein and Leber at rallies, in lectures and in articles,[91] and as early as 1919 Theo Haubach wrote an article, ' Foundations of a Socialist Policy in Europe ', in which he virtually repudiated any revision of the peace treaty. It was not by the shifting of frontiers that Europe could be led out of ' the anarchy of Versailles ', wrote Haubach, but only by a new order based upon genuine understanding; this would automatically solve the question of what concessions must be made to Germany – a link-up through the Corridor, for instance.

Above all, however, Franco-German and German-Polish understanding was ' for us Socialists more than just a temporary elimination of difficulties; it is the stable foundation, created to last, of a future Europe '.[92] In this conception there was no room for the idea, which was indeed explicitly rejected, of a Central European *Grossraum* grouped about a reexpanded German nation state. This was brilliantly expressed in 1938 by Hermann Brill; though not a member of the Kreisau Circle, he formulated in a pamphlet the programme and aims of the socialist group, the ' German

Popular Front ', which differed very little from the foreign aims of the Kreisau socialists. Either France could rule over a fragmented Germany – which had been the Napoleonic solution – or Germany could dominate Central Europe in order to weaken France – which had been Bismarck's solution. ' Both were nationalistic. Both failed. . . . But there is also a European solution . . .'[93] Leber's demand that the principles of economic co-operation and of democratic internal policy should also determine international relations was based upon the same outlook.[94] The idea central to both is the rationalisation of European foreign policy so that Europe might become a community of pluralistic states prepared to settle conflicts in a rational spirit, instead of a collection of powers whose arbitrary moral standards could only lead to irresponsible action.

Socialists have a natural tendency to think along these lines in matters of foreign policy and accordingly Social Democrats such as Leber and Haubach were representative of the marked progressive elements in the Kreisau group. But those of the Kreisau Circle who, because of their origin, were true ' notables ' also possessed an independent tradition. Fritz Fischer is surely right in protesting against the use of the word ' Resistance ' as it is understood today to describe Bethmann Hollweg's conflict with the High Command and other ' imperialist ' political elements in the German *bourgeoisie* during the First World War; two such utterly dissimilar situations cannot be covered by the same term.[95] Yet Bethmann Hollweg and his circle initiated a move towards sanity in foreign policy whose conception no longer derived from the issue of the war, but from the war itself. Although Greater German nationalism with its striving for a place in world politics and a leading position in Central Europe remained predominant, the foundations had been laid for a tradition of modern ideas in foreign affairs which was handed down to the middle- and upper-class Kreisau Circle. Bethmann Hollweg, whatever assessment may be made of his conduct in the early years of the war, was yet able from his experience as Chancellor to realise that fundamental reform in matters of foreign policy and in the system of international relations was now inevitable. ' This, the most tremendous of revolutions ever to have shaken the world ', he wrote in

January 1918 to Prince Max of Baden, ' cannot cease, the nations cannot be exonerated from all the frightfulness they are perpetrating before God and the world unless humanity, having firmly turned its back upon the conditions which engendered this war, considers what should be put in their place.' The imperialism and nationalism which ' in the last decades have determined the broad lines of every country's policy, have set up goals which individual nations can pursue only at the cost of a general confrontation.'[96]

In 1920 Kurt Riezler, Bethmann's one-time secretary, drew yet other conclusions from this insight.[97] After criticising with merciless and irrefutable logic the war aims of the German ' Military Party ' – which would have been intolerable to Europe and could only have been sustained by the most brutal use of force – he refuted with equal severity the return of France to major power politics and to her ' supremacy in a Balkanised Europe with the connivance of the British '. Since he regarded the peace of Versailles as the expression of this French policy and as a regression into the more or less reactionary concepts of prewar foreign politics – just as Leber did – he concluded that there could be only one answer to the question : ' What must be done?' and that was the formation of a European federation preceded by economic union. It must become ' the general European conviction that its major interests are common to all nations in Europe ', and that conviction must in turn lead on to ' a pan-European frame of mind '. Nor should it be difficult for a conquered Germany to realise that therapy for Europe was also therapy for herself. Following the ' terrible aftermath of immature dreams ' Germany must ' now, and for all time, pursue no policy other than the pan-European '. And many of his passages presage a concept which later was to be developed, more especially by Moltke, namely, that if thinking was to be Europeanised, it could only be on the basis of a changed concept of the state. ' Everything through the state, everything for the sake of the state, the spectacle of a stupendous achievement – but an end in itself, an achievement attained at its own cost and eventually self-destructive.' Such was the ' tragedy of the state ' which the war revealed.

Obviously the Kreisau ' notables ' continued this tradition.

Theodor Steltzer, one of the earliest members of the Circle, may be regarded in a sense as representative of the Bethmann-Riezler school of thought. As early as the autumn of 1915 Steltzer, himself a General Staff officer, gave a lecture to the General Staff in which he demonstrated that Germany could not win the war, and it must therefore be settled politically. He went on to suggest that the war should be conducted on the basis of a defensive strategy.[98] To express such a view publicly, at that particular time and place, testified not only to his exceptionally courageous thinking and to his faith in his own ideas,[99] but also to his recognition – if still somewhat nebulous – of the wider political contexts. It was therefore logical that after the war he should continue to press for a ' departure from the politics of force ', for the end of German power politics and for understanding with France.[100] The statements he made at this time may be summed up as follows : Versailles was no cause for indignation, since the French had merely repaid the Germans in their own coin; what it did represent was a reason for spiritual and political conversion having as ultimate goal the ' community of free peoples '. It is significant, too, that in the autumn of 1939, when Trott was in the United States, he entered into close relations with Riezler.[101]

Yet the younger members of the Kreisau Circle did not merely attach themselves to a ready-made tradition; they developed and added to what was already there with discoveries of their own. Rothfels has pointed out that after the war, at universities like Breslau and Königsberg, fundamental questions were posed in lectures, seminars and students' associations on the subject of a border zone ' in which Germans and non-Germans lived so inextricably intermingled that the Western concept of the sovereign state and the nineteenth-century political concept of the nation could seem nothing more than a reactionary wraith. Federal and supranational solutions were also earnestly debated.'[102] It is in this soil that the opinions of Lukaschek and van Husen were so firmly rooted. Moltke, above all, was deeply preoccupied with minority problems, upon which he intended to write a thesis. He recognised at an early date that the minority question was not merely a German, but also a Central and East European problem; it is characteristic of his attitude that as early as 1928 he was criticising the way in which German minorities in Poland were allowing themselves to be governed from Berlin.[103] In this spirit, relations between Germany and Poland could be assessed without national connotations, and in 1930 van Husen ventured to assert that 'the survival of Poland and good relations between Poland and Germany' were a 'European necessity'.[104]

In the case of Trott, there can be no doubt that his early contacts with socialist circles and his experiences during his long period as an undergraduate at Oxford were decisive.[105] His existing interest in the problem of the relationship between national sovereignty and international order – his thesis concerned Hegel in that very context[106] – took, under these influences, a definitely supranational turn. In 1931 he was already suggesting that 'within the community of peoples, the function of the nation resembles in some sort that of the family within the state'.[107] A few years later, in 1934, in a letter to his father, he said that he was no longer thinking along the lines he had pursued in his thesis, but was endeavouring to 'define rather more closely my previously somewhat generalised ideas, and better still to compare them with English ideas on civic mentality and on the development of an international cooperation beneficial to all'. This had led him into ' so vast an empirical field that to survey it is beyond my powers '.[108] His ideas thus turned increasingly towards ' a world situation in which it would someday be possible to achieve a system of legal international relations '; this had been regarded by Hegel as Utopian, but to think in such sceptical terms ' is now tantamount to regarding as Utopian the absence of the otherwise necessary self-destruction of the nations '.[109] Indeed, Moltke had gradually come to think quite naturally in international terms, and as early as 1935 his assessment of the political aspects of the First World War shows that he had become totally independent of the traditional historico-political outlook of his own caste. To deny the need for, indeed the existence of, an international order, he said,

seems to me quite patently to contradict the evidence of the last war. This was, to some extent, a war of sanctions waged by allied powers against another power which, probably as a re-

sult of inaccurate information obtained by the Allies, was held
to have broken the unwritten laws – or rather, the unwritten
conventions – of international behaviour.[110]

Hence, like Leber, Haubach and Reichwein, these later members of
the Kreisau Circle, *bourgeois* in the widest sense of the term, had
even before the Second World War, evolved conceptions no longer dominated by 'vital national questions', but by one 'vital
international question' – how to discover the basis for and the
means to achieve rational European cooperation.

There were, of course, differences. Moltke had cast off all
nationalism and through his ideas on domestic and social policy
had arrived at a radical, and in many ways necessary and practical, repudiation of the concept of state hitherto predominant in
Germany; he denied the 'idol of the state'. His idea of Germany
was of a country divided into small, autonomous units in a federal
pattern that should be extended to comprise all Europe; there
would be no sovereignty save that vested in the total European
state. Yet it is clear that the development of his theory must eventually lead not only to the complete abolition of sovereignty, but
also to the territorial dissolution, if not the total fragmentation,
of the European states; it is equally clear, however, that such
ideas represent a Utopia which, though logical, is somewhat surprising. Later, in the formative period of the Kreisau Circle, it
still had some currency, but failed, naturally, to impose itself.
And while Trott himself was certainly no nationalist in the true
sense of the word, he nevertheless had a deep-rooted national
feeling and a high sense of the special contribution, both spiritual
and political, which his people and fatherland, by reason of their
essential nature and their strength, could and should make to
the general culture of Europe – a contribution he described as
'indispensable'. Closely connected with this was the fact that,
so far as the domestic and economic political structure of Germany was concerned, he was not advocating the wholesale adoption of Western – i.e. Anglo-Saxon – principles and forms, but
a combination of the 'personality principle of the West' with
the 'reality principle of the East'.[111]

He now believed, however, that the age of unrestricted national sovereignty had run its course and must come to an end, since the existence of non-restricted states would inevitably lead to war and to the ' self-destruction of the nations '. For their own protection, indeed if they were to survive at all, he maintained,[112] the peoples and states had no choice but to renounce full sovereignty. Conversely, the intellectual and political independence of Germany and her rôle as intermediary between East and West must be safeguarded; hence the country could not do without a political basis and political delimitation. From this twofold need for protection he evolved his conception of a European federation consisting of already extant states but with restricted sovereignty, a federation whose form would thus enable it to fulfil the twofold protective function for which it was designed. It was not an unrealistic plan from the point of view of the means available for its realisation. It was precisely because he saw them as ' necessary institutions ' that Trott, better than Moltke, understood that the existence and sovereignty of states are realities which can at most be exploited, but not simply liquidated. ' It is pointless to say that national sovereignty is a false principle . . . it is the only tool that will enable us at present to return to some degree of international order ', he wrote in the summer of 1937. In another letter he said of this problem, which greatly preoccupied him : ' For states are not simply vast masses of power, but instruments which, whatever their doctrine, require for their survival a certain degree of cooperation which they will promote after their own manner, and which would be impossible if states did not exist.'[113]

Yet Moltke, in his moral, intellectual and political radicalism, was able to see more realistically many individual aspects of the situation and its development than was Trott, whose grasp of the total conception, however, was closer to reality. In his talks with English politicians during the 1930s, Moltke always put forward the view that too much stress had been laid on Versailles in accounting for the rise, the success, and the practical foreign policy of National Socialism. For this reason, he told Lord Lothian in 1935, any policy of appeasement would, by definition, be mistaken; it would be far better to defend the existing rudiments of international order.[114] He never shared the opinion that concessions to Hitler would strengthen liberal forces in Germany by depriving Hitler of his ostensible grievances, but insisted instead that diplomatic victories would only mislead the Führer into basing his foreign policy upon the speculation that Britain would remain neutral in the event of war in Europe.[115] At the beginning of 1939 it was already patent to him ' that it is no longer a case of how to carry on until the fall of the dictatorships, but in fact of how to prevent the other countries of Western Europe either becoming the prey of those régimes or evolving similar régimes themselves.'[116] And in the summer of 1940 he energetically opposed a renewed inclination, even in members of his own circle, to exploit politically the victory over France and what was now her evident ' willingness to enter Europe on the basis of the *fait accompli* '.

In a letter to Graf Yorck at this time, he wrote : ' We would be destroying the spiritual ties with the best elements in other countries, if we sought to reconcile them with a situation which obviously cannot be allowed to endure . . .'[117] His comment that the ' demolition expert ', Hitler, had ' facilitated rebuilding . . . by his removal of the façade ' sought to express the feeling that the campaign had shown traditional European power politics to be utterly unworkable : the claims of one power had been swept aside with almost casual ease, while the triumph of the victorious power had done nothing to alter fundamentally the political relations between the two peoples.

Trott, on the other hand, counselled his English friends and political acquaintances to adopt a firm attitude towards Hitler. Yet, like Goerdeler, he seems to have long considered as both right and necessary the voluntary concessions, including territorial ones, made by the British to German national susceptibilities.[118] Obviously he was not unfamiliar with the idea that a Germany whose justified national demands had been satisfied would be better prepared and better situated to revolt against Hitler. Thus in November 1939, when he was in the United States, he communicated this conviction to an American friend : ' . . . If a solution had been found to Danzig, there would have been no further aggression – because the anti-Nazi mood in Germany would have been able to crystallise . . .'[119] That he himself was not interested in territorial goals – and in this he differed deci-

sively from Goerdeler – is shown by a lecture he gave at this time
to the Yale Club in which he described it as absolutely necessary
for the Western powers publicly to guarantee the German frontiers of 1933, if the German generals needed for the *putsch* were
not to be scared off.[120] For a long time he went on hoping that
the spiritual and political crisis in Germany, which was so intimately connected with the National Socialist movement, would
provide opportunities and footholds for socialist development,
or at least prepare the way for it; the fermentation that was in
process might, he thought, produce results. Since he also had an
unerring faith in the qualities of the German people, he constantly urged in his correspondence and conversations with Britons and Americans that the Anglo-Saxon world should erect a
' strong bulwark against war ', including rearmament, and at
the same time display ' an attitude of solidarity with the urgent
unrest in Germany '.[121] While able to understand the increasing
identification of ' National Socialist ' with ' German ' – ' I see
clearly enough why this is so ' – he indignantly repudiated it as
' basically false '.[122] He further condemned as provocative,
attempts by London to organise a system of alliances against
the aggression of Berlin.[123]

It should not be forgotten in this connection that Trott regarded
Anglo-German collaboration – not without emotional motivation – as spiritually and politically crucial to the pacification and
unification of Europe; for this reason the increasing gulf between
Germany and Great Britain, between individual Germans and
individual Britons, was agonising for him, and he sought des-
perately to combat it. Doubtless, too, he was deeply hurt by the
gradual change which he noticed in the attitude of some of his
English friends towards himself. Moreover, during 1938 he was
not in Europe at all; this was the year of the most active appeasement policy, the year in which Hitler's policy of blackmail in
foreign affairs was at its most blatant – in other words, the twelve
months preceding the war when international politics were in
a state of crisis. This period in England saw that change in the
psychological climate which brought her to adopt a more intransigent policy towards Germany. During that year Trott was,
geographically speaking, remote from all that was going on and

was thus unable to assess the full extent of the strain on Britain's readiness to make concessions. But if his statements during 1938 and 1939 sometimes betray considerable irritation at Anglo-Saxon moral and political self-righteousness, he nevertheless continued to adhere to his vision of a close Anglo-German friendship; and if he waxed vehement in the face of unjust criticism of the German national character, he denied with equal vehemence that the motives and arguments for his defence were inspired by nationalism. He saw no less clearly than Moltke that a system ' that has threatened or which already holds sway over the whole of the rest of Europe and which cannot be changed from within, can only be regarded as a régime of force, and it would mean surrender on the part of Europe were she to accept this as final '.[124]

Again, in 1939, during his negotiations with Anglo-American politicians, Trott had put forward a clearly defined European concept. In a memorandum written for Lord Halifax towards the end of 1939, he pleaded for cooperation ' for a constructive European future ', and it is significant that in this memorandum he ascribed to the German working classes a special aptitude for politics within the total framework of Europe; firstly, because they had been alienated from Communism by the Russo-German pact, and secondly because they still maintained a ' strong tradition of international cooperation and rational politics '.[125] Notes written at this time reveal his idea of Europe's future.[126] This would approximate to ' the example of the United States of America whose common national frontier and whose customs and currency union have *prima facie* excluded the possibility of internal armed conflict '. He was fully aware of the problem inherent in the superior German industrial system and, to relieve the resultant stresses, he proposed ' common European action for economic development ' which would be ' something along the lines of the League of Nations' loans to Greece and Austria ', Africa, the Far East and South America, ' organised on the basis of large syndicates '. Undertakings of this nature would further bring about ' changes of outlook ', so leading to cooperation elsewhere: this, introduced as the motive for European unification, presages the development aid of later decades. He further suggested that there should be a ' pan-European civic status, and a common supreme court of law ', as well as communal European fighting forces. His formulation was based on the assumption of inevitable German defeat, and his warnings against a ' super-Versailles ' after the war are emphatic. A harsh peace would only serve to activate the German ' persecution complex ', provide material for demagogues, and put obstacles in the way of the incorporation of Germany into a new Europe; there was even a danger that, were the Germans again to be humiliated by the Allies, they would take refuge in Bolshevism or even ' National Bolshevism '. Thus it was of great importance to announce moderate war aims well in advance : the Allies must assure Germany that she would be granted an ' equitable basis for national existence ', and that her frontiers of 1933 would be respected.

It might be said that with these plans Trott was not only obeying the impulse of reason, but was also putting forward a wholly acceptable proposal for translating that impulse into practice. The question of whether his programme as a whole was realistic – leaving aside the somewhat implausible idea of European citizenship and European fighting forces – cannot, however, be answered. And whereas the ideas propounded then and later by the National Conservative Opposition would not only have impeded Europe's progress in political and spiritual matters, but would indeed have meant retrogression, Trott's ideas were remote from the reality of Europe, probably because they were too much ahead of their time. But it is equally possible, given the hypothetical case of a new government imbued with such a concept, that relief from the pressure hitherto exerted by Germany, and the repudiation of the European situation which had been partly responsible for this state of affairs, would have engendered sufficient momentum for a general movement towards European coalitions. Moltke's ideas at this time – he adhered to them at least until 1941 – were Utopian then, and would still be so today. In his memorandum written in 1941, *Ausgangslage, Ziele und Aufgaben* (' Initial Situation, Aims and Tasks '), he briefly described his fundamental concept of ' a pan-European state divided up into smaller, non-sovereign state structures ' which, quite aside from the ideological elements and those relating to constitutional law, presented few real possibilities for Europe.[127] But what is of vital significance in these European plans is not this or that fantastic detail nor the occasional botched outline; such failings are common to all preliminary plans. What is of significance is the recognition, repeatedly formulated by Trott and Moltke, that in Europe the end of the politics of force, of nationalism and of the concept of race if it had not already arrived, must be induced, and that, to make European federation possible, the ' preponderance of the former major states of Germany and France must be abolished '. These men had thus correctly grasped the fundamentals of the problems besetting Europe at that time, and had they been able to translate their insight into practical politics, there might have been a real chance of reshaping the European order, whatever concessions reality or the political self-determination of other European states might justly have demanded. At the very least, a Germany governed by such principles would have been far more acceptable to Europe.

## Plans for a Postwar Europe

Until the end of 1941, the Kreisau Circle exerted little or no influence upon the National Conservative Opposition group. But with the growth of closer contacts, the impact of Kreisau's ideas, especially on foreign policy, was unmistakable. Between the time of the Polish and the French campaigns, Beck had clearly inclined to the conviction that Germany's new position of hegemony should be preserved in a non-National Socialist state. Yet before the Wednesday Club in June 1942 – a year and a half after Popitz's lecture on the imperial concept – he spoke of ' areas . . . which could not be made into living members of the national state ', and went on to say that God had created peoples ' without any predetermined order of rank, and no cultural people could be wholly self-reliant '. Though, in the future, competition between states was inevitable and would lead as it always had done in the past to disputes, such questions must be decided by bodies ' recognised as the overriding authority '.[128]

A particularly clear instance of this development is Goerdeler. Whereas in the spring of 1941 he was still proposing to the British government that it should sanction European coalitions on a regional basis – the virtual recognition, that is, of a Central Europe organised by Germany, and hence the recognition of German leadership on the continent[129] – he proceeded to whittle down his claims until finally, in the middle of 1943, he wrote that the peoples of Europe must ' find their way freely and independently towards a lasting, peaceful federation in which neither Germany nor any other state would claim supremacy '.[130] With characteristic impulsiveness he set full sail for Europe and had already begun to prepare a European Economic Ministry, a European Army and a European Ministry of Foreign Affairs. With equally characteristic optimism he suggested that ' it would not be difficult to agree as to details '. In going on to demand not only the survival of national states but their full ' independence in all decisions ' he appears to be unaware of any contradiction. A few months previously he had expressed the same kind of ideas in a memorandum destined for the generals.[131]

Needless to say, the leading National Conservatives were not wholehearted converts to the Kreisau outlook. Some of the remarks in Hassell's diary reveal a certain uneasiness behind his approbation of the younger men's ideas of future foreign policy, and even something of the irritation felt by men like Hassell and Goerdeler at the reckless jettisoning of values and concepts which to them were by now almost second nature.[132] Hence it was psychologically impossible for the old National Liberal, Goerdeler, to surrender the idea of the sovereign German nation state derived from the national claims of 1848 and Bismarckian politics; nor could he voluntarily renounce territory which he regarded as German and as part of that nation state. Yet it may be assumed that as Chancellor in 1943 or 1944 Goerdeler would not have allowed this or that territorial demand to stand in the way of peace negotiations. In his memoranda in those very years, however, he clung with avowed tenacity to every claim that he had ever put forward as ' a vital German question ', while at the same time sincerely declaring that within the European federation ' internal European frontiers would play a progressively smaller rôle'.[133] Had it ever come to talks between the British government and the German Opposition, Churchill could not have attached any credence to such statements, uttered as they were by a man who, almost in the same breath, promised Lithuania to Poland in order that Germany could demand the eastern frontier of 1914. It should not, of course, be forgotten that Goerdeler was a man whose sense of justice and reason led him to demand certain frontiers because he did in fact regard them as reasonable and just. Finally, it should be remembered that his generation had experienced certain disputes, such as that between Sudeten Germans and Czechs, as serious conflicts which had arisen quite independently of Hitler and would therefore still require a solution after the latter's departure.

Since the solution which was actually put into practice in 1945 was probably beyond the range of his imagination – he had only considered resettlement for areas of very mixed ethnic groupings[134] – the question as he saw it could only be settled by the determination of frontiers. Seen in this way, his territorial claims were intended to have a therapeutic function with a view to a permanent postwar order. It apparently never occurred to him that his reason and justice were orientated exclusively towards German interests, and that it was German wounds alone that he sought to heal. In a report written while he was under Gestapo arrest, he was still able to write, ' Germany remains a Reich ', and then proceed to advocate the territorial demands of that Reich as the panacea for European pacification.[135] Indeed he never quite lost the sense of the strength Germany had acquired between 1939 and 1942. Significantly, he never desired a German-Polish agreement regarding the eastern frontier; rather, he sought ' to negotiate an understanding with the British government " over " Poland '.[136] And in a memorandum of December 1942 he delineated the frontiers of the Balkan states which, though he expressly repudiated the Vienna award as a ' farce ', were yet wholly in the spirit of that award.[137]

For Hassell, then as always, Bismarck's Reich was the crux of his political thinking. It is true that, with his knowledge of foreign affairs, he did not, like Goerdeler, harbour any illusions about the harshness of the peace terms that would be imposed on Germany, whatever her government,[138] but for a long time he clung to the hope that he would succeed in salvaging ' at least the rudiments of Bismarck's Reich '. He was no doubt able to envisage

E

more clearly than any of his friends the European community of interests, but as a diplomat thinking in terms of spheres of interest and zones of influence, he probably looked with a sceptical eye on the possibility, envisaged by Moltke and Trott, of a political realisation of those common interests on a basis of voluntary unification. Again, even more than Goerdeler, he was interested in the preservation of a specifically German internal structure, and he therefore immediately understood Trott's concept that Germany's special character and her rôle of intermediary between East and West required political safeguards. Whereas a short while before he had regarded Germany as the ' heartland ' of Europe, a magnet exerting a determining influence upon the states within its field, some of the passages he now wrote might well have been by Trott himself. Germany should assert her claim ' not only to political but also to spiritual independence ' if she was to exercise her unifying function in Europe; hence she must commit herself ' neither to the East nor to the West '.[139] In this sense, too, he wished to preserve the Reich, even in truncated form.

Thus the tactics by which Goerdeler and Hassell sought ' to extricate the Reich from war on two fronts '[140] were determined entirely by the concepts and methods of traditional European statecraft. They themselves felt that the Soviet Union was the most threatening of outside dangers. It was a threat wilfully conjured up by Hitler in 1939 by his pact with Moscow; at that time it was still in some degree latent, and moreover Hitler's rapid victory in France had seemed partially to vindicate his policy. But his attack on the Soviet Union, after the failure there of the *Blitzkrieg*, had turned a latent threat into a very acute danger. Now in 1939 the National Conservative Opposition had postulated in the British the same need for a bulwark against Russian aggression as they felt themselves and had sought to use this as a platform for German-British understanding. What could be more natural than to assume that with every military victory by the Soviet Union, London's anxiety would increase as did that of Germany? Was it possible for liberal, Christian, democratic England to accept the fact of a Bolshevist Germany? Must not the British, for reasons of state, wish to prevent the balance of Europe being destroyed,

as it would be by a Soviet victory? And was not therefore the survival of Germany as a viable country, if not as an ally, now more
than ever before, of vital interest to Great Britain? After the fall
of Hitler, this would form the point of departure for the government of a Germany restored to sanity and decency.

These ideas predominated in Hassell's thinking, and upon them
Goerdeler rings the changes in his memoranda, whether destined
for British readers or for German generals.[141] They recalled the
British policy of appeasement, which was partially directed towards the exclusion of Russia from Europe, and also the fact that
during the 1920s Britain had already intervened to prevent too
great a debilitation of Germany by France.[142] Precisely because the
situation was now far more dangerous and Germany's defeat
would involve infinitely more serious consequences, they argued
that the chances of cooperation were proportionately increased.
Further, there were three additional reasons making, at least, for
an improved tactical position. Since France was now completely
eliminated, England need no longer take account of the Quai
d'Orsay. The neutral states, on the other hand, could not be left
out of consideration, and it was these latter who, because of the
special nature of the Soviet threat, would throw in their lot for
the preservation of the Reich.[143] Above all there was the Polish
question which had been ignored in 1939. For Poland, on whose
behalf Britain had after all entered the war, was more exposed
than any other country to Russian expansionism. Yet Britain could
not protect her, and only the German Army stood between Moscow and Warsaw. If a new German administration were to guarantee the 1938 eastern frontier of Poland, and if it were to declare
itself ready to defend that frontier by force of arms, the British
government would be bound to accept such an offer, if only because of moral pressure by the Free Polish Government.[144] Thus
in Goerdeler's memoranda intended for the military at this time
the predominating demand was that action must be taken against
Hitler so long as the army was capable of holding the eastern
frontier of Poland.[145] It is particularly ironical historically that
the very country on whose account Hitler had involved Germany
in hostilities was now to serve the Opposition as a pretext to
extricate the Reich from that same war. Again, it might be seen as

a variant, but one with a positive slant, of the pledge concept as applied to Belgium in the First World War. The whole idea amounted to an offer, for British consumption, that there should be in some sort a return to the customary policy of a balance of power and that Germany should serve Britain as a ' Continental sword '.

All the communications addressed to England by this Resistance group were either determined or inspired by the political recipe outlined above. In order to impart these ideas to politicians in Britain, Hassell even made a kind of open avowal. In September 1943, an article had appeared in *Nineteenth Century* which strongly advocated the retention of the traditional British balance-of-power policy in Europe, rejecting equally strongly the division of the continent into Russian and Anglo-American zones of influence; instead of this, there should be a return to ' middle Europe ', by which the writer no doubt understood the *cordon sanitaire* of prewar days. To this Hassell replied in the December issue of *Auswärtige Politik* in which, after an ironical allusion to the ' sympathetic ' treatment given to France in the English periodical, he suggested that ' the writer does not hesitate to toy with the possibility – which he twice mentions, though in guarded terms – of a revision of British policy towards Germany, i.e. of falling back *faute de mieux* upon Germany to counterbalance Russia '. He followed this up with the comment : ' A naïve outsider might go on from this conclusion to formulate the audacious idea that it was but a short step from such a view to the realisation that a strong and healthy nucleus would be needed to maintain a balance in Europe, and that that nucleus was Germany.' Yet even a more sober and less optimistic attitude to what was in fact the policy pursued by Britain would inevitably lead the reader of the article to conclude that were the ' organised " central zone " to prove impractical, it must then be recognised that a Germany with unimpaired powers would be the only antidote to a Europe falling progressively under Russian influence '. Somewhat ominously, Hassell then continues : ' It is in a way an amusing thought, and one which it would be fascinating to pursue, that conversely a strong and healthy Germany would be for Russia the only effective antidote to overwhelming Anglo-American ascendancy.' With this he comes to the heart of the matter and makes a formal proposal :

> European balance? Agreed! . . . If it is correct – as the writer of the article asserts – that the object of the ' new ' balance of power policy is to create a new order in Europe dependent on its own inner strength, no objection could be raised . . . But even from a purely physical standpoint, balance on the Continent demands that the point of gravity must be sought in the proper place, that is, at the centre. All efforts to achieve a balance which is not centred upon a strong and healthy German nucleus are doomed to failure . . . This has nothing to do with German supremacy, but only means an order which corresponds to the nature of things and one which is therefore to the advantage of all concerned. We are in complete agreement with the writer in so far as he says that the nature of the peace must be determined by the permanent factors of the European situation.

But why, Hassell concludes by asking, ' is there absolutely no indication that responsible men on the other side might be prepared to draw some sort of conclusion from the recognition – apparently shown by the writer of the article – of the Russian threat to the " central zone " and to the whole of Europe?'[146]

In an introductory note to Hassell's article, Friedrich Berber, the editor of *Auswärtige Politik*, wrote that though this should have appeared rather earlier, it had certainly lost none of its topicality in the meantime. Thus Hassell's article, appearing as it did in a semi-official publication, might even be regarded as a kind of peace-feeler from the régime. No doubt Hassell assumed that his name would exclude any such misunderstanding. Indeed the somewhat despairing concept it represented did remotely resemble certain hopes nourished by Hitler and his entourage, in that it involved speculation on tension and conflicting interests among the Allies. The essential difference was that the conspirators offered as partner a Germany without Hitler, a Germany prepared to make a reasonable peace. Goerdeler knew well enough that ' it would be childish to dream that the two powers [Britain and the Soviet Union] might part company during the war '.[147]

But given these two prerequisites, it was believed, the laws of European politics which Hitler's existence had suspended would again come into force. The assumption was, of course, false, and failed to take into account either the political influence and aims of the United States or the fact that Hitler had turned the war into total war, in as much as he had stabilised what was surely an unnatural alliance between Communist Russia and the capitalist West, an alliance upon which the latter, at any rate, pinned its hopes for a comprehensive and enduring postwar order.

The practical outcome of this, kept constantly before the eyes of the German Resistance by their American contact, Allen Dulles, was that ' one war ' could only be followed by ' one peace '.[148] Anyone living abroad, like Gisevius, was able to grasp this fact. But within Germany the National Conservative Opposition was increasingly haunted by the threatening spectre of 1918, the memory of which had already played an important part in the Sudeten crisis; now the spectre was beginning to acquire the substance of flesh and blood, assuming the form of a super-Versailles, revolution at home and, with the advance of the Red Army, Bolshevisation. All this might possibly be averted, as long as there remained any capacity to act and any strength to fight. In such situations people will clutch at straws. Thus in the summer of 1944 Goerdeler, Hassell and Beck clung to their concept in spite of the demand for unconditional surrender, and sought desperate alternatives as the room for tactical, let alone strategical, manoeuvre dwindled. Finally, they were debating whether they should merely open the sluices in the West, so producing sufficient pressure to reinforce the dam in the East. Beck and Goerdeler, however, had already realised by the spring of 1944 that they could no longer reckon without Moscow. The proposal they transmitted at this time to Dulles dealt with special negotiations with the Western powers and the simultaneous or immediately consecutive occupation of Germany from the West, whereupon the Western Allies would assume the function of intermediaries with the Soviet Union.[149] During the final days before the 20 July plot, they seem to have become resigned to the view that after the *coup d'état* they would have to begin negotiations both with the West and with Moscow.[150]

Their plans, then, were concerned with salvaging the German state. That was altogether to be expected and was neither morally nor politically indefensible. The duty to commit political suicide cannot be postulated, even if a people's name has been heavily burdened with guilt. Yet there also took place a profound change in their idea of Germany's relationship towards other countries and towards Europe. It was not only that, as from the beginning of 1942, they withdrew the claim they had temporarily put forward to the leadership of Central, if not the whole of, Europe; Goerdeler himself had reverted to being, as he had been in the twenties and thirties, the revisionist politician in the ' Greater Germany' tradition (although now on the defensive); and Hassell had again become the advocate of the ' Lesser Germany' Reich concept. But alongside this return to the normality of prewar European politics, we find a new, forward-looking idea. Whether as a Greater or Lesser Germany, they are now ready to incorporate the Reich into one great entity, the community of the states of Europe. Goerdeler had held with obstinacy to the imperial concept and to the boundaries of 1914, but once having grasped the concept of European federation in which Germany, forfeiting all claims, would be incorporated, he adhered to the latter with no less tenacity. Hence the change indicated not only a return to the former European normality, but at the same time entry into the normality of a future, then still hypothetical, Europe.

While this is a clear demonstration of Kreisau influence, the members of that circle themselves experienced a change as a result of their contacts with the Conservative National Opposition. After what must clearly have been violent clashes on the desirability of retaining the Reich concept,[151] the Conservative leaders were able to impose their ideas in the teeth of the Socialists, and probably also against the convictions of Moltke himself. In *Grundsätze für die Neuordnung* (' Principles for the New Order '), drawn up in August 1943, there is a significant formulation: ' The Reich remains the supreme leading power of the German people.'[152] Even though this was immediately followed by the declaration that the Reich must be incorporated into the ' living community of European peoples', the adoption of the Reich concept was bound to have political consequences. The ideology of the Kreisau Circle acquired, as it were, some of the nationalist ballast. Of the members of that circle, Trott was most open to these ideas, for he had always insisted upon the necessity to safeguard the essential Germany and her special internal structure by means of a strong political carapace. It is, indeed, characteristic that in a comparatively late memorandum he demands a peace in which there should be neither surrender of territory nor any occupation of Germany.[153] It is even more characteristic that in the autumn of 1939 he still held the German frontiers of 1933 to be acceptable, whereas in a memorandum written in late April 1942 he advocated the restoration of free Polish and Czechoslovakian states, but ' within the framework of their ethnographic frontiers '. Thus between those years he had come to adopt Goerdeler's claim to the Sudeten areas and to at least some parts of West Prussia.[154] He too was looking for ways, not only of salvaging Germany's existence as a nation, but also of avoiding unconditional surrender; thus, in tactical matters of foreign policy, he found himself speculating on the antithesis between the Western powers and the Soviet Union – and that along very similar lines to Hassell and Goerdeler. If, as before in 1939, he sought to use the threat of German Bolshevisation and gradual political reorientation towards the East – for which the intransigent attitude of the Western Allies was partly responsible – to convince the Allies of the necessity to help the German Opposition against the East, he was clearly unaware that such a threat must detract from his own argument for an alliance between the Opposition and the West, namely their common spiritual and political view of the world. Were the threat not taken seriously, it would necessarily be ineffective, and if it were seen to be real, there could be small belief in any community of interests. He himself, like the other members of the Opposition concerned in the *putsch* of 20 July 1944, had never, and indeed never could have, considered what might be called an ' eastern solution '.

The feeling of kinship with the West was altogether genuine, especially against the menacing backcloth of Russia, even though Trott and his friends – and also Stauffenberg with his very similar views – desired to sustain the 'German way' in domestic affairs and to guard it against foreign intrusion; right up to the end, indeed, their political planning was based on their hope of a change in British policy. Even when in April 1944, in conversations with Dulles' intermediary in Switzerland, Gaevernitz, he depicted the Soviet threat in lurid colours, Trott was far from announcing or even threatening recourse to an 'eastern solution', as Gisevius supposes;[155] what he was trying to convey was that the German Resistance Movement, in order to obviate the need for an 'eastern solution', must effect a shift to the left. Again, his request that the Western powers should proclaim their readiness to welcome the inclusion of socialist leaders in a future German administration, would seem to have been a renewed attempt to induce the Allies to promise cooperation with a Resistance government.[156] Yet since the end of 1942 he had known at heart that unconditional surrender was inevitable[157] and he must, at an early stage, have given up his ambition of retaining Germany's territorial gains; eventually he must also have realised that Austria and even East Prussia had been lost.[158] Furthermore, despite his objection to any talk of collective guilt, he had declared as early as 1942 that he and his friends were ready to 'accept our due share of responsibility and guilt'.[159] Above all, he and other like-minded conspirators had always stood for a concept of Europe identical in content to his ideas of 1939 and connected with, but not dependent on, the hope of saving the Reich.

Thus it is not possible to draw a clear moral, spiritual or political distinction between the more radical members of the Kreisau group. Because the interests of the Kreisau socialists lay more in the direction of social policy, they were less sensitive to the surrender of external powers and to losses of territory, and hence were earlier prepared to recognise their inevitability. Leber, Reichwein and Leuschner, too, went on hoping naturally enough, until halfway through the war, that it would be possible for Germany to retain her territorial status of 1937. Yet to them there was no question of retaining Hitler's conquests, and it would appear that Leber showed little patience with discussions about the Sudeten territories and the eastern frontier of 1914.[160] It was further relatively easy for the Kreisau Circle, with its wholly Christian outlook, to accept the idea expressed in 1942 by Bonhoeffer in Sweden, namely that the immeasurable guilt accruing to Germany through the National Socialists no longer admitted of ' foreign-policy solutions ', and that action by the Resistance should and should be seen to be an ' act of repentance '.[161] Those who were unable to grasp this idea and who, in fact, looked for ' foreign-policy solutions ', were not in a position to understand that they were rejecting the only attitude that held any prospect of success in foreign affairs.

In an extreme situation the totally unpolitical thought may well be the genuinely political thought. It was, at any rate, early plain to Leber as well as to Moltke that Germany, even with a Resistance government, would have to reckon with unconditional surrender and considerable territorial sacrifices. They were quite familiar with the idea of political ' reparations ', and as a Silesian landowner Moltke had in 1943 already resigned himself to the loss of Silesia.[162] Not that this attitude indicated passivity in regard to foreign affairs. Moltke actively and purposefully sought contact with Resistance groups in occupied countries, looking upon this as ' practical European politics ', and as service in the name of a larger concept. Writing to an English acquaintance in 1942, he said that not only were he and his friends prepared to help the victors to ' win the peace ', but added the assurance that they also wished to help win the war. His relationship with the European *Résistance* should be seen in this context; furthermore, towards the end of 1943 he was to make some definite proposals to American contacts in Turkey. He told them that the group he represented held ' an unequivocal military defeat of Germany and her subsequent occupation to be absolutely essential on moral and political grounds '; proceeding from this premise, he considered the Allied demand for total surrender to be justified, in which event the prior negotiation of peace conditions must necessarily be precluded. Since, too, he and his friends believed that they were fundamentally in agreement with the West on spiritual and political matters, especially with reference to the future of Europe and Germany, future cooperation was assured more certainly than by formal guarantees which, as circumstances were then, could in any case not be made.

On these grounds, he and his group proposed full military co-operation with the Western Allies. Should the Allies be in a position to land in France and to follow up the operation immediately with the invasion and occupation of Germany, the group was prepared as soon as the Russian troop reached the Tilsit-Lemberg Line – always supposing that the eastern front could be held – to support the operation with all the means in their power, by withholding, for example, larger German formations. At the same time they would form a ' provisional anti-Nazi government ' which would be responsible for the non-military aspects of co-operation. This course of action would presuppose, however, that the operation be carried out at high speed if the German nation as a whole was to tolerate it, and even to see it as a justified and ' daring patriotic deed . . . comparable to General Yorck's Convention of Tauroggen '. In this case both military cooperation and the composition of the new German government could be discussed in advance. But if the Allies were planning an attack that would proceed as slowly as the Italian campaign, then the whole scheme would have to be dropped, because in that event ' German help could have no decisive effect on the war . . . but would only lead to the growth of another stab-in-the-back legend, while seriously compromising the German circles involved and rendering them incapable of future action '.[163] This plan, too, was a rescue attempt, a rescue from Communism, and quite apart from its military impracticability, it demanded of the Western Allies a policy towards Russia similar to that demanded by Goerdeler and Trott; furthermore, the cooperation of the German commanders in France was far from certain at this time, even though Stauffenberg sometimes thought otherwise; it is not even clear how many of the Kreisau Circle knew of and sanctioned the plan. Moltke was absolutely right, however, in his assessment of the group's own moral and political situation, and in his assessment of the contingencies arising from it.

Kreisau's view of Europe, then, was the Europe of the future. The roots of the National Conservative leaders were undoubtedly embedded in the old Europe. They had started out as representatives of a normal and – in the Europe of the thirties – inevitable nationalist revisionist policy but, their demands having been met (by Hitler), they did in fact revert to a form of power politics familiar to Europe but no longer suited to her needs. Their thinking, like their emotions, was centred on the Reich. Led astray, not by Hitler but by the unfolding power of Germany, they saw the Reich for a brief moment of time as the power that would lead and order Europe, and in this they were confusing Germany with Prussia and Europe with Germany. But even before the last phase of the war they had become aware of their error; their tragedy lay in the fact that, at the precise moment when they sought a *rapprochement* with Europe, Europe recoiled from them while they in turn believed that they could not act without European help. This was neither their fault nor yet that of Europe. Hitler had repulsed the Continent and the world, not from himself alone but also from Germany. Thus these men were unable to save the Reich from its destroyer whom they looked upon as a mere parasite having no real community of interests either with themselves or the Reich. No one with a sense of history could fail to be moved by the scene in Bismarck's friedrichsruh when, a few days before 20 July 1944, Ulrich von Hassell took his leave of the Reich – ' all the time on the verge of tears at the thought of the work that had been destroyed '. But they had already been able to link their own values and their own world to the concepts and ideas of a new epoch which found its most forcible expression in the Kreisau group. Thus in the final analysis, whether their *putsch* succeeded or failed, they were not without hope for a new Germany in a new Europe, and their action testified to their faith in that hope. For they had ended up by confirming everything that Trott had written as early as 1939 : ' Europe is something far deeper and more living than an ethnic or aesthetic dream image, and her spirit will emerge all the more clearly for her crushing self-surrender.'[164] That such a spirit could survive in Germany under Hitler's rule, and that eventually a group of patriots sought to put an end to his rule in that same spirit, gave to political thinking in Germany, in spite of the action's failure, an impulse which must never be allowed to fall into oblivion.

# Social Views and
# Constitutional Plans
# of the Resistance

HANS MOMMSEN

## Sociology of the Resistance

Helmuth von Moltke professed the conviction that the task confronting the opponents of National Socialism would not be fulfilled simply by eliminating all outward signs of tyranny; its main object must be a radical restructuring of the principles of social and political life. ' Only in this way ', he wrote to Lionel Curtis,[1] ' can we hope to persuade our people to rid themselves of the dominion of fear and horror; only if we are able to present them with a picture of what lies beyond the horror and the fear of the immediate future '; and this must be a picture worth working for, one that would justify a fresh start. To ' set up the human image in our fellow-citizens' hearts ' was to Moltke a ' question of religion, of education, of occupational and family ties, of the right relation between responsibility and justice ' – as also, we would add, a question of the social constitution. The realisation that the struggle against the National Socialist régime of force must be conducted on the basis of an independent social and political philosophy was not restricted to the Kreisau Circle. All those groups which can be regarded as belonging to the Resistance came increasingly to realise that, over and beyond a change of régime, there would have to be comprehensive social and political reforms.

The question of the social and political ideas of the Resistance touches on their historical and political origins – the Opposition was not merely a radical moral protest against lawlessness and violence. It further relates to the problem of whether there was any *real* alternative to the corruption from within of the German tradition of state, which terminated in the satrap-like rule of a clique of dishonest politicians subservient to an effete dictator who, in his bunker, was totally cut off from the realities of the Reich; that tradition owed its existence, perhaps, to German society's deep-seated aversion for the pluralism of 'natural' social systems. If there was such an alternative, it must manifest itself in the German Resistance. Indeed, the circles involved in the conspiracy of 20 July have been regarded as a political élite, a clandestine leading caste.[2] Their political thinking was representative of those elements in German society whose task it was to adapt that society to the conditions of a technological industrial civilisation – without any radical break in historical continuity – and also to provide an appropriate political constitution.

Such a possibility, however, is expressly repudiated by George K. Romoser[3] and Hannah Arendt,[4] who see in the German Opposition merely the continuation of the anti-democratic opposition to the Weimar Republic. The view held by a number of writers that the essential political nature of the Opposition was 'reactionary' argues against the hitherto predominant theory: the Resistance was the direct precursor of a restored democracy in Germany and hence the progenitor of the Federal Republic; alternately – and basically this is no different – the Resistance was a Communist contribution to the national mission of the DDR. It is not here proposed to deal with the second thesis (although it would be possible to show that it was true only in a restricted sense, even in the case of Communist-affiliated Resistance groups). Our concern here is to analyse the non-Communist Resistance, bringing in only Communist participation in the general German Resistance movement.

Not only Romoser, but also his opponents and supporters, have succumbed to the temptation of making retrospective judgments unrelated to the historical circumstances; in this way they eliminate the historical dimension to which the political thought of the Resistance in regard to modern pluralistic democracy belongs. But an historical analysis should endeavour to see the German Opposition in the general context of European crisis – a crisis arising from the transition into a modern, highly industrialised society. Further, it should enquire into the historical perspective and the antecedents of the movement, yet avoid the straitjacket of the terms 'progressive' and 'reactionary'.

We are not concerned in this enquiry with determining the frontiers between 'inner emigration' and political abstinence

on the one hand, and active resistance on the other, or with an-
swering the exceedingly difficult question of where, exactly, collaboration goes over into uncompromising opposition, or with the
degree of political importance to be accorded to the respective
political and religious centres of the Resistance. We shall restrict
ourselves here to those groups either directly or indirectly concerned with 20 July, thus excluding the Communist Resistance as
well as groups that were active abroad, whose social and political
ideas differed basically from those which evolved in the ambience
of the totalitarian state and out of the determination to effect
political reorganisation from within.

Advocates for the Resistance have repeatedly stressed that it
comprised people of all political persuasions and from all ' walks
of life '. Yet the lower middle class, almost unanimous in its support of the National Socialist experiment, was virtually unre-
presented. The conspiracy of 20 July, in spite of the active collaboration of leading socialists, was wholly unrelated to the mass
of working people; their reaction to a *putsch* could only be sur-
mised, and enquiries instigated by Delp revealed a disheartening
lack of support. The general view of the Kreisau Circle was
reflected in Trott's memoranda on foreign affairs up till 1944, in
which he spoke of widespread passivity among the workers.[5]
A determining factor was the early and effective decimation of
the illegal socialist and Communist organisations; this had led
Theodor Haubach to decide that underground activity could not
continue except on the basis of personal contacts.[6] Leuschner's
description of Germany as ' one enormous prison ' makes it easy to
understand why the Resistance lacked popular support. The
political thinking and planning of the Resistance in Germany –
as opposed to the *Résistance* outside – was much influenced by
the uncertainty of how the population, most of whom for most
of the time supported Hitler, would react.

The social structure of the active Opposition was comparatively
homogeneous. Its members were predominantly upper-class and
regarded themselves – unlike the ' dilettante régime ' which they
combated – as personally qualified to assume a leading rôle.
There was no significant distinction between ' *bourgeois* ' and
' socialist '. Reichwein, Mierendorff and Haubach were not merely

F

typical Social Democrat intellectuals, Leber was the complete opposite of a socialist official, and Leuschner and Maass had succeeded in discarding inhibitions of class as a result of their political activities and their experience under National Socialism. The group of former trade unionists, however, occupied a somewhat special position if only because, from the very beginning, they had taken an uncompromising stand against National Socialism; the same could not be said of the other conspirators, except in a few individual cases. The distinction between civilian and military, as also between aristocracy and middle-class was of little significance as regards the social structure of the Opposition; the large majority of the officers were middle-class ' notables ' in the best sense of the word.

With the exception of Leuschner, there was no one in the Opposition who could be regarded as a typical representative of the Weimar Republic. The socialists in the movement had nearly all opposed the official leaders of the Party and had strongly criticised the Weimar party system during the last stages of the republic. Political planning was crucially affected by the fact that, apart from Leuschner and Leber, there were no experienced parliamentarians either in the central group or in those immediately surrounding it, a fact which can only partially be accounted for by the political persecution and elimination of this section of the population. For professed or potential opponents of the Weimar Republic were remarkably numerous, and for this reason only can Romoser's contention that the Opposition represented the continuation of the ' conservative revolution ' be regarded as justified.[7] The utter disrepute attaching to the Weimar Republic even in the eyes of its one-time supporters – and this applies equally to those persons who were intimately connected with the Weimar coalition parties – contributed to the lack of enthusiasm manifested towards active resistance. But in all fairness to those supporters of the Republic, who continued to resist passively in the face of not inconsiderable reprisals, it should be said that it was far easier to go over to active resistance from the camp of the collaborators than from the camp of the acknowledged Opposition, and this both on psychological grounds and because of the control exercised by the police state.

Active resistance, in so far as it involved widespread conspiracy, demanded both disengagement – such as Max Weber postulated for the professional politician – and at least minimal material security. In this respect the preponderantly conservative or bureaucratic upper class was a nursery well adapted to the formation of an underground resistance and the potential exploitation of social and political positions of power. Until the war this class was less exposed than the middle and lower classes to the inroads of totalitarian coordination. Nor, during the time of the Republic, had its monopoly of the Diplomatic Corps, the administration and the army been broken; and while the upper class was not exactly exclusive socially, it preserved certain social attitudes which rendered it in some degree impervious to political pressure and demagogy. Its inherent solidarity can be seen, for example, in the fact that while opposition to the régime was freely expressed, word of this did not spread beyond those circles. The men who belonged to the nucleus of the Opposition had been socially in contact with each other either directly or indirectly before they ever thought of conspiracy. Their personal aversion to National Socialism was at the start a matter less of political conviction than of good taste, and the callous cynicism shown by National Socialist officials at all levels in their disregard of conventions must have appeared all the more repulsive in that it was combined with incompetence and corruption. The widespread disapproval of, and disassociation from, certain aspects of National Socialism evinced by well-informed circles where such reactions seemed entirely natural, as also by those whom disillusionment had turned into opponents of the régime, were of great significance in camouflaging active resistance. Hence the Gestapo was generally inclined to ignore hostile utterances as far as it was possible to do so, and only took action where there was little risk of political repercussions.

On the basis of the real if relative freedom enjoyed by the upper class in the formation of political opinion, Dahrendorf has described the early years of the régime as authoritarian rather than totalitarian.[8] The Opposition's much-criticised indecision, their failure to convert their words into deeds, as well as their often overoptimistic assessment of the chances of overthrowing the régime, is explicable as much by this upper-class integrity which proved ever more illusory as it is by the marked hostility and deep mistrust which they had to endure from the National Socialist *parvenus*. The social matrix of the Opposition partly accounts for the fact that – unlike the *Résistance* or the rudimentary ' German Popular Front '[9] – it never formed as it were a cumulative movement, nor did it ever acquire a label; the term ' German Freedom Movement ' was not adopted. It was not till 1944 that attempts were made to form a more comprehensive popular movement. Thus the Opposition was not a political ' movement ' with the avowed object of winning the support of unvoiced public opinion or the majority of the population which it would then, at least in theory, represent. It was as sincere and upright individuals that members of the Resistance groups approached the Allies, as ' notables ' invoking the support of institutions of which some, such as the General Staff (even if only under the *imprimatur* of Brauchitsch), were still extant and others, such as former parties and trade unions, were in abeyance. They saw themselves as a political leading caste, and their claim to represent ' the whole ' as legitimate simply by reason of their social position and concomitant political responsibilities.

Indeed it is quite evident from their proposed constitutions and the proclamations they had drawn up that the problem of legitimation was not of primary importance to members of the Opposition. Their discussions on the subject of the future new order in which, significantly, a corporative system figured, were no more concerned with the possible convocation of a constituent assembly than was Leuschner with the possible objections of future trade union members to the executive he had planned. The proposal impulsively put forward by Goerdeler in 1940 that a revolutionary government should at once be legalised by plebiscite met with determined opposition from the conspirators, who did not share his ' sanguine hopes ' as to the outcome of the voting. As in the case of the later coalition policy, the idea was to legitimise the new administration by including all those political elements thought to be relevant, excluding however Communists in general or those dependent on Moscow. On the other hand Popitz, with his strong and fundamentally *étatiste* views, was sharply critical of what he regarded as Goerdeler's parliamentarian 'coalition negotiations', although these were essential if things were to be kept under control after a successful *coup*. The conspirators were themselves inevitably compelled to attempt a 'revolution from above' by the very nature of the totalitarian state; in 1944 there was still considerable doubt about the extent of the support this might receive from a 'revolution from below' and whether the former would need legitimation by the latter.

The Opposition's social and political planning was influenced by the internal situation in the Third Reich in as much as this restricted effective resistance to an upper-class group integrated by personal ties, together with a few trade unionists who continued in opposition despite persecution, and an appreciable number of members of the officers' corps which had remained unaffected by coordination. Following the ruthless steps taken by the National Socialist government, with the support of the Conservative coalition partners, against their opponents of the left, it was predictable that the Opposition would rally round centres which might be described as 'residual' and which had largely or wholly survived the National Socialist policy of coordination because of their strong traditional ties with the Wilhelmian and Bismarckian eras. The relative homogeneity resulting from this allows us to build up, from the memoranda, plans and personal statements of the active Opposition, a model of its view of society which, in spite of many points of contention, shows in its main outline an astonishing consensus. Yet the underlying ideas were largely developed independently, and internal divergencies were sometimes so great as to be barely reconcilable. It is a view of society characterised by its comparative lack of concern for public opinion, by its idea of an 'organic' body politic which would not allow social and ideological antagonism to come to a head, turning them rather into an impulse beneficial to the community, and finally by its notion of a government that would be 'free of conflict'. This social image that contrasts with the principles of parliamentary democracy and modern group pluralism would seem to be representative of political thought as it evolved clandestinely in National Socialist Germany. It was completely in

thrall to the concept of an independent ' German way '; none
the less, there can be no doubt that it agreed on many counts
with the programmes of the Resistance movements outside Germany.

## Overcoming Mass Society

Ralf Dahrendorf has pointed out that all the Resistance groups –
with only one exception, the Communists – ' could be described
as defenders, wittingly or unwittingly, of the *ancien régime* ',
and that this ' insurrection of tradition ' was also an insurrection
of ' the retroactive illiberalism and authoritarianism of the
past '.[10] Nowhere, he believed, had morality and liberalism diverged so far as in Germany, and it was legitimate to ask whether,
had the Resistance succeeded, this would not have led to an
authoritarian form of government. The question raised by
Dahrendorf is crucial in the assessment of the Opposition, yet
it would seem to be one less of conflict between liberalism and
authoritarianism than of conscious or unconscious orientation
towards a ' society devoid of conflict ', to use the term applied
by Dahrendorf to the German political tradition. The social
image of the active Resistance was not, as Dahrendorf implied,
inspired by the desire to restore the ' values and institutions ' of
the Weimar period; all groups rejected, at least in theory, the
idea of returning to an earlier *status quo*. Underlying the political thinking of the Resistance was the endeavour to find new
solutions, enabling Europe as a whole to recover from her spiritual
and political crisis, but their search for these solutions was conducted largely in the field of historical experience. What distin-
guishes this thinking from mere reversion to the past is its particular blend of traditional elements and socially Utopian ideas,
but it is nonetheless thoroughly conservative in the sense of Karl
Mannheim's distinction between conservative and liberal.[11]

Again, it would not be admissible to identify the Resistance
with the intrinsically problematical concept of the ' Conservative
revolution '.[12] For the Resistance represents a broad current that
had absorbed the cultural criticism of the twenties, not only from
German, but from what was already beginning to be pan-Euro-

pean thought, and hence does not fit into any pattern of ' right and left '. The Youth Movement, experience in the trenches, Nietzsche's philosophy and neo-Kantianism were as instrumental in determining the character of the Resistance as they had been in determining the psychological and historical preconditions for the National Socialist breakthrough. Of comparative insignificance are the differences in outlook as between the generation which had known imperial Germany and had felt that the 1918 fiasco was the beginning of the end, and the generation which received its formative political experience in the period when the traditional party system appeared to be in course of reconstruction as a result of the reformative efforts of groups as different as the Popular Conservatives and the Social Democratic internal opposition. The conflict which arose during the final weeks before the attempted *putsch*, and which derived from their different historical and political points of departure, was overlaid by the shared experience of enforced inactivity, or rather of fruitless activity. Throughout their writings – whether in Bonhoeffer's *Rechenschaftsbericht* (' Rendering of Accounts '), in Haubach's and Leuschner's letters, or in Leber's diary – the conspirators reveal the tormenting awareness that they, an ' intermediate generation ', must wait, and wait perhaps in vain, for a future that was their responsibility but was still obscure – and this at a time when all the talk was of ' attack ' and of ' action '. Kreisau thinking, like that of the Socialists, was concerned with the form this future would take; what they wanted – and upon this the generations differed – was a new beginning, a clean break with past history. Moltke wrote of ' starting time anew ', and Schlange-Schöningen declared : ' We must build up the new state, not so that the infernal cycle of German history repeats itself, but so that we *begin a new* history. It is not true that the era of dictatorship is beginning; it has ended . . .'[13] The determination to begin anew is most clearly evident in the substitution of European solutions for the old thinking in terms of the nation state; it is found in Leuschner, Haubach, Mierendorff and Leber, as in Moltke, Yorck and Trott, and these men compelled the one-time *Völkisch* or Nationalist Conservatives to think again.[14]

Nevertheless, socio-political thinking turned mainly upon the

unresolved German antithesis: traditional social order and un-
differentiated mass society. That criticism which had formed the
basic impulse of the Youth Movement, and which condemned the
impoverishment of social and spiritual life by technology and
faceless administration, imposed the question as to what constructive forces could be mustered in the social field to combat
' fragmentation ' and ' collectivisation ', the ' big-city mentality ',
the tyranny of ' imagined consumer requirements ', the loss of
a ' feeling for quality ', the ' struggle for position ', the ' cele-
brity cult ', the senseless ' hurry ' of modern life, and finally what
was felt to be a superficial ' *bourgeois* way of life '. While all
the Resistance groups differed in their interpretation of the causes
underlying the social consequences of extreme industrialisation,
they were unanimous in condemning those consequences, which
they described as ' stereotyping ' (*Vermassung*); they were concerned with finding a means of protecting the forces responsible
for shaping society from being overwhelmed by the autonomous
development of the worlds of technology and big business, and of
preventing the suffocation of the individual sense of responsibility, and the personal mode of existence by ' hydrocephalous
organisations ' and anonymous undertakings.

Cultural-critical reflexions of this kind found total confirmation in the social reality of National Socialism, which had originally made use of the same irrational and retrogressive currents,
and had been lauded for having vanquished the forces of destruction in the ' life of the people '. The massed parades, the frenetic
applause of crowds drunk with propaganda, the paramilitary
organisations in which stereotyped social behaviour was enforced
in the guise of comradeship, seemed to justify apprehensions of
a ' mass existence '. The former socialist, Theodor Haubach, saw
in Breughel's paintings ' a premonition of the consequences of
the mass age ' which causes the ' masses, having escaped the control and discipline of religion, and alone and alienated from their
gods, to degenerate into grotesques, monstrosities and ghosts '.[15]
Stereotyping as the cause of religious, cultural and political decline seemed to be related to the increasingly ' materialistic ' attitude and to the surrender of all values transcending the purely
utilitarian. Dietrich Bonhoeffer, who declared that the alternative

lay between ' proceeding towards an age in which the best would be selected, that is, an aristocratic order ' or towards ' uniformity of all outward and inner circumstances of human life ', spoke of a process of ' vulgarisation in all classes of society ' and believed that the real task lay in the ' rediscovery of buried qualitative experience '. Only in this way, he maintained, would it be possible to oppose ' every form of stereotyping '; the task of the church was not to impose the principle of equality, but to reaffirm the ' sense of human distinctions '. Nor was Bonhoeffer afraid to incur odium for his allegedly ' unsocialist mentality '.[16]

Thus the ' de-massing of the Masses ' (*Entmassung der Masse*) – to borrow the slogan-like title of Gerhard Ritter's memorandum written for the Freiburg circle – was the central theme of all the political and social plans for reform. ' A human type of the old school, upon whom his daily round leaves its indelible stamp,' wrote Einsiedel in his memorandum for the Kreisau Circle,[17] ' confronts a highly unstable mass type ' whose activity in modern industry no longer gives him inner satisfaction. The liberal thinking of similar-minded politicians, such as Goerdeler, recognised as one cause of the crisis the increasing ' soullessness of work processes ', and König saw progressive ' depersonalisation ' and the ' breeding of mass man ' as the result of over-precipitate and anorganic industrialisation. All these things, which can be summed up in the Marxist concept ' alienation ', led most of the Kreisau group to think in terms of ' personal socialism ' and to demand that the material and ideal existence of the working classes be safeguarded. ' It is time the twentieth-century revolution ', Delp wrote, ' was given a definitive theme, and the opportunity to create new and lasting horizons for humanity ' – namely, social security and the prerequisites for individual intellectual and religious development. So long as man's existence continued to be sub-human and without dignity, he would remain the victim of circumstances and be incapable either of prayer or of thought.[18]

Indeed the process of levelling and the concomitant breakdown of traditional social stratifications were of crucial significance, because those whom it affected were unable to keep pace and could not therefore adapt to their changing social rôles. The

majority of the Opposition saw this as a process largely conditioned by spiritual-historical factors, beginning with the breakdown of historically evolved social structures and proceeding inexorably towards the Bolshevist nightmare. In the eyes of the
Kreisau Circle one of the basic causes was man's loss of religious
certitude. Steltzer criticised modern man's ' secularised unpolitical individualism ' which, in intellectual matters, rejected all that
was metaphysical and sought to base human civilisation on purely
rational grounds.[19] It is interesting to note that ' unpolitical ' is
used in the sense of ' anti-social ', and equally that Steltzer, in his
study *Geborgenheit der Masse* (' Security of the Masses ') perceived in the collectivisation of the masses, and in the dominion
of ' mass undertakings ', the counterpart of rational individualism. Similarly, Gerstenmaier declared that secularisation had
brought about the decline of ' the natural community structure '.[20]

Delp, perhaps the most fertile of the Kreisau intellectuals,
saw this as a more complex process. He attributed it to two related developments; the first was external, that of the ' technical, social, scientific and economic world ', whose demands had
been too heavy for man, wholly preoccupied as he was in effecting an internal shift of emphasis; secondly, Delp suggests, the
process of rationalisation has thrown man back upon his own
individual resources, which are insufficient for him to escape
manipulation from without. Thus man, in so far as he sees himself merely as *Ens vegetativum* or *sensitivum*, must be brought
back to awareness of his ' person ' and must learn to take himself
seriously as ' part of the ordered scheme of things '. In individualism – the ' inner shift of emphasis in man ' – Delp perceived
an inherent historical logic and consistency; in this he differed
not only from Steltzer but also from the Cologne circle round
Otto Müller, Letterhaus, Gross and Jakob Kaiser, whose traditional reading of Catholic social teaching postulated a ' Christian
community and a general order of life ' that savoured of authoritarianism.[21] To Delp, a mere return to religion, to the ' Christian
state ', was no real solution; the only means towards man's integration into community and people and his return to religious
sensibility was the rediscovery of himself in the truest sense, so

as to embrace every aspect of life – the casting-off, that is, of his self-alienation.

Moltke and Yorck ascribed the problem of ' stereotyping ' to the disappearance of medieval universalism and the ever-greater encroachment of the modern rational bureaucratic state whose logical outcome was totalitarianism and which had successfully asserted its claim to the ' whole man '.[22] The hypertrophy of the territorial and national state involved the concentration upon the latter of all loyalties and ties, while all the energies that should have been devoted to the needs of smaller communities had been harnessed in the service of the state order, an order that, to the individual, was but a faceless, bureaucratic machine, thus destroying ' his inner allegiance to his country '. It was a process Moltke considered to have been reduced to the absurd in the totalitarian state, which had become the sole mediator of forms of expression such as art, education, language, and had rendered all normative values relative; its necessary collapse must also involve the ' destruction of the idol of state ' and leave behind a vacuum which would demand the creation of a new political cohesion on the basis of ' the greatest possible number of the smallest possible communities ' where man as an individual would be taken seriously. To Moltke, recovery from mass existence meant the elimination of the state in its modern, mechanistic, hypertechnical form, and the creation of non-national areas to be occupied by spontaneously formed communities and autonomous bodies, after the manner of subsidiaries.

This conception, which is reminiscent of Proudhon, demands the reintegration of the isolated individual into manageable groups where there can be a reawakening of a sense of responsibility and where true fellowship can flourish. In this way, Moltke believed, the revival of self-discipline would be linked to religious and metaphysical values by means of which the claim of the state upon the individual would be limited and made relative. ' An unbelieving mass ', wrote Moltke in 1939,[23] ' will sell itself to any politician, but a class of believers will not.' In formulating this concept, Moltke went beyond the traditional German Protestant line of argument; and in just the same way Delp was critical of the hierarchic bureaucracy of the Catholic Church for having lost sight of the fact that man is the *raison d'être* of church life. These two men formed the poles of the Kreisau discussions, and it was from them that the circle's thinking received its distinctive imprint.

Thus the sum of the Kreisau proposals was the overcoming of mass existence, not by a return to liberal individualism, but by the creation of a synthesis which would give pride of place to man as a member of a community. ' The key to their common endeavour is the desperate attempt to preserve the core of personal, human integrity ', wrote Trott in his memorandum in late April 1942.[24] ' The restoration of the inalienable, divine, and natural rights of the human being is their fundamental aspiration.' Delp expressed the personalist idea more profoundly than any under the concept ' theological humanism '. But similar trains of thought are to be found in nearly all the groups of the Opposition. At this time Leuschner was in close communication with Elfriede Nebgen and Jakob Kaiser through whom he came to know the ideas of Ludwig Reichhold,[25] which were then held to offer a valid solution. In 1942 Leuschner remarked that the age of individualist man had been followed by the age of collective man, and added : ' But there is yet a third, beyond individuality and collectivity. It is not a compromise but something higher, something different: the person.' This expresses the Kreisau formula exactly.

Leber, by comparison, was more pragmatic. He did not believe in government by the masses and argued strenuously against the ' truly grotesque ideas about mass rule ' held by his own Party, for he regarded authority and firm leadership of the masses as indispensable. He, too, however, was no less unequivocally opposed to the anonymity of a bureaucratic political machine which would exclude the ' militant personality ', and considered that Marxist evolutionary fatalism represented the basic error of socialist theory. ' For in it the value of the individual character must perish, organising ability, not creativeness, now being the desirable accomplishment'; the socialist concept of the ' masses ' overlooked the fact that man was not a calculable entity. Both Marxism and liberalism erred in their underestimation of man's irrational ties.[26] Like Kreisau, Leber demanded room for the development of personality; unlike them, he enjoyed an unbroken relationship with the workers; he was wholly without Kreisau's almost hostile mistrust of the masses, perhaps because he did not overestimate them, and he did not make use of the overworked slogan of ' stereotyping '. Yet by temperament, and in his forward-looking aspirations, he resembled the members of the Kreisau Circle. In the same way that Leber unsparingly criticised the failure of his own Party, Delp reproached the church with having missed the opportunity of personal leadership. '. . . . This law, whereby the leadership is nameless and faceless, has been no less conducive to the stereotyping of our lives than has the anonymity of business, or the anonymous administration of party, state and economy.'[27] Thus, too, Trott demanded that ' new, personal forces ' should prevail.

With its basic assumption that the well-worn tracks of a departmentalised political machine must be abandoned and class restrictions eliminated from social action, the Opposition was carrying on the work begun in the twenties. In November 1931 Trott suggested that a new philosophy was needed that would not, like Hegel, grandiosely adumbrate a superannuated image of the world, but would start off with ' the realisation of a new idea of human personality '.[28] This implied the rethinking of the whole concept of state.

Although Goerdeler started from a very different political premise, he too deplored the ' fragmentation ' of man in modern society, attributing it to religious atrophy in everyday life, to the ' overrating of the material way of life ', to increasing specialisation and to the ' alarming growth of urbanisation '. He believed that progress in natural science and in modern technology had brought about a weakening of emotional ties and had destroyed the unity of mind, body and soul. He sensed, if not very clearly, that this called in question his patriarchal-liberal state image but failed to attribute any responsibility to the tradition of state itself. With the loss of feeling for the totality of the human being, he thought, the foundation for a harmonious policy that would engage equally all elements in the nation had also been lost. Hence the restoration of the political and social order which, since Bismarck's day, had been going awry, was essentially an

anthropological problem. In his political testament,[29] Goerdeler
asserts that man's existence must be organised on a broader basis,
and never for a moment did his fundamental optimism allow him
to doubt the feasibility of his idea – a man religious, nature-lov-
ing, unsophisticated, practical, energetic and ready to assume
public responsibility.

In one of his memoranda Goerdeler wrote: ' The question is
not that of capitalism or socialism, it is that of individualism
or collectivism.' His own answer to that question was in favour
of individualism, but it must be an individualism based upon
the location of the person in the community. His liberal credo –
and he rightly held the current expression 'liberalistic' (*liberalis-
tisch*) to be ' a catchword without any apparent meaning ' – was
combined with a strong, indeed patriarchal, sense of duty in
regard to social welfare. He unhesitatingly advanced social views
of Darwinian stamp when he declared that life was a struggle,
and held that it was one of the merits of National Socialism to
have brought this into evidence; yet it was, he said, ' a struggle
ennobled by obedience to God's commandments ',[30] and at heart
what he longed for was a harmonious order devoid of conflict.
The ordered, Christian family seemed to him the private model
for public life; it is not surprising that he should have advocated
education towards a ' sense of national community free of class ',
and have talked of ' reconciliation with the people '. The fact
that while in prison he reproached himself with neglect of his
family is indicative of the tragic contradictions he represents,
contradictions that are also discernible in the conflicting tendencies of the period to which he belonged. Goerdeler was closer
to the personalist thinking of Kreisau than his terminology might
at first suggest, though he had a much stronger tendency to look
for the solution to social problems in the historical experience of
the nineteenth century, which to him seemed ' happy ' experience.

## National Socialism and Bolshevism

The Opposition aimed, by diverse means, at a national and social
order based upon the autonomy of man; its extreme antithesis

was the Bolshevist system. This the Opposition regarded as the expression of total dehumanisation in all social and human relations. Nearly all the conspirators used the term Bolshevism as a synonym for complete and anarchic stereotyping, and their assessments of Stalin's Russia are full of clichés borrowed from right-wing and Nazi propaganda. But even those of them who had at first welcomed the advent of Hitler whom they regarded as the conqueror of Communism, soon recognised the similarity between the National Socialist and Soviet dictatorships. 'What in Germany is dirty brown sludge', Trott declared, 'is invested in Moscow with a harsh, Asiatic brutality.'[31] They saw National Socialism as the revolution from below, in radical opposition to the Western, Christian tradition, and as the destructive power whose avowed aim was the ' atomisation of the masses ', in the words of Schulenburg. It was not the authoritarian aspect of the National Socialist oligarchy which was the main object of criticism, but rather the parasitic nature of the system. Thus Beck, and after him Goerdeler, coined the term 'totality of policy' to counter the slogan 'total state' (*totaler Staat*) and Goerdeler regarded the system mainly from the viewpoint of 'fragmentation' and thus succeeded in assessing it more correctly than was often the case in theories of totalitarian dictatorship.

The extent to which the equation of National Socialism and Bolshevism influenced the thinking of the conspirators and turned them into advocates of natural social order is apparent from the fact that they grossly overrated the true political significance of the Russo-German pact of September 1939. Towards the end of that year, Commander Liedig wrote a memorandum[32] which throws light on the views of the Oster circle in the *Abwehr* and which is also representative of Beck's and Halder's political ideas. The writer paints a gloomy picture of a Bolshevist Germany. The NSDAP (National Socialist German Workers' Party) he maintained, was well on the way to effecting a second revolution, its machinery only a 'mask for subverting old national orders', while official ideology had degenerated into mere demagogy, and anti-Bolshevism had become an empty formula. For it would not prevent Hitler from succumbing to the attraction of the 'nihilistic conceptual vacuum outside the European com-

munity of nations'. Liedig further prophesied that National
Socialism would be absorbed '. . . intellectually no less than geo-
politically, into the Russian Asiatic zone that had now been thrown
open to it '. Hitler himself could only survive as ' Stalin's satrap ',
his ' Russian governor in Soviet Germany ', while the country
itself would ' at best become a Russian satellite, and at worst a
nation of helots under Russian domination '.

This prediction, born of hatred and depreciation of the adver-
sary, was accompanied by a rather more relevant analysis of Hitler's political system. ' He has but one political trick up his
sleeve – a revolutionary dynamic subversive of all those historical
ties and all the cultural associations that have in the past been the
pride and honour of Europe.' This ' Bolshevism ' cliché, however, led the writer to conclude falsely that Hitler had now taken
the decisive step towards ' dynamic coexistence ' with Bolshevist
Russia, thus finding himself compelled to proceed ' in the near
future from the first revolution to the second, from National
Socialism to Bolshevism '. The idea was proved wrong, at any rate
so far as foreign policy was concerned, by Germany's attack on
Russia. Hassell, on the other hand, had forecast an inevitable
clash between Hitler and Stalin. As regards internal affairs, however, the idea was of some political relevance, for fear of
' national Bolshevism ', whatever its cause, was a determining
factor, above all in the case of the Conservative Opposition and
the army. In Kordt's and von Etzdorf's memorandum written
at the end of 1939[33] we read that Germany had ' never been
so close to chaos and Bolshevism '. In Scheffler's[34] memorandum
to the Department of State, written at Trott's instigation in late
1939, there is express mention of the danger of revolutionary
repercussions resulting from Nazi-Bolshevist fraternisation, and
the writer expresses the hope that these might be avoided by
means of a *coup*. Fears of this nature lent strength to the determination of the group round Beck, Hassell, Popitz and Goerdeler
to bring about Hitler's downfall, but they were also used as an
argument for the setting-up of an authoritarian régime after
the *coup*. Dietrich Bonhoeffer saw in the Bolshevist threat emphatic confirmation of the need for a postwar administration
that would be ' authoritarian but not Fascist '.[35]

We should be presenting a distorted view of the Conservative Opposition's attitude if we failed to point out that beneath these fears there lay a sense of social resentment which doubtless led to strong inner tensions within the active Resistance. Hassell's remark concerning the inevitability of 'inner Bolshevisation' of the National Socialist system was an allusion to the elimination of the Russian upper class by the Bolsheviks, and he further expressly stated that the 'Hitlerian form of socialism' was aimed at the disruption of the upper classes and at reducing the church to a collection of insignificant sects.[36] Such trains of thought were conducive to the kind of *bourgeois* anti-Communism which had facilitated Hitler's rise to power and the undeniable acclaim he received at the start; indeed, it would be difficult to overestimate the significance of this mentality, which was to paralyse the Conservative forces until well into the war. A few days after the death of Hindenburg, Halder wrote to Beck that Hitler's 'genuine intention, propelled by an idealistic impulse' was, in practice, being vitiated by the activities of a group, speciously sheltering behind the Führer's authority, which was opposing the formation of a political front and preparing to 'overthrow existing values'; this group personified the 'Communist threat'. For this reason Halder regarded the Röhm affair as 'only *one*, and that not the most serious, abscess' in the German body politic. Here, he believed, Communist forces were at work; thus he failed to distinguish between the social revolutionary forces in the NSDAP and the Communists, a *simpliste* view that is typical of his political thinking.[37] In 1938 Beck himself was still of the opinion that common action on the part of the General Staff could rid Hitler of 'Cheka and party-boss rule', thus preventing the 'resurgence of Communism'. The passivity of the general in face of the June murders is in large measure explicable in terms of this trite confrontation of traditional 'idealist' values and Communist 'materialism', an oversimplification of social-political problems that was not peculiar to Beck and Halder alone. It further throws light on the fact that the generals of the Opposition, with but few exceptions, only made up their minds to unconditional action when the Bolshevist danger threatened to become a military reality.

G

Rejection of the Bolshevist system necessarily entailed the question of what attitude should be adopted towards anti-Communist Socialist elements. Whereas Hassell was content to dismiss the problem of socialism as ' another Nazi cuckoo in the German nest ',[38] Adam von Trott believed that a compromise between socialism and tradition represented a crucial question of domestic policy and, indeed, of foreign policy. He early became preoccupied with the elimination of class differences, and his attempt to evolve a socio-philosophical theory that would supersede the Hegelian tradition of state aligned him with socialist groups – as also with Communists; with the former he was to establish close contacts both before and after 30 January 1933. In February he admitted to his father that for him ' the positive rights of the individual ' could only endure if the rights of the proletariat were ' held sacred ', though there seemed little prospect of this under Papen and Hitler. Writing to Margret Boveri, he suggested that Hegel's ' right to free will ' must be superseded by the ' right to work ' – self-realisation in the widest possible sense of the term.[39] This reveals a great measure of agreement with Delp's ' personal Socialism ', and, together with the *rapport* established by Josef Furtwängler between the ideas of Trott and Moltke, would therefore seem to show that he had been instrumental in shaping the Kreisau proposals.

In 1933 Trott expressed the fear that any neglect of the rights of the masses would have ' serious repercussions', and in the spring of 1937, after reading a paper by Felix Morley, he still believed there was a real possibility of a popular rising – a strange though not fortuitous misinterpretation of internal conditions under National Socialism. Like Schulenburg, he doubtless felt a certain affinity for the Strasser faction, and he believed that the conflict between the Socialist elements of the National Socialist movement on the one hand, and the rising *petit-bourgeois* mediocrity of Nazi officialdom together with the capitalist beneficiaries of the system on the other, had yet to be resolved. From his own standpoint a proletarian rising was undesirable since it would render social stabilisation even more difficult. In this context he also feared that international conflict would either inhibit or completely block any solution to ' the social and economic crisis in

Germany ', and he showed a tendency to underestimate Hitler's political aggressiveness. As a result of the clumsy conduct of the victorious Allies at Versailles the German people had, he thought, been driven into a radicalism which was now at fever-pitch; war would therefore lead to total catastrophe.[40] In Trott's view, National Socialism was as much the result of national frustration as of social and economic crisis, and he believed that this could be dealt with from within if the Western democracies adopted a firm yet in no way aggressive attitude; but a repetition of the external situation of the twenties could only drive the proletariat into ' national Bolshevism '. For reasons of domestic policy he was a strong advocate of appeasement. What was happening in Germany, he wrote in 1938, was a European phenomenon, and he showed a certain degree of national sensitivity in his repudiation of critical generalisations from abroad. It was his conviction that totalitarianism was a general phenomenon of crisis, from which the democracies were not excluded, and which derived from lack of social integration among the masses. ' It is my view that the sterile and cynical defeatism underlying the spiritual chaos in Europe is attributable to democratic no less than totalitarian misuse of the instinctive aspect of human consciousness.' The customary exploitation by all political systems of the emotional malleability of the masses, and what he regarded as the cynical policy of manipulating the public will by propaganda and appeal to the instincts, was regarded by Trott as the distinctive symptoms of crises, not only in German society, but in that of Europe at large. He therefore doubted the practicability of realising the ideal of individual freedom, even in a democratic system founded on capitalism. ' You have not properly answered my objection ', he wrote to a close friend, an American journalist, ' that capitalist and imperialist democracy perhaps makes use of freedom only as a screen for a policy based on purely compulsive measures, whereas some aspects of authoritarian systems might admit of what is basically a more honest guarantee of human right in the modern industrial society.'[41]

Trott's conviction that the formal democratic principle of freedom was unrelated to the degree of social freedom realised, and

that a liberal régime was no safeguard against individual vulner-
ability to potential political manipulation, led him to reject all
forms of plebiscitary rule. The history of the past ten years, he
reflected towards the end of 1939, had shown that ' amorphous
faith in popular intuition is no good . . . In one way or another
popular movements have always led to despotism.' Trott proposed
a return to conservative principles and a firm, constitutionally-
based authority; every socialist state must be authoritarian in
some degree if it was to survive. ' Why not write a paper on
tradition and Socialism?' he asked Julie Braun-Vogelstein.[42]
Thus Trott was very far from advocating the application of
Western democratic principles to Germany. In this his views resembled those of the socialists; Leber was contemptuous of
the men of the 1918 revolution who had had absolutely no idea
of what the new German community should be like, and had
allowed themselves to be guided by the example of the Western
democracies ' without realising that their inherent nature no
longer corresponded to their outer form '.[43]

Modern social conditions induced Trott — who rightly sus-
pected that the American ideal of the pioneer had no lasting practicability — to break fundamentally with what had become a
meaningless *bourgeois* ideology, and to seek a new social order
with a European basis, an order that would stand for ' the freeing
of the proletariat from economic need ', while at the same time
incorporating it into an authoritative order permeated by the
Christian spirit. He advised against publicly advocating the principle of individual freedom, for this would be to do violence to
' given realities, whether national, historical, geographical, cultural, or confessional '. And in a memorandum of November
1943[44] he wrote : ' A purely rationalist upbringing has led us to
misunderstand both human nature and the social facts of mass
existence as well as the uncontrolled forces to which the stereotyping of man has given free rein.' Trott's formulation contains
the basis of the German Opposition's reflexions on social and
constitutional policy which testify to the fact that the serious
crisis of liberal democracy underlying the Fascist and National
Socialist victories had also affected the supporters of democracy
and induced in them the conviction that the principle of liberal

parliamentary democracy was doomed to founder in the age of the industrial society.

## The Agrarian Question, Regional Planning, and Middle-Class Politics

The thinking of the Opposition was moulded by its orientation towards tradition, the desire to preserve historical continuity and rejection of an antagonistic society. Their fundamentally defensive attitude in the face of social levelling is most clearly expressed in their treatment of questions of agrarian policy. The fact that Kreisau was much preoccupied with these is understandable, for landed property formed the background of the founders of the circle. Yet other groups of the Opposition showed no less interest and, indeed, the agrarian crisis, especially as it affected landed property east of the Elbe, was an important contributory factor in the decline of the Republic. It was an interest, however, that was intrinsic to their fundamental outlook. ' Questions of agrarian policy', wrote Einsiedel in a memorandum drawn up for the Kreisau Circle,[45] ' must always form an integral part of any discussion of national construction.' The elimination of ' stereotyping' which must be a basic factor in the new European order would demand the creation of a consciousness ' which affirms the value of personality and the existence of a free individual sphere, at the same time linking them organically to a natural communal sense'. In rural districts the roots of organic life had not been so much impaired, for there ' the natural foundations of a self-sufficient life-cycle' had been preserved, and the feeling for personality had not yet succumbed to mass consciousness. For this reason, Einsiedel concluded, great importance must be attached in the new order to ' a strong, self-sufficient rural population'.

Views of this kind were common to nearly all groups of the Opposition. In the ' preliminary basic state law' drawn up by Popitz, agriculture was described as ' the nation's most important source of strength', and in Mierendorff's proposed programme for ' socialist action' the ' peasant's security of tenure of his land' was accounted a prerequisite for social justice and freedom. Goerdeler stressed the need to maintain a healthy farming community ' both on sociological and biological grounds and for reasons of domestic policy'; in this he, like Schulenburg, subscribed to the problematical conception of the peasantry as a political asset both as regards population and ethnology. ' It is imperative for the German people to have a viable rural population, not so much on grounds of national security as on grounds of health.'[46] All groups showed a tendency to contrast neo-romantic idealisation of the ' back to nature' variety with a highly organised view of society. Thus Einsiedel wrote: ' Industrial-capitalist development, like fascist organisational experiments, tends to uproot the national life from its organic condition and to transplant it into an organised condition; in this way human life becomes split and a man's work degenerates into a technical activity determined by division of labour within the overall rational scheme of work.'

The anti-rational and anti-individualistic basic attitude, clearly apparent in Einsiedel and which had already become manifest in the thinking of the Opposition in their discussions of the causes of ' stereotyping', is no isolated phenomenon; Goerdeler, too, often contrasts ' organic' formations and artificial ' organisations' which he suggests are typical of the National Socialist system. Einsiedel no less than Delp, Gerstenmaier and van Husen betrays the influence of the romantic concept of ' *Volk* ' and Max Hildebert Boehm's doctrine of the ' self-reliant people'. The phraseology is significant. ' The citizen-compatriot [*Staatsbürger-Volksgenosse*] ', we are told, ' is no longer an organic part of a living body politic having a congruent political order; he is a mechanical component in a materialistically orientated and rationally directed state machine.' Steltzer, who had been influenced by Friedrich Naumann's National Social programme, expresses very similar views, and within Stauffenberg's close circle ideas of this nature were also deliberated, Wilhelm Ahlmann having been especially preoccupied with the question of ' the future of the farmer in industrial society', as Fahrner has pointed out.[47]

There were varying degrees of rejection of industrial and

technological progress. Einsiedel even went as far as to warn against excessive technical development in farming lest it destroy the ' unhurried and placid ' rhythm of a life dependent on the seasons. He showed strong aversion to any application of ' economics to rural life '; similarly, Mierendorff's demand in his political programme that farming should be protected against the danger of ' becoming a pawn in the capitalist game ' is essentially a demand for the exclusion of the liberal principle of competition from the agricultural sector. The view was generally shared that the countryside must be spared the noxious influences of urbanisation. Hence cultural institutions, and more especially schools, must remain independent and must not be adapted to urban conditions. Thus the aspirations of the twenties in the field of public education, brilliantly represented by Reichwein in the Kreisau Circle, were resumed, if now with a somewhat problematical ideological slant.

One of the chief bones of contention was the problem of large estates. These were defended by Einsiedel on the grounds that they favoured the formation of natural rural centres. ' The representation of rural values of life ' must be the responsibility of independent, highly cultured men ' who must be able adequately to counterbalance other sections of the population, especially in industrial economy '. Here opinions were divided, however. Moltke had set an example of voluntary renunciation in dividing up part of his estate, and according to Fahrner, Stauffenberg had been contemplating a similar step. The idea no doubt derived from Schwerin-Schwanenfeld and would seem to have been responsible for far-reaching schemes of property and land reform.[48] Goerdeler and Trott were both emphatic advocates of the partition of great estates, as Leber had shown himself to be in his criticism of large estates east of the Elbe. At the beginning of 1944 a broadcast prepared by Goerdeler contained the promise that there would be no restoration of an unjustifiable system of land tenure at the expense of rural health and that ' account will be taken of the German people's settlement requirements . . . if necessary at the expense of estates of unhealthy dimensions '; the same demand had been made in a broadcast by Leuschner, and Trott went ever further with his idea of comprehensive land reform and ' rural Communism '. His attitude to landowners east of the Elbe was distinctly hostile, and he bluntly informed Yorck that he rejected ' the whole aristocratic business '.[49]

On the whole those elements predominated which advocated the widespread introduction of the medium-sized holding, though they were never to gain a clear majority over those who wished to maintain the rural *status quo.* In particular Steltzer combated the *Erbhofgesetz*, a law affecting the sale of entailed land, because it favoured large as opposed to medium-sized holdings.[50] Moltke proposed that when the time came for demobilisation, precedence should be given to working farmers and agricultural labourers. Fritz Dietlof von der Schulenburg demanded widespread land settlement, which he compared with German colonisation in the east, though this did not mean that he was a declared opponent of landed property. Nor could it be said that he was opposed to industry, but he certainly harboured ideas on agrarian policy that were distinctly romantic, one of his suggestions being that senior civil servants should be tied to the land by the loan of agricultural state property. It was also his view that a healthy tradition and attachment to the soil were prerequisites for a stable political order and that these could only be formed in the course of generations and in rural areas. His ideas on land settlement were closely related to those found in National Socialist ideology, but they were hardly in keeping with the concept of a ' new feudalism ' to be based, not on the desire for gain, but on the consciousness of public responsibility. The rural élite of which he dreamed was to hold the land in fief and administer it in the service of the community. Schulenburg must surely have come to realise that all this was unpleasantly reminiscent of the method (its precedent the Neudeck estate affair) adopted and successfully applied by the Third Reich, of buying the political allegiance of the leading classes, and that the artificial restoration of what in fact was a predominantly aristocratic upper class was wholly unrealistic.[51]

The concrete measures proposed by the Opposition were principally concerned with combating the flight from the land, especially since it was considered that the rural population must not be allowed to fall below a certain level in relation to the rest of the country. It was proposed to slow down the flight from the land: firstly by measures that would bring about constructive improvements – the building-up of rural cultural institutions, housing for farm labourers, the encouragement of skills, and protection of small and medium-sized undertakings; and secondly, by raising the price of agricultural produce and the level of agricultural wages so that the latter were on a par with those of industrial workers. It would appear that they did not go into the question of how this was to be reconciled with the conception of an economic policy based on the ' ability principle '. Goerdeler, who combated autarchic ideas and proposals for state subsidies with equal vigour, believed that this problem could be automatically solved by the imposition of tariffs to protect agricultural produce, without any apparent awareness of the incompatibility of this plan with his proposals for close European cooperation on the Stresemann model.[52] The energetic policy advocated by Popitz in regard to the rural population, by which it was intended to effect the stabilisation of the agrarian sector's interest in the total economy, was no more specific as regards practical detail; it would seem that within the framework of its European concept, the Kreisau Circle was aiming at a European economic community isolated from the world economy, yet whose total agricultural production would be below the calculated consumption. Hence it did not appear necessary to limit German agricultural production.

The Opposition's overall conception of agrarian policy corresponded to its programme of regional planning and had similar social and political motives. The negative aspect of this programme was the prevention of concentrations of population in a few industrial centres, its positive aspect the creation of healthy living conditions by means of settlements and the building of homes. ' In spite of increased prosperity due to the modern industrial economy ', there had been a concentration of population in cheerless industrial quarters which had not been conducive to ' a healthy national life ', declared the writers of a memorandum on economic policy for the Kreisau Circle.[53] The wholesale destruction of big cities and the migration of a large part of their inhabitants provided an opportunity for comprehensive reform.

This became the conscious aim of Schulenburg, in particular, and was related to his work at the Ministry of the Interior. He believed it would be nonsensical to rebuild the shattered towns which for so long had developed in an unnatural atmosphere divorced from the healthy roots of life. The task must not, he held, consist in ' restoring cities which are responsible physically for the biological death of the people and intellectually induce those stereotyping phenomena so favourable to the political opportunism of any demagogue and which can only bring about a progressive cultural decline '.[54] Goerdeler, too, rejected urban culture on biological and mental grounds : ' The family is ruined by prolonged residence in the big city.'

The Opposition's ideas about the measures to be taken were unoriginal, in many instances immature, and frequently only realisable, if at all, by means of unlimited government intervention; yet they contain a number of constructive proposals which have still not been superseded. This is true of Schulenburg's idea of building rings of satellite towns, as also of Goerdeler's proposal to locate the principal centres of administration in medium-sized and small towns, thus initiating a change of structure that would bring about decentralisation. Goerdeler rejected on practical grounds the suggestion that big cities should be only partially rebuilt, since the tremendous investment in drainage and power networks ought to be exploited despite the destruction; he suggested, however, that building should be less concentrated and that slums should make way for healthy blocks of flats. Schulenburg, Goerdeler and Popitz were further all agreed that the growth of cities should be kept within reason by a ban on new industrial undertakings in towns of a specified size (the figures varied from 100,000 inhabitants to 400,000). It was a typical proposal in its underestimation of social and political contingencies, but it is not without parallels in Western European countries. Schulenburg envisaged the removal of large concerns, and Goerdeler the licensing of all undertakings having more than 100 employees. Both dreamed of ' a reconstruction of German industrial areas along the lines of Württemberg '; Schulenburg had sought to realise this goal in his East Prussian plan and again during his time in Silesia, and in the Ruhr district he had achieved some successful results in the field of regional planning.[55]

These measures for improving the political structure would, it was hoped, be effected by means of state legislation and administration. In addition there was to be a comprehensive scheme of resettlement, and of urban and rural housing, a scheme that was supported not only by Kreisau, but also by the Goerdeler group, and which found expression in the programme for a new order prepared by Bergstraesser for Leuschner. Schulenburg regarded the building of small holdings and workers' settlements, the provision of 'individual homes' and the preparation of land for allotments as 'among the most important economic and national requirements'; Goerdeler was deeply concerned that man's new relationship with nature should lead to a resurgence of moral and other forces beneficial to the community. It was a programme corresponding to the regional planning policy of the NSDAP between 1933 and 1939 – a policy, however, which never got beyond the early stages and had to be sacrificed to compulsory rearmament. The housing and land-settlement policies had also had to be abandoned in favour of the construction of motorways and of cheap blocks of flats for workers. It was in this connection that Goerdeler remarked that the funds provided for motorways would have been better employed in the settlement programme.

The general tenor of the proposals for political reorganisation outlined above was the restriction of the undesirable manifestations of modern industrial society, on the one hand by assistance to areas that had been deliberately isolated from urban life, and on the other by large-scale dispersal of urban concentrations and the removal of industry and trade into areas which had been predominantly agricultural. The endeavour to avoid, in so far as this was possible, anonymous concerns and mammoth undertakings within the industrial sector, resulted inevitably in an actively middle-class policy. Goerdeler repeatedly drew attention to the harmful consequences of closing down private concerns during the war, stressing the fact that the 'middle classes' were the natural reserve for the leading caste and hence represented the nation's greatest asset.[56] Goerdeler's markedly *bourgeois-*

liberal ideas were in agreement with Moltke's conception of 'small, manageable communities' and the creation of a large class of people having economic security. Moltke, too, suggested measures to protect the small firm or workshop along lines similar to the agrarian programme which proposed the creation of a large class of independent farmers. Indeed the basic constitutional principle put forward by Goerdeler, Schulenburg and the Kreisau Circle postulated the creation of a whole new class of notables.

In their discussions of questions of regional planning and of reconstruction, the Opposition groups notably endeavoured to grapple with an urgent set of problems which the National Socialists had never seriously attempted to solve. The latter's lack of ideas on the subject is evident from a questionnaire based on Schulenburg's long memorandum which was submitted to Goerdeler and Popitz while in prison, and in the answers to which the Ministry of the Interior probably had a very material interest. Both the Secretary of State, Stuckart, and his deputy, Ehrenberger, had for years worked in close contact with Schulenburg, and it is noteworthy that Himmler himself was proposing to make use of the Opposition's suggestions. The internal crisis of National Socialism and its system is clearly revealed by the fact that it was forced to resort to the ideas of its most determined foes for its own political plans.

## Economic and Social Policy

As often happens in times of transition and crisis, there was a large measure of agreement between men of varying political outlook when it came to criticising the social realities of industrial society. The Kreisau programme, as has been shown, combined a conservative desire for reform with socialist trains of thought. The symbiosis they sought to achieve was expressed by Delp in his concept of 'personal socialism'. Both liberal and *étatiste* elements were equally critical of mass society, as is evident from the extent to which Goerdeler's aims corresponded to those of Schulenburg, and from the common stand made by Popitz, Hassell and the Kreisau group against liberal economic policy in the traditional sense. The crucial difference here was that the ills arising from industrialisation were traced back to liberalism as, indirectly, were the procedures of a planned economy which were interpreted as an attempt to escape from the economic anarchy that liberalism had unleashed.

This conclusion was reached by the Kreisau Circle in ascribing to liberalism the responsibility for the triumph of ' purely materialistic utilitarian ideas '. Moltke took for granted the state's fundamental right to intervene in economic matters; it seemed merely a question of expediency whether the state decided to adopt measures of economic freedom or measures of economic control. Everyone was agreed that ' a return to the same un-restricted economy as before, if not to all lack of restriction in the sense advocated by extremist economic theories ' was quite inconceivable. Indeed the complete freedom of the individual in economic matters was rejected, if only because it appeared incompatible ' with the major organic tasks confronting us '.[57] At the same time they declared themselves opposed to any form of ' collectivist ' economy which was destructive of ' the living forces of the personality '. Basically they were looking for a constructive principle in economics by which they might steer between the Scylla of *laissez-faire* and the Charybdis of a planned economy, to arrive at new forms related, as Schmölders' memorandum had it, to ' the level of personality and social con-sciousness lying above material utilitarian ideas '. Schmölders con-ceived of a ' system of social advancement ' that would make ' ability the criterion of social standing and political respon-sibility ', a construct which, as will be shown, adopted Moltke's ideas and drew a distinction, difficult indeed to apply in prac-tice, between the ' acquisitive drive ' and the ' drive for prestige '.

It was in accordance with Kreisau principles, whereby econo-mic positions of power either for individuals or for groups must be prevented and avoided, that the state economy should be at the service of individual interests. All forms of lobbying were therefore rejected. In order to be able to implement its plans for structural change, especially in regard to comprehensive regional planning, the state must be allotted considerable powers even though it would seek to achieve its object largely by indirect control of the economy by means of economic and fiscal measures. This was entirely in accordance with Goerdeler's views. 'General economic policy' he declared in *Das Ziel*, 'must aim at keeping within bounds in so far as possible all cartels, syndicates, combines, trusts etc., or at breaking them up so as to form independent undertakings in order to make way for the individual creative personality and its sense of responsibility '.[58] Goerdeler was no less determined than Kreisau to prevent unjustified profits which were not the fruit of real ability and were made at the expense of the national economy or to the detriment of communal interests. In spite of his connections with Bosch, Goerdeler was extremely critical of industrial magnates; he was constantly drawing attention to their habit of demanding help from the state in time of crisis and of eschewing general economic responsibility. Nobody could censure more severely the omnipotence and featurelessness of managing directors whom Goerdeler contrasted in some sort as a class with the owner of the capital, and it is typical of him that he viewed limited liability companies with the utmost suspicion, expressly demanding of them that they give their employees the right of co-decision.

'Property is the responsibility of the whole.' To this formulation of Schulenburg's Goerdeler was able fully to subscribe, taking for granted the social responsibility which property involved. 'We are determined to obviate all possibility of the abuse of capitalism, in whatever form, for monopolistic, political or other purposes not connected with business ', he wrote in the broadcast speech he had prepared in 1944. To this extent Goerdeler regarded state intervention as justified and necessary, but it was his belief that the state must set a good example to industry by a clear-cut and restrained fiscal policy. He held the normal financial and tax machinery to be adequate for the realisation of the principles of an ordered competitive economy, but in all other respects he repudiated state-directed industry. An economy could only grow and prosper where ' the state or some other complex leaves as many risks as possible to the individual and deprives him of as few risks as possible '. But as Goerdeler only envisaged a gradual departure from the National Socialist planned economy, it would be improper to speak of fundamental differences between his ideas and those of the Kreisau Circle. In both cases the aim was to base the economy on the ability principle, to effect partial socialisation and to restrict state intervention to indirect measures.[59] Nor was there any difference of opinion as regards cartel and monopoly control; neither side denied that cartels had a useful task to perform.

Yet in 1943, as we learn from Hassell and Gerstenmaier,[60] there were heated arguments between Goerdeler and the Kreisau Circle which provoked Hassell in a temporary *volte-face* to remark that Goerdeler was 'really rather reactionary'. This sudden increase in tension cannot be attributed to Goerdeler's economic objectives, which were not fundamentally different from those of the Kreisau political economists – Schmölders, Blessing, Abs or von Trotha; its causes were, rather, terminological. Goerdeler's idea that the state must bow to what he regarded as the principles of 'natural law', (i.e. liberal principles), and Moltke's view of the state as the 'master of the economy' were obviously incompatible even though, in practice, both would produce much the same results. For if in this dispute Popitz and Hassell acted as go-betweens and, by and large, declared in favour of the Kreisau point of view, it was no natural alliance; both they and Schulenburg harboured ideas that were distinctly *étatiste* and whose logical realisation would be a comprehensive form of state socialism, itself a radically authoritarian solution.

A compromise was rendered even more difficult by the fact that Goerdeler's antagonists had had practically no opportunity of gaining experience in an economy that was not of *dirigiste* complexion and therefore tended to overrate the rôle of state intervention in economic matters within a system dependent on individual initiative such as both sides desired. This would seem to indicate a fundamental inconsistency in the Kreisau proposals arising from their endeavour to combine considerable restriction of state programmes in the social and political sectors with the widest possible state authority in matters of political economy. As regards regional planning and measures for structural improvement, the decentralisation of industry and above all agrarian policy, which Goerdeler also expressly excluded from the field of free enterprise, both sides were in relative agreement. According to Gerstenmaier, Goerdeler's 'dogmatic obscuring of the issue' acted as an irritant;[61] in fact, Goerdeler's was too open a nature for him to exploit differences of principle as a tactical weapon; in his eyes, either these did not exist at all, or they were due to his partners' lack of experience.

The differences between Goerdeler and the Kreisau representatives were not, however, essentially irreconcilable in regard to practical social policy. Goerdeler objected to the term ' social policy ', preferring the expression ' equalisation policy '; this clearly demonstrates his inclination to iron out social conflict. He believed the existing social legislation to be adequate; what remained to be done in the social sphere could, he thought, be achieved by measures for constructive improvement, and he opposed social security legislation that was too far-reaching on the grounds that it would have a debilitating effect on personal initiative and would lead to a false sense of sufficiency. These were questions upon which Goerdeler was relentlessly dogmatic, continuing to hold to those views he had expressed in 1932 and which were almost entirely in accord with Brüning's policy.[62] In this, he adopted a patriarchal, autocratic attitude quite out of keeping with his other views, and one which showed a complete lack of understanding for the basic causes of class conflict. What Goerdeler regarded as social policy was the morally requisite ' equalisation of hardship ', and not a deliberate reordering of the relations between capital and labour. The only remedy he could devise for unemployment was to lengthen hours of work without a corresponding wage-rise, and it is characteristic of the political naïvety embodied in that conception that he also proposed to implement what he regarded as the essential social building programme by lowering the wages of building workers.[63]

The tenacity with which Goerdeler held to the belief that unemployment – to his mind, at least partially unavoidable – could only be combated by means of lower wages and longer working hours, is apparent from the scathing criticism to which, in his *Gedanken eines zum Tode Verurteilten* (' Thoughts of a Condemned Man '), he subjected the New Deal, the Beveridge Plan, and what he called the ' Marxist theory of the eight-hour day '.

He persisted in holding, at least in part, to his idea that the workers must themselves be liable for unemployment benefits, and he worked out a complicated system, regressive as compared with existing legislation, whereby the state would benefit at the expense of self-insured workers and occupational groups. These conceptions, which Ritter has shown to have been politically unrealistic even in 1932,[64] explain Goerdeler's leanings towards the trade unions, for even at that time he advocated the formation of work associations comprising all the trade unions of the various occupational groups, or alternatively occupational bodies based upon compulsory membership and possessed of autonomous powers, which would be responsible for social insurance including unemployment benefit, so that in this way they would deliberately ' help to bear the burden of state '.[65]

Thus Goerdeler, as Ritter has pointed out,[66] surrendered even the principle of Bismarckian social policy, but persisted in the belief that social advancement in the modern industrial society was possible for the workers, even though this might not happen within the course of a single generation. The remedy he proposed, as may be seen from his ' Economic Primer', lay in the better economic education of the masses; this relates his thought to that of Leuschner, who believed that lack of education was the main reason for the insulated condition of the working classes. These views were also shared by Haubach, Reichwein and Jakob Kaiser. But the alliance between Leuschner and Goerdeler was of a temporary nature; like the Kreisau Circle, Leuschner believed that the provisional cabinet would soon outlive its purpose and would have to give way to a ' second wave ' which would bring about a Socialist majority. For there could be no thought of political compromise in questions of insurance, or in regard to Goerdeler's demand for payment by result (i.e. piecework), in questions of the length of the working week or of wages policy.

Yorck responded to Goerdeler's ideas on social policy by calling him ' reactionary'. Goerdeler retorted by describing the Kreisau group as ' drawing-room Bolsheviks'. The Kreisau proposal that a firm's employees should have a share in its profits and growth seemed absurd to Goerdeler, because it ran counter to his fundamental principle of the allocation of responsibility.

H

He accepted with some reserve the idea of partial nationalisation, but essentially only in respect of the power industry which he supposed could for the most part be vested in local authorities. He felt more sympathy for Leuschner's suggestion for trade union-administered concerns – on the model of the Workmen's Cooperative Production Society – so long as these operated under the same competitive conditions as private business.[67] At the same time Goerdeler inveighed against ' undue returns ' on capital and strongly criticised the management of heavy industry prior to 1933. He was a man of the ' middle-class centre ', and was one of the few later to acknowledge a debt to Stresemann's policy and personality which, in their liberal conception, so much resembled his own. What distinguished him from Stresemann and aligned him wholly with Brüning was the ' apolitical ' quality of his ideas, which were entirely determined by the demands of financial reconstruction. This was the one point upon which the otherwise divergent views of the Resistance were agreed : whereas Goerdeler was incapable of appreciating the antagonism of political and social interests, so that his thinking continued to be determined by the idea of an order ' devoid of conflict ', the Kreisau members thought in terms of a new social order which would rest on the association and not the liberation of pluralistic forces.

## The Community, the Concept of Leadership and the 'New' Elite

The dualism characteristic of Germany's internal development was a dualism of state and society which, after 1918, had prevented the democratic parliamentary system from taking root, but which the Nazi revolution appeared to have vanquished with its slogan ' *Volksgemeinschaft* ' (' People's Community '). It was a dualism that was decisive in regard to the Opposition's thinking, and this in two ways : firstly because it had not been resolved by the political ideology of the Weimar period – not even by Carl Schmitt's irrational constructs – and this meant that the conspirators were to a great extent thrown back upon authoritarian solutions; secondly because they felt if obscurely perhaps, impelled to overcome this dualism both politically and socially. A typical, though theoretically unsatisfactory, attempt in this direction, was Beck's and Goerdeler's theory of a ' total policy ' which would harmoniously combine *raison d'état* and morality, economic interests and spiritual needs. In the principle of ' unity of party and state ' the Conservative Opposition at first saw what it believed to be the long-awaited demise of dualism, but it was to realise all too soon that, as Goerdeler put it, the anti-thesis between state and multi-party rule had been replaced by the even less manageable antithesis between state and party.[68]

The extent to which the thought and the actions of the majority of the conspirators was governed by the idea of restoring unity in both political and social fields is immediately evident from the records of Gestapo interrogations; the constantly recurring motive for resistance was that Hitler and the other National Socialist leaders had betrayed the principle of *Volksgemeinschaft*. This concept of community, which had already been current before 1933, and not only among the adherents of right-wing politics, was also taken up by Hitler's Conservative opponents. In a memorandum written for Hitler's benefit in 1934, Goerdeler demanded ' the setting-up of a genuine, undoubted people's com-munity '; and in *Das Ziel* he wrote of the ' class-free feeling of the people's community '. Here we see the terminological origin of the political objective, which relates it to Tönnies' famous distinction between society (*Gesellschaft*) and community (*Gemeinschaft*). It is significant that the term ' society ' is used only occasionally, most often by Trott.[69]

The concept of a ' new community ' found in Goerdeler's memorandum *Praktische Massnahmen zur Umgestaltung Euro-pas* ('Practical Measures towards the Reorganisation of Eur-ope '), was used in a variety of ways by all groups of the Resis-tance. Schulenburg hoped to see Bolshevism and ' parasitic capitalism ' overcome by means of a ' new communal order '; he described the officers' corps as a ' self-reliant, detached, and there-fore genuine, community ', possessing the intellectual and moral force to give unified direction to the masses, thus rescuing them from the formless law by which they were governed. This confron-tation of organic ' community ' and amorphous ' mass society ' which was a natural product of Schulenburg's Prussian socialist thinking, was in harmony with the ideas of the whole Opposition. Steltzer defined politics as ' community work ', Gerstenmaier spoke of ' natural community structures ', Yorck and Moltke sought ' right community within the state ' (a formulation which clearly delineates the dualistic problem), Leber used the expression ' new German community '. Reichhold, perceiving in the victory of the totalitarian state the revolution of the ' community ' against class, deduced that the labour movement could not reply in terms of ' class politics ', but must now see itself as a part of the communal whole – a part having equality of status.[70]

The concept of community implied the idea of a natural, graduated order postulating the free, self-sufficient personality. The complete absorption of the individual into the community as demanded by the totalitarian state was definitely repudiated, as was an education aiming at spiritual and ideological uniformity.[71] The idea, upon which was based the whole concept of a given, unified, organically structured society deriving from historical tradition, resulted in the definite repudiation, not only of class differences, but also of all social pluralism. The conception that it should be possible by means of a sensible social and political structure ' harmoniously ' to reconcile divergent interests in the political sphere, and at the same time to resolve the dualism of state and society, was formulated by Yorck in a somewhat imprecise rendering of Kantian views, as follows : ' Right community is achieved in a state when there is so powerful and steady an insight into the nature of the task to be performed that recourse to ethics is necessary only for the purpose of correction '.[72]

Community involves leadership – and it was perfectly logical that leadership selection and the formation of an élite should occupy a central position in the thinking of the Opposition. ' The German problem ', Steltzer declared in 1944, ' is exclusively one of leadership ', and he believed that the National Socialist catastrophe was attributable to the absence of an adequate leading caste. The experience of the Weimar Republic, and the idea of leadership that was so much in evidence in the twenties, were instrumental in shaping this thinking, and this is particularly true of the socialists. In 1930 Mierendorff had turned against ' a system of formal democracy that is wide open to political pressure by organised power groups, so that neither strong government nor real democratic rule by and with the people is possible'. Haubach believed that 'our movement must learn to realise that there is nothing undemocratic about ceremonial, about command or disciplined leadership'. What Leber demanded of the 'statesman-like leader-personality' was ethical character and inner faith, and he expressed the conviction that these contained the seeds of all true authority. He also cited Max Weber, who said of the old Social Democracy that it evinced no sign of any Catilinarian will to power.[73]

The men of the Opposition were unanimous in attributing Germany's decline to lack of leader-material and absence of desire for leadership. Beck's study of Ludendorff was basically concerned with this problem, and Goerdeler's favourite historical theme was the failure of political leadership in the Reich since the departure of Bismarck. Schulenburg joined the NSDAP because he believed 'party politics' to be the opposite of true political leadership, which he saw personified in Otto Strasser. Steltzer stressed the failure of the 'old leading caste', by which he also meant the military, and ascribed this to the same causes as had been responsible for 'stereotyping'. Goerdeler believed that the reason why 'political leadership had ceased to be a whole and had been arbitrarily split up and departmentalised both in the geographical and the administrative sense', was the failure in Bismarck's constitution properly to allocate responsibility, and also the lack of proper leadership on the part of the Weimar Republic. He was a supporter of the presidential system and later regretted that he had not complied with Brüning's request to join Papen's cabinet. As adviser to Hindenburg, he had advocated a temporary Enabling Act, and in 1941 he was still able to describe as 'wholesome' the idea of 'a short-term imposition of sanity by dictatorial measures'.[74]

Basically this criticism went deeper, and here Goerdeler was representative of the large majority of the conspirators. He blamed democracy (as he understood it), and the parliamentary principle for the decline in political leadership, and in 1932 he deplored 'the unsettling effect upon Reich politics of the *Land* parliaments', demanded the coordination of Prussia on behalf of the president of the Reich and ' of his ministers ', and stressed that the original function of the parliaments had been ' supervisory '. Democracy he decried as ' rule by the masses ', and went on to say that England was not a true democracy since her electoral system enabled a minority to appoint the cabinet. But he also pointed out that Britain, too, was short of notable leaders, attributing this to the ' democratisation of the nation which had brought with it a decreased sense of responsibility, a greater manifestation of personal vanity and a growing need for present popularity '.[75] Leadership, he believed, must be based on trust, but whence that trust derived he did not seek to explain, though his experience as an influential *Oberbürgermeister* should have enabled him to do so; he did, however, express the doubt that elections served to foster it. ' We need the stabilising ballast of state leadership unhampered by elections ', he wrote in his memorandum *Aufgaben der deutschen Zukunft* (' The Future Tasks of Germany ').[76]

It was partly a result of dualistic thinking that Goerdeler, although so much preoccupied with the leadership problems of the Wilhelmian epoch, never asked himself the question how a system in which the key positions would come to be held by able and responsible men was to be achieved. Nor was he alone in shirking the issue. Max Weber's works, in which the need for selection in parliamentary leadership is discussed, were unknown to those – always excepting Leber – whose concern was a new German constitution. ' The right people must be put at the top ', was the inept reply to the crucial problem posed by the constitutional state, and it was a reply characteristic of the mentality then prevalent. Schulenburg, Hassell and Popitz believed that senior state officials would make natural leaders. Schulenburg, an opponent of bureaucracy – like Popitz and Goerdeler, he welcomed the Civil Service Law of 7 April 1933 – gave at least some thought to the idea of the civil service as a training ground for a leading élite, in much the same sort of way as ' shock-troop leaders ' had received training during the First World War. The proviso in nearly all the constitutional plans whereby the civil service was declared ineligible – Kreisau incomprehensibly restricted this to political, i.e. electoral, officials – reflects the aversion felt towards a civil service that was politically involved in the parliamentary sense. Not only must there be no civil servants who were Nazi Party members, there must be none belonging to any party, so that political organisations might have no opportunity for jobbery. Goerdeler continued to insist, as he had done in 1932, that 'firm steps must be taken to eliminate politics from the civil service', as was already the case in the army.[77]

The qualities demanded of the leading caste consisted in wholly apolitical, practical abilities and characteristics. This is apparent from a typical exchange between Moltke and Yorck about the kind of man a 'statesman' – they did not use the word 'politician' – ought to be. Goerdeler did little to alter this picture, except that his chosen source for the leading class was local government. In his view, as in that of Steltzer and of many others, local government was the sphere of practical decisions and ought therefore to be kept as free as possible from the confusing and nefarious influence of party politics and status-seeking. This conception, of very similar stamp to Brüning's politics of 'practicality' and reminiscent of Freiherr von Stein, of whom more presently, was indeed self-contradictory, since it postulated that both local and national civil servants should be independent of party, while at the same time stipulating that they should have political qualifications, such as good repute, trustworthiness, a gift for leadership and good political judgment. Goerdeler, in fact, had little understanding of the machinery of central state government, which is not comparable with local government, and hence was unable to perceive the difference between bureaucratic administration and political leadership. This is apparent from the disputes that arose upon his joining the second Prices Commission and from his proposal for the amalgamation of ministries, his criticism of specialisation in administration, and his suggestion that there should be permanent (specialised) secretaries of state, while the ministers' personal private secretaries should be mobile.

It was a peculiarity of the Opposition's constitutional thinking – again with the exception of Leber – that they should hold that plebiscitary components in the modern constitutional state are symptomatic of decline and, indeed, tend towards ' the rule of mediocrity ', as Hitler's example seemed to show.[78] That this theory applied, not only to the National Socialist system, but to all forms of parliamentary selection of leaders, is demonstrated by the use of this phrase of Edgar Jung's as a slogan against the Weimar Republic. When it came to formulating a definite solution to the problem of how an élite was to be formed, very marked differences became apparent. The Popitz-Hassell circle never for a moment doubted the mission of the old upper class from which their own group derived, and even Goerdeler, who thought along lines that were much less aristocratic, agreed with Hassell's oft-repeated lament that Nazi propaganda was guilty of hateful diatribes against the aristocracy and the upper classes. The view put forward by Popitz in 1934, when speaking before the Wednesday Club, that it was essential to establish a ruling class, the complaints made in statements to the Gestapo of the persecution of the nobility and intelligentsia and, lastly, Stauffenberg's view that consideration should be given to the nobility's historical achievements, all point to a distinct tendency to seek the restoration of a socially and politically dispossessed leading class. Even the ' Red Count ', Schulenburg, was no exception; in 1941 he was still speaking of the nobility's ' right to existence ' as a politically responsible class, and he alway remained an advocate of historically-based élites, even where they had been artificially created by the acquisition of new estates.[79]

The men of the Kreisau Circle stood in direct opposition to these views, and stressed the complete failure of the old upper class. Hence they definitely rejected the inclusion of Popitz in any future cabinet. Yet both Moltke and Yorck thought along markedly aristocratic lines, and it was significant that Yorck talked to Alexander Graf Stauffenberg of the élite's historical guilt in having ignored the social question.[80] They were the opponents of inherited privilege and tended to the idea of an ' open élite ' based upon spiritual rather than social factors. Dietrich Bonhoeffer expressed the Kreisau conception and the circle's view of itself most aptly in the following words :

In the midst of a very far-reaching approximation of material and mental living conditions among men, the feeling for quality which nowadays cuts across all social class and permits the appreciation of the human values of justice, achievement and courage, might succeed in creating a new élite comprising those to whom the right of strong leadership will be conceded.

His following remark strikes a slightly discordant note: the 'recognition of historical justice', he says, will make it 'easy' to renounce privileges.[81]

Incontestably, Kreisau's plans for a new order fall down when it comes to the question of institutions for their realisation, for the views they express are full of social Utopian elements. Yorck and Moltke dreamed of a global élite and a state of affairs in which 'divisions and schisms between the inhabitants of this planet would be of only secondary importance because mankind wholly comprised within one party', would be so imbued with, and united by, the same values that 'even enemies would agree in essentials'.[82] This conception is explicable psychologically only in terms of the total intellectual isolation of groups whose illegal nature cut them off from the world around them, yet it was a conception that was to be a determining factor in Kreisau thinking. Another manifestation of this mentality can be seen in the regret expressed by Steltzer at the gradual disappearance of the intellectual élite which had become indistinguishable from a society 'whose destruction we are now witnessing', and is again apparent in his hope that there might be, throughout the world, a class of people who would be permeated by 'a new and whole vision of the world and of mankind'. Bonhoeffer also subscribes to this idea when he writes of 'the birth of a new, noble mentality, combining in one circle people from every walk of life.'[83]

Though the Kreisau plans respecting a new élite had a markedly social Utopian flavour, they were nevertheless an essential part of a total political conception. In the first place they accorded with the circle's idea of itself as an élite *vis à vis* other countries, a position it was seeking to legitimate, and also with its intention to assume responsibility in the event of Hitler's fall. In the latter case what was contemplated was not so much an actual cabinet – although Kreisau also concerned itself with the possible composition of a future government – but rather a form of political trusteeship, in respect of which they used words such as 'regent' or 'administrator'. The constitutional plans do not specify the nature of the relations between this élite and the political leadership; it was the undoubted task of the élite to represent the national conscience and to infuse spiritual and religious values into political and social life. Hence it must on no account lay itself open to the charge that it was seeking positions of political leadership.[84]

The same orientation is apparent in Haubach's proposal for a council of elders consisting of men unconnected, or no longer connected, with political life; the council would be responsible for ensuring that public affairs were properly conducted. A similar idea was that of Hielscher, who proposed setting up alongside the government an advisory council of enlightened men (*Bund der Bünde*). This is an indication of the continuing influence exerted by what had been a basically apolitical Youth Movement. According to Fahrner's account there was also talk in the Stauffenberg circle of the 'leading protagonists' need, in their deliberations and their actions, for the participation of uncommitted men not themselves holders of office, such as enlightened governments in the past had always sought by various means to gather round them.'[85] Even though Stauffenberg himself probably thought along more realistic lines, the Opposition was to some extent influenced by that German neurosis, particularly rife in the Stefan George circle, deriving from the fear of 'political monkey-business', and also by a longing for wise statesmanship that would transcend politics. And both these factors represent a flight from the conflicts of political interests in the pluralistic society.

The social Utopian flavour of this élite concept derived from the strongly religious orientation of the Kreisau Circle. It postulated a general Christian revival, comparable to the national revival among the peoples of Europe at the beginning of the nineteenth century and demanded that man should once again become aware of his transcendental ties. Thus it represented a return to a view of man which, the circle believed, had existed in Europe before secularisation, individualism and the modern idea of state had brought about the disintegration of the Western community, and before the old European economy had been undermined by liberalism and capitalism. The contacts sought by Bonhoeffer, Schönfeld, Gerstenmaier and Trott with ecumenical organisations, and Reichwein's and Poelchau's proposal to form a 'German Christian community' to overcome denominational differences, were both determined by this way of thinking. Steltzer's endeavour to give concrete political content to the concept of 'brotherliness' is indicative of the élite's twofold function, that of a responsible intellectual community without institutional ties, and that of a moulding force in practical, political policy-making. Underlying this was the theorem of an order that would integrate all divergencies of interest and political opinion and invest society with meaningful wholeness, a theorem rooted both in the German idealist tradition and in the Catholic doctrine of natural law.

Moltke's programme of 'small communities' was intended to put the ideas about an élite into practice. For outside the administrative sector there was to be as large a number as possible of spontaneously evolved communities which would also be nurseries for an élite. These 'small, manageable' communities were to grow out of the 'individual's natural affiliations' and must be linked to family, parish, home, profession and trade; they must not have the character of a 'mechanical, artificial' structure, nor of an 'organisation' ordered from above, but must, on the 'subsidiary principle' be groups forming naturally from below. They must be moulded by the will for common public responsibility, each serving the common good within its own limited sphere of activity. Originally Moltke had in mind the granting of political privileges to the 'small communities' and their members, and he considered the possibility of making franchise and eligibility, as well as admission to public office, dependent on the exercise of certain activities beneficial to the community – e.g. work in social institutions, work camps, parish and church councils, associations, study groups, university and school clubs. Except in connection with communal activities, there was, at first, to be no freedom of association or assembly.

Moltke was quite aware of the practical difficulties inherent in the realisation of these ideas. Which kinds of community should receive recognition and by whose authority, proved an insoluble problem, especially since Moltke envisaged granting them considerable rights, including the raising of taxes, police and supervisory functions and even compulsory powers over their members. Again, the idea that members of communities should, on the basis of public services rendered, be granted political privileges and 'special advantages with regard to the policy-making of higher authorities' contained a fatal flaw, namely that by laying down a mode of procedure, the spontaneous nature of the 'small communities' was immediately invalidated since they would thereby become institutions responsible for political policy-making. That Moltke's reflections on these matters were not merely peripheral is evident from the fact that Goerdeler – not to be outdone – also discussed these ideas: 'As with the selection of spokesmen in a firm, so groups which have distinguished themselves by exceptional ability and performance should be rewarded with qualified suffrage.' He added, however, that this 'must not be allowed to lead to privileges of property, school and higher education' and that the only basis of privilege must be the ability and performance principle.[86]

What characterises these proposals is not only the implied rejection of the egalitarian society but, above all, the contradiction inherent in the idea of an 'open élite' and its sanction as an institution. For it was quite clear that the 'ability and performance principle' would soon be replaced by traditional and social sources of legitimation. Such a conception was bound to lead to misunderstandings, though this was not at all Moltke's intention, and it is not really surprising that the socialist Mass should have gained the impression that the 'Counts' group', and Moltke especially, intended 'to restore and maintain the privileges of one particular socially restricted group of persons'.[87] The granting of privileges to a socially differentiated élite was not only impossible in practice but questionable on principle, because the state, of which the organic basis was to be these subsidiary groups holding sovereign rights, would itself and in its own turn need them as a regulator; furthermore, there was the diffi-

culty attendant on the use of compulsory constitutional measures
to ensure the readiness of citizens to act in common for the common weal. Yet Moltke's idea has a certain attraction. With it
was combined the proposal to replace the national states of Europe by a large number of smaller territorial units, some of them
of multiracial character. Europe must become a federation of
'autonomous bodies, themselves now historical' so that the problem of hegemony which for centuries had disrupted the peace of
Europe would cease to exist. The partition of the German national
state which this would necessitate, however, met with some opposition in Kreisau, especially from Delp, Gerstenmaier, Steltzer
and van Husen. That this had been the subject of argument is
evident from the formulation found in *Grundsätze* ('Principles'): 'The Reich *remains* the supreme leading power of the
German people.'[88] But it is noteworthy that in Moltke's plan he
succeeds in reconciling federalism and the principle of autonomy,
and indeed Kreisau as a whole drew no distinction between autonomy and democratic political practice. These proposals would
have entailed on the one hand considerable erosion of centralised
authority in accordance with the socialist idea of a self-governing society; on the other hand they represented, within what was
a fundamentally bureaucratic outlook, the most progressive
attempt to institutionalise the pluralistic forces in society and to
allot them their own place in the graduated structure of the community, thus turning a power that might have endangered the
existing order into a stabilising quantity. Moltke's conception
was in certain respects a conservative version of the soviet principle, combining direct democracy with élitism. Its antecedents
were the conscious tradition of the Prussian nobility which regarded itself as the equal of the state, if not indeed as its main-
stay, and the anti-liberal nature of political romanticism.

Moltke denied that his proposal could be misconstrued as an
attempt to 'atomise' the body politic, and he was emphatically
opposed to anything that would weaken 'the central power in
its own fields' as, for instance, in the sphere of economic planning. Here he stumbled on the dilemma, however, which socialism
had failed to surmount before him, namely, the incompatibility
of political autonomy and economic centralisation. It is true that

Moltke hoped, by means of decentralisation and self-government
on the one hand, and the formation of an autocthonous élite on
the other, to counteract the harmful omnipotence of the state,
for he regarded the illicit normalisation of the latter as the basic
ill of the German political tradition. ' To see the state as a moral
entity is, in my opinion, to set foot on the path which leads, by
way of Hegel, to the idolisation of the state.' Hence Moltke considered it to be exceedingly dangerous to give the state ' a religious interpretation and a religious substructure' and wished to
see it regarded as an essentially amoral institution in order that
' no one should try to hide behind the state '.[89] Accordingly he
demanded the complete segregation of church and state and like-
wise endeavoured to persuade Cardinal Faulhaber of the necessity to annul the Concordat of 1933.[90]

The radical stand taken by Moltke on this question was due
in no small part to the insight, gained as a result of his professional position, that the realisation of the National Socialist terror was only possible because of the legality arrogated to state
action. It recalls Radbruch's phrase ' living lie of the supreme
state '. In turning away from the Lutheran concept of state
Moltke was fundamentally at variance with Goerdeler who,
although he may have spoken of the ' poison of state idolisation '
by which the German people had been infected, never for a
moment doubted the liberal state tradition contested by Kreisau.
The state was, he believed, a divinely ordained system, but at the
same time he expressly declared : ' The state is not an end in
itself, but only a means towards orderly living and the welfare
of its citizens.'[91] While he tended at times to be authoritarian
and patriarchal, his position differed basically from that of Hassell, Popitz, Schulenburg and Beck. For these men had never got
beyond the magic circle of political authoritarianism, as is
apparent from Hassell's expression ' state-conscious Germany ',
and that of Schulenburg, ' the continuance of Prussia's demand
on the Reich ', or again from Popitz's conviction that the German state must be a ' national state which keeps a firm hold on
all the essential elements of political life '.[92]

The differing attitudes to the state corresponded to the various
ideas on the composition of the leading caste after the revolu-

tion put forward by the three Opposition groups. First there was the Hassell-Popitz-Beck-Schulenburg group which proposed the retention of the existing ' politically responsible ' élite; secondly Goerdeler, who wished to place the responsibility for the social and political order in the hands of a class which had proved its ability in the practical field of public law and local government; and lastly the Kreisau Circle, with its idea of the new intellectual aristocracy, formed of men from all social strata, united by their common basic values.

The constitutional political plans and objectives of the individual groups were materially determined by their respective concepts of state and the nature of the élite which they supposed would be qualified to exercise political power in that state. In the endeavour to replace mass society by some form of ' community ' with a social scale that would give expression to ' personality values ', they rejected political policy-making by plebiscite in favour of an institutionalised system for the formation of an élite, a system which, depending on the method proposed, indicated whether the fundamental attitude of those advocating it was reactionary, or whether it was conservative.

## The Authoritarian State

The fact that the German Opposition's constitutional proposals are based on the quite definite rejection of the Weimar ' system ' shows the total discredit into which the first German republic had fallen. Events seemed to have invalidated the parliamentary system that was believed to be ' Western ', and the plebiscitary tendency of the party state had apparently led straight to dictatorship. Hence in drafting their constitutional plans, the Opposition looked back to the traditions of the nineteenth century, and more especially Stein's political thinking reinterpreted in an organisational and national sense. Where they differed was in the emphasis laid on the national, the liberal and the conservative aspects respectively of the historical tradition deriving from Prussian reform. The first, chronologically, were the authoritarian, reconstructive plans, but the basic conceptions of the later groups differ little in their essentials, although there were compromises as between varying shades of opinion within the opposition.

The constitutional plan worked out during the summer of 1938 by Oster, Schulenburg and Heinz envisaged the restoration of a ' German monarchy '; it also combined ethnic-national objectives with Prusso-German socialism and certainly went back to ideas earlier than Friedrich Naumann's conception of a ' democratic Kaiserdom '. Similarly the constitutional programme drafted towards the end of 1939 by Erich Kordt and Hasso von Etzdorf had strongly authoritarian characteristics. It demanded that the political structure should conform to ' decency, cleanliness and true Prussian tradition ', envisaged ' that the people should have a say in the making of public policy, as befits the free German citizen ', and aspired to ' a just and truly German (Prussian) socialism ' as well as to ' a Christian, moral revival '. The rule of law (*Rechtsstaat*) would be ensured by means of a *habeas corpus* act. But significantly, the problem of effectively controlling the power of the state was not raised.[93]

The next contribution to the Opposition's proposals took the form of a memorandum from the *Abwehr* circle in which the post-revolutionary political order is discussed.[94] It contains Etscheid's comment on ' the real authority ' now needed by the people, in place of the ' blind obedience ' demanded by Hitler, and further expresses the conviction that the ' remaining middle classes ' as well as ' all those workers and employees not formerly under Communist organisation ' would be prepared to accept even harsh and unexpected decisions if they felt certain that ' our people will not be thrown into the melting pot, along with 180 million Bolsheviks, to be subjected to yet further political and social experiments '. The proletariat, he believed, was gradually becoming aware that the National Socialist régime had come to grief, a régime previously tolerated on the grounds that ' it had seemed that the chaos resulting from the war could only be cleared up by concentrated work and disciplined organisation, a task in which other politicians, parties and movements had failed '. There was, he went on, an ' uneasy feeling that the democratic, parliamentary institutions of other countries do not represent the right form of government for the German people ', while on the other hand ' absolute dictatorship, whether by an individual or a small, closed group' was not capable of solving internal and external problems. 'This has inevitably brought the realisation of the need for conservative institutions and measures to preserve the state, a realisation which, in conversation, often finds expression in the somewhat drastic demand for Friedrich Wilhelm's just, if heavy, stick.'

This demand for a return to previous methods, based upon a questionable analysis of proletarian morale, demonstrates the extent to which the *Abwehr* Resistance group was deluded by ideas of class and by its links with the Prussian tradition of state which precluded any close relation with the Republic. A characteristic of its general political attitude was a marked anti-Communist bias, and this too explains the support given to Hitler's régime in the early years; it also led Etscheid to conclude that, if it were possible to gain control for only a few days of 'the powerful German propaganda machine', it would be easy to make the German people understand that the only possible course was 'to adopt a plainly belligerent attitude towards Bolshevism'. This was in keeping with the identification of National Socialism and Bolshevism mentioned earlier. Once they had recognised this situation, the memorandum continued, the people would be ready 'to accept a strict and even disagreeable form of authority' if this were to guarantee justice and 'security of existence'. The reiterated argument of the generals, especially Halder, that the people were not ripe for revolution was countered with the statement that of course 'a broad popular movement was preferable to revolution from above'; but that would presuppose military intervention necessarily embarrassing to a 'military leadership then enjoying the maximum power and confidence' and would prejudice the necessary internal and external prerequisites for a revolution. Etscheid took the view that the Opposition should act without consideration for existing popular opinion. In general it would be possible to postulate

the readiness of the masses to accept the decisions of responsible men who take the initiative in exceptional situations of this sort, as also the possibility of representing, by the skilful use of propaganda, the motives and aims of a successful action

I

as being in the interests and therefore in the name of the whole people . . . The more determined and ruthless the intervention, the readier would its opponents be to recognise the sense of authority and qualities of leadership it revealed.

This was to shelve the dilemma presented by a revolutionary attempt. Nothing definite was known about the possible reactions of the people, but considerable opposition was anticipated, an opposition which, it was presumed, could only be overcome by means of a strict authoritarian system. It was in this sense that Beck later put forward the view that the Opposition's actions should ' not be too much influenced by consideration for the moods of the people '.[95] Hence it would be expedient to ' carry over, for permanent retention in the reconstructed state, an appreciable amount of what had been achieved by National Socialism '. This was in conformity with the suggestion in Hassell's constitutional plan, which appeared some months later, to the effect that NSDAP institutions, such as the NSV (National Socialist Popular Welfare), the *Arbeitsdienst* (Labour Service) and the *Deutsche Arbeitsfront* (German Labour Front), as well as the organisation of the economy, should be retained, at least in principle. This implied a partial recognition of the social coordination brought about by National Socialism; the remark that in this way ' a synthesis of hitherto divergent forces would be effected ' further contained a fundamental rejection of plurality of interests and of the political party system in favour of a unity of social forces established by the state.

The memorandum put forward reasons, including reasons of foreign policy, for a ' conservative administration ', an idea which originated in a suggestion of Hassell's, who believed that Britain was in favour of a conservative régime, and that she had shown interest in the restoration of a constitutional monarchy.[96] A restoration was not, indeed, expressly proposed in the constitutional programme drafted by Hassell after consultations with Beck, Popitz and Goerdeler in January and February 1940, but such a solution is implicit in the intention to entrust the supreme power to a regency of three men. ' Monarchy is highly desirable, but this is a problem for the next stage ', Hassell remarked at the end of

February. The idea derived from Popitz who, Hassell went on to say, wished to leave the question of a monarchy ' until later ' – unlike Goerdeler who, as always, was all for putting his cards on the table. While Popitz had been responsible for initiating the programme, it was also supported in all probability by Schacht, Oster and Witzleben. It is significant that Planck, whom Hassell wished to include, was turned down by the generals as a supporter of Schleicher.[97]

Hassell's programme expressly stated that only a temporary solution would be sought ' until such time as it is possible to set up a normal constitutional existence ', but he certainly did not mean by this the restoration of parliamentary democratic institutions. The brief of the constitutional council to be set up by the Regency was ' to organise the unified German state along political and economic lines that take special cognisance of historic tradition so as to ensure both the cooperation of the people in the political life of the Reich and a control of the state based on local and corporate self-government.'[98] In an age of popular sovereignty, the expression ' cooperation of the people ' is something of an understatement. In fact there was no thought of a central parliament; Hassell spoke of ' control of the state by some kind of occupationally based organisation ', and called the proposed régime an ' organic, constitutional state with controls '.[99]

A good deal is known about the origins of the constitutional programme. Those mainly responsible were Hassell and Popitz, and the former once noted: ' Popitz and I are still agreed.' Goerdeler's proposal to hold a plebiscite after the revolution was vigorously opposed by the two partners. What Popitz demanded above all was ' immediate Reich reform ', that is, the realisation of a radical centralisation programme expressed in a clause whereby the provincial governors were to be dismissed and the executive power in the *Länder* handed over to the military commanders. The clause concerning the ' need to reconstruct the state on the basis of local and corporate self-government (by a system of filtration)' derives from Hassell. It was an idea he had discussed a short time before in an article on ' Stein's Organisational Concept of State ', in which the whole complex of problems raised by the Stein revival in the German Opposition becomes apparent. The constitution must take into account the particular characteristics of German development; in his memorandum written shortly afterwards on the subject of a new order in Europe he postulated ' effective control of political power by the people exercised in a manner appropriate to the nation concerned '. Similarly Popitz demanded that ' Christian morality based upon German tradition must be our guiding star '.[100]

A notable item in the constitutional programme is the clause concerning the reinstatement of career officials, a clause undoubtedly aimed at the NSDAP; but it retained the essentials of the Civil Service Law, namely suppression of the influence of political parties and rejection of a political civil service. It is not fortuitous that there is no mention of the formation of political parties or associations; on the other hand we find, in connection with censorship, the all too well-known phrase ' protection of state and people ', but with a characteristic change of emphasis; and of the press it said that ' after the war there will be new regulations formulated on the basis of the freedom of the press within the framework of state security '. Certainly this constitutional programme, drawn up at the beginning of 1940 with the revolution in view, contained no elements permitting the reconstruction of the state as a democracy under a monarchy, as in Britain, nor was there any provision for general elections. The programme indicated a departure from the parliamentary principle and could only have been put into practice by the use of direct political compulsion. Goerdeler cooperated closely in its preparation but, as will be shown, his ideas were only in partial agreement with those of Popitz and Hassell from which they differed radically in intention. The early 1940 programme presented no real alternative to Hitler; it would have meant a military dictatorship of the kind that had been dreamed about in 1934.

The same criticism applies to later plans made by this group, more particularly to the ' law for the reestablishment of order in the political and legal spheres ' drafted by Popitz on the basis of discussions with Hassell, Jessen, Planck and Beck.[101] It followed closely on ' Hassell's programme ', and its substance derives from the deliberations of 1939/40. Here, too, we find a promise of an order conforming to the character and history of the German people, and the 'collaboration of all classes of the population' in a definitive constitution. This implies occupationally based representation and, together with the later statement that the government must be close to the people (*volksnah*), seems to indicate that the proposed régime would be of a highly conservative nature. Unlike the 'programme of 1940', it does not expressly commit itself to any future constitution, aside from stating that after the stabilisation of the German people's general living conditions, arrangements would be made for 'representing the people on a *broad* basis' – not, that is, on the basis of general elections.

The 'preliminary basic law of state', as this plan was called, was not intended as a short-term measure for the first few months following the revolution but, as this provision implies, was meant to last. It provides for the nomination *and* the dismissal of the Reich Chancellor and lays down that the members of the Council of State are to be appointed 'for a term of five years'. The basic law of state, incorporating far-reaching preliminary decisions of a practical kind on constitutional politics, is transitional only in the sense that it leaves open the possibility of a restoration of the monarchy, and envisages a constitution. The provisions it contains, which are reminiscent of a state of emergency, nevertheless represent normal conditions over a period of years, while the situation immediately after the revolution is to be regulated by an emergency law promulgated at the time.[102] Ritter rightly described this plan as absolutist;[103] besides the ruthless implementation of centralist principles, it provides for the prohibition of political association and a general clause that every German must so conduct himself 'as not to prejudice the common weal or to besmirch the honour of the German name'. The context of this general clause is a statement on the need 'to avert operations from without and subversion within', and the wording was no doubt chosen with intent, since Popitz was a distinguished jurist. The clause invalidates the initial guarantee of a number of basic rights which, however, do not include freedom of assembly, secrecy of post and telephone, freedom of speech or of the press. In contrast to Hassell's programme, science, teaching and

the exercise of the arts are, to quote the ominous wording, only to
be restricted 'in so far as is requisite for external and internal
security and for the respect due to the nation's spiritual and moral
tradition'. That there is more than a terminological resemblance
to National Socialism is evident from the fact that the purging
of the civil service must be carried out 'in accordance with the
Professional Civil Service Law of 7 April 1933'. It is true that
the paragraphs of that law specifically concerning Adolf Hitler
and the NSDAP were to be invalidated, but the regulations
relating to the treatment of Jews and to hereditary health were
only to be suspended 'pending the final settlement'.[104]

The basic law of state gives unlimited power to the 'supreme
head of state' in his capacity as Regent of the Reich. While the
Regent must have the counter-signature of the Chancellor or
of the competent minister, he himself is responsible for nominat-
ing the Chancellor after consultation with the government, and
for appointing the ministers after consulting the Chancellor. Not
only is he in supreme command of the armed forces but is also
responsible for the discharge of the government's fiscal policy.
He presides over the Council of State whose members he appoints
in accordance with the suggestions of the Chancellor. The Council
of State generally has to approve bills before these are passed,
but has no right of decision and resembles very closely Reich
minister Frick's proposed 'Greater German Senate'. Thus the
suggested régime is a dictatorship made palatable by constitutional assurances; it is the 'people's leader-state' (*völkische
Führerstaat*), without Hitler. There can be no doubt that Popitz's
plan was fully in keeping with his fundamental outlook and
cannot be explained in terms of tactical adjustment to an exceptional situation. Popitz's strong opposition to general suffrage,
his declared aversion to the multi-party state, his deliberate
advocacy of a presidential solution to the question of parliamentary principle, and his demand for a second chamber in the form
of an upper house, had already placed him on the extreme right
even before 1933.

In this connection it is of special significance that Popitz, just
like Carl Schmitt whom he so often cited, vigorously repudiated
every form of pluralism, or 'polycracy' as he called it. In a lec-

ture before the Wednesday Club in the spring of 1933, he welcomed National Socialism as having overcome ' the pluralistic forces bound to material interests ' and looked forward to the rise of ' a master class based upon knowledge and responsibility, and serving the people to which it is allied '.[105] He advocated a constitutional structure in keeping with the German character. His own ' social ' outlook, which he himself stressed, was basically a defensive one; at any rate he failed to rid himself of the Bismarckian error of political patriarchalism involving the belief that equal political rights for the workers were unnecessary if they were given social welfare instead. He rejected Goerdeler's plan for a single trade union for he saw in it, not altogether without reason, a ' centre of power of the first order,' and a ' state within the state '. Until the end he continued to warn Stauffenberg, through Jessen and Hassell, against Goerdeler's plans. His support of the factory unions was tactically determined, for basically he thought in terms of ' professional ' solutions along the lines of the Third Reich, adopting, however, a more positive attitude towards the Kreisau proposal for profit-sharing employees. His fiscal policy, too, was aimed at raising the standard of living among the lower classes of the population.[106]

As an opponent of all forms of federalism, he was prepared to accept some degree of autonomy but – and in this he resembled Schulenburg – not Goerdeler's programme as a whole. It is significant that Goerdeler's proposal to abolish the office of district president led to considerable ill-feeling between the two men. Again, when Popitz declared before the Gestapo that a strong unified state was needed to combat ' the internationalism and the Judaisation of the Weimar régime and the intolerable convulsions of the parliamentary parties ', it is unlikely that he did so merely to ingratiate himself. In questions of foreign affairs, too, his ideology was not unlike that of National Socialism. He spoke of the ' mission ' of the German state in Central Europe, and demanded ' a national, homogeneous people imbued with the consciousness of community '.[107] Thus his political outlook cannot be described as simply traditional. For Popitz, as Rothfels has pointed out,[108] and as is shown by the fact that he established contact with Himmler, wished to make use of the Third Reich's Praetorian guard. For this reason, Kreisau roundly contested his suitability for inclusion in the eventual cabinet, although Goerdeler was willing to overlook differences of opinion for the sake of Popitz's expert qualifications. The constitutional proposals of Popitz, Hassell and Jessen in no way represent a ' conservative ' reversion to the constitutional monarchical régime of the Bismarckian epoch; their nature is predominantly fascist, so that they are rather a continuation of than a return to Papen's proposed presidential dictatorship, and postulate the complete subordination of society to the state.

## The Constitutional Proposals of Carl Goerdeler and the Kreisau Circle

We have just seen that the markedly authoritarian constitutional programmes drafted by Hassell, Jessen and Popitz, as also at first by Beck, were intended to consolidate the existing upper class (in so far as it had not been compromised by active participation in the criminal National Socialist régime), in its leading rôle, and in no way envisaged any kind of democratic selection of leaders. By contrast, the two most important constitutional programmes produced by the German Opposition, Goerdeler's circumstantial plan, and *Grundsätze für die Neuordnung* (' Principles for a New Order '), drafted by the Kreisau Circle, are the expression of specifically socio-political objectives, revealing the whole gamut of the political influences that were at work in the Resistance; at the same time they have a homogeneous character which makes them clearly distinguishable from the proposals put forward by Popitz and Hassell.

Goerdeler's constitutional plan, which first appeared in his memorandum *Das Ziel* written towards the end of 1941,[109] was partly the result of contacts already established through Hassell with Trott, Yorck and Moltke; it was not till after the writing of the memorandum that he became well acquainted with Leuschner. Early in 1942, Goerdeler submitted his draft to Hassell and his friends; it earned the manifest approval of Beck (some of whose ideas it incorporated),[110] but an opposite reaction from

Hassell and Jessen, who regarded it as ' a pointless attempt to cancel an existing state of affairs '; indeed, they saw in it a kind of ' reactionary' document. Their view was consistent in that Goerdeler was not prepared to take over lock, stock and barrel the institutions of the *völkische Führerstaat* and this Hassell, Jessen and Popitz interpreted as a desire to return to ' parliamentary' forms.[111] Certain authoritarian aspects of Goerdeler's constitutional model may, therefore, be attributed to his endeavour to comply with the ideas of this group; on the other hand it should be emphasised that to a very great extent Goerdeler had succeeded in shaking off ' reactionary' political thought.[112]

*Grundsätze für die Neuordnung* was drafted by Moltke and was based upon the discussions held at the first and second Kreisau meetings; it was inspired chiefly by the ideas of Moltke, Steltzer, Yorck, Trott and Delp. While the draft contains no definite constitutional plan and is capable of various interpretations, it must be considered within the context of the circle's conceptions of social and political affairs as we have already described them. Like Goerdeler's plan, they are based upon the suppression of egalitarian elements in the democratic system, with strong emphasis on the subsidiary principle and that of self-government, as also on the transfer of political policy-making into the more manageable sphere of local and communal autonomy.

The anti-egalitarian nature of their ideas on constitution is most evident in the clauses on franchise and electoral procedure. Both advocate universal franchise, Kreisau setting the voting age at 21 and Goerdeler at 25 (24).[113] Both plans also envisaged plurality of votes for fathers of families. Kreisau proposed a supplementary vote in respect of each child below voting age, and Goerdeler, two votes for fathers of families having at least three legitimate children. This was in keeping with the emphasis put upon family life as the basic unit of the state. The age of eligibilty was set by Kreisau at 27, and by Goerdeler at 30 (28) for parish and district councils; at 35 for election to the *Reichstag*; in both plans members of the armed forces were declared ineligible, as were political officials for election to *Landtag* and *Reichstag*; Goerdeler excluded officials in general and clergy of all denominations; naturally the ban did not in this case extend to officials of local self-governing bodies. These provisos reflect the endeavour to keep politics out of the civil service and to prevent the infiltration into representative bodies of centralist elements. Kreisau also regarded women as ineligible. Schulenburg's proposal that eligibility to local councils should also be made dependent on property and marriage failed to find acceptance.[114]

These clauses evince the tendency to favour the type of the ' notable ', that is to say, the independent, socially integrated, respected citizen who deserves well of his community; this derived in Goerdeler from the basic idea of Stein's urban system, and in Kreisau rather from the idea of ' small communities '; in Steltzer and Delp, however, great stress is laid upon the Steinian autonomous tradition.[115] Goerdeler's endeavour to lay down a residential qualification for eligibility in order to obviate the nomination of ' outsiders ' by supraregional associations is not specifically referred to by Kreisau, but the latter's stipulation of a quorum of candidates was intended to fulfil the same purpose. In both cases the main concern was that those seeking election should be known to the electors and that the electoral districts should be ' manageable ' units.

The unfortunate experiences of the Republic with proportional and party-list representation led to the latter's unanimous rejection by all groups of the Opposition. Leber summed up the arguments against these methods as follows : ' Far from doing justice to its true function of ensuring the selection of suitable men and of establishing confidence between rulers and ruled, it simply carries over into politics the vicious circle of party hierarchy.' Proportional representation prevents ' the formation of broad streams of opinion ' and gives rise to multi-party fragmentation.[116] For the same reasons Bergstraesser, in a constitutional plan drafted for Leuschner, recommended vote by personal merit.[117] Goerdeler's and Steltzer's critique went even further. Proportional representation, they maintained, compelled the parties to stress programmes and not personalities and relieved representatives of all sense of responsibility towards the electors; Bergstraesser objected to the denigration of the ' democratic compromise ' implicit in such statements. The paradox inherent in the demand on the one hand for parties having ' pure ' ideologies and the condemnation on the other of ' ideologisation ' of politics is characteristic of the mentality of Leber, Goerdeler and Steltzer.

Relative majority representation, implicit in the Kreisau plans and explicitly demanded by Goerdeler, was to guarantee the ' organic connection ' between electors and elected and facilitate the formation of small electoral districts. Kreisau therefore envisaged the splitting-up of the councils of larger municipalities into a number of representative bodies having equal rights; in cities, the town council would be elected from these by indirect suffrage. It was not explained how this would be done in the case of communes, in so far as they were unequal in size to the *Länder* which, it was planned, would have from three to five million inhabitants. Nor were the Kreisau plans explicit on the subject of candidate nomination, though the intention was obviously to hand over these tasks to the ' small communities '.

Difficulties of this kind arose because the plans were concerned with obviating interference by political parties, at least in the earliest elections. As Steltzer pointed out, ' corporate self-government is a safeguard against the predominance of centralist parties which inexorably introduces political strife into the smallest village and thus destroys the sense of corporate responsibility '.[118] This was in agreement with Goerdeler's view, for during his time of local government he had invariably found the parties to be a disruptive element.[119] The solution he sought resembles in principle that of the Kreisau Circle. He went beyond the idea of small circles of electors by recommending that a quarter of the representatives be chosen by the whole community, not by party list representation, but by the relative majority of most of the electoral districts, another quarter being chosen by the Trade associations. Later he repudiated this scheme, limiting to four the number of candidates each district might put up. These were to be nominated by occupational groups, the ' German Trade Union ', and the ' political movements '. In this he differs basically from Kreisau, which sought to obviate the participation of ' organisations ', and more particularly that of a centralised organisation such as the ' German Trade Union '. In practice such a restriction of nomination rights would have been intolerable; it followed from the consideration that relative majority representation would foster the formation of a few large parties, whose existence it in turn presupposed. Now since the associations responsible for the nomination of candidates were democratically founded in Goerdeler's sense of the term, this proposal was basically no more than the translation of the Kreisau concept into social reality; the enfranchisement of occupationally conceived associations corresponded to the enfranchisement of the small communities; 'small' district elections would be replaced by association elections.

Hence the question of candidature in communal (for Kreisau also in district council) elections was of crucial importance, because it was envisaged that election to the higher-ranking assemblies would be by indirect vote. According to the Kreisau plan, members of the *Landtage* or of their equivalent, the municipal assemblies, would be elected by the district councils and by the municipal representative assemblies of those towns or town divisions not forming part of districts. These would in turn be responsible for electing the *Reichstag*. Goerdeler's system was more complex, involving a threefold election, first from the communal representative body to the district council, then from the district council to the *Landtag* (*Gautag*) and finally from the *Landtag* to the *Reichstag*. Thus a sort of vicious circle would be formed, in that the procedure would lead to the restriction of those available for representative functions to a comparatively small group, especially since Goerdeler, in order to ensure the selection of an able executive élite, postulated that candidates for the *Landtage* should have spent five years as communal deputies and as members of a district council, and that candidates for the *Reichstag* should have held public office for a similar period. Kreisau succeeded to some extent in avoiding this error by stipulating that half of the *Landtag* members should not belong to one of the electoral bodies. From another aspect this clause also had its drawbacks since it meant that in practice a subsidiary election would become cooption. As regards election to the *Reichstag*, this was to be only a 'provisional' measure simply because there was no other way of forming a constitution. Goerdeler's plan, similar in principle but differing in method, proposed that half the *Reichstag* deputies should be elected by direct vote. The personal merit of the candidate was ensured by the fact that nominations could only be made by four privileged associations and by the clause that the deputy must be domiciled in the electoral district and must have proved himself in public service. This reveals a distinctly centralist mentality, whereas Kreisau deliberately envisaged the use of the *Landtage* with their federalistic structure as organs of decentralisation.

In practice, however, there was considerable agreement between the two plans. Goerdeler made his departure from the conception of a liberalism based upon ' notables ', and Kreisau from a doctrine of organisational hierarchy. Ultimately this amounted to the same thing. Both plans sought to avoid rule by professional parliamentarians, to replace the ' functionary ' and demagogue with the man firmly ensconced in the local ' community ', and to achieve a ' harmonious ' condition of political policy-making. There were to be no large-scale election campaigns, for elections would be confined to the selection of trustworthy representatives who must first present their individual programme to the electors, a programme related to communal and district matters. Both plans combined the representational principle of classical liberalism with a kind of direct democracy at the lowest level, though in Goerdeler's case this was virtually invalidated by the clause that representative assemblies including the *Landtage* were to be convened only at certain intervals. In communes with more than 12 deputies and in districts and *Länder* respectively, central committees were to be elected; these would act as advisers to executive authorities and also have right of decision in certain matters, thus representing yet another grade of indirect voting at all three levels. Their sessions were to be *in camera*; communal representative bodies were to meet every quarter, the district councils twice a year and the *Landtage* only once a year, more especially for the discussion of budgetary matters; resolutions relating to expenditure were conditional on simultaneous resolutions providing for reimbursement. This followed immediately from the proposals put forward by Goerdeler to the Reich President in 1932. They were in keeping with his dislike of large assemblies which inevitably tended towards parliamentary forms, and with his habit of basing political decisions on personal discussion; at the same time they revealed unmistakably the full extent to which Goerdeler based his views on monetary policy – so aligning himself with Brüning – as also the dominant rôle played by local government in his constitutional thinking.[120]

Goerdeler was inspired by the idea of promoting civic interest in self-government, but his irrepressible *dirigiste* tendencies led him into extremes. Fearing that parliamentary forms would permit ill-informed, ' demagogic' elements to determine political decisions, he was reduced to plans whereby the people's representatives, once the government had been elected, retained only advisory functions. He repudiated ' uncontrolled, over-democratic parliamentarianism ', but in fact the government he envisaged was in no way answerable to parliament, and the system he devised would have exceeded Papen's wildest dreams. The Reich Chancellor would at first be responsible for directing policy in the cabinet of which the ministers, as in Bismarck's constitution, would not be answerable to parliament; however the *Generalstatthalter*, or Regent, must dismiss both Chancellor and ministers if requested to do so by a two-thirds majority in the *Reichstag* or by a simple majority in both the *Reichstag* and the *Reichsständehaus* (second house). The Regent must then propose a new government. The government would at all times be empowered to enact decrees in lieu of laws, with the exception of budgetary and fiscal legislation and the conclusion of foreign treaties; such decrees must be annulled or withdrawn should this be demanded by a majority in both houses, one of them a two-thirds majority.

This meant the application of Article 48 of the Weimar Constitution as a state of normality and also, by analogy, its application to the formation of the government, the latter being wholly in the hands of the Regent. This procedure, which relieved parliament of all initiative in the choice of Chancellor and the formation of the government, leaving it only the function of a constitutional ' brake ', has been wrongly construed as a ' constructive vote of no confidence ' and regarded as a parallel of Article 66 of the Basic Law of the Federal Republic. Parliament could not, furthermore, compel the Regent to nominate the government of its own choice; where there is no vote of confidence there cannot be a vote of no confidence. Now the *Reichsständehaus* consisted partly in leaders of a variety of occupational associations, union representatives and employers' representatives, and partly in notables appointed by the Regent; it was unlikely that a house so constituted would, in practice, decide to enter into open conflict with the government on crucial political issues, so that in every case parliament would need a two-thirds majority if it was to rescind legislation or bring down the government. Thus in principle the government might be a minority cabinet; the two-thirds majority required to bring about its fall meant virtually that in accordance with the article the proposal of a new Chancellor would also require a majority of sufficient size to effect a constitutional change; this, together with the Regent's right to dissolve parliament, meant the effective abolition of parliamentary opposition. The *Reichstag* had no independent legislative rights; in order to pass laws it required the assent of the non-elected *Reichsständehaus*. Legislation with financial implications could only be enacted with the assent of the Chancellor. ' Thus the head of state is able to impose new political measures by changing his ministers or the Chancellor . . . or by a renewed appeal to both Houses, or by fresh elections.'[121]

The Kreisau system – in so far as it is apparent from their draft – is by contrast far more flexible; the second chamber (*Reichsrat*) which in principle is similarly constituted, has no share in legislation. The authority of the *Reichstag*, unlike that in Goerdeler's plan, is not restricted. But the circumstances governing the formation of the government are similar. While the Chancellor – but not the ministers – is appointed by the Regent with the assent of the *Reichstag*, the Regent can dismiss the Chancellor at his own discretion, provided that he immediately appoints another; the *Reichstag*, on the other hand, has the right, if it has a qualified majority, to demand the dismissal of the Chancellor provided that at the same time a new Chancellor is proposed to the Regent. Here too we find applied to the formation of the government the construct upon which Article 48 of the Weimar Constitution is based, and which deprives parliament of its primacy in legislation – again with the disadvantage that in case of conflict the Regent would be in a position, through his right of dismissal, to compel the acceptance of a Chancellor of his own choice.

It may seem otiose to discuss in terms of their practicability plans which had not yet been fully thought out and had necessarily remained somewhat fragmentary. Yet by doing so we are able to assess their position in the history of German thought. Their lack of precision derives in part from the fact that no one had any very clear idea of the practical function or potential effects of the constitutional principles that had been put forward. Hence it is only possible to discuss tentatively what specific forms the intended régimes would have assumed. Steltzer spoke of a 'modified parliamentary system ',[122] but the expression is only partially true of the Kreisau plan. The position of the Regent, appointed for a term of 12 years by the *Reichstag* at the proposal of the *Reichsrat*, is so strong that at best sovereignty can be said to be shared between parliament and the head of state. Parliament is deprived by the indirect vote of the support of public opinion represented by the major parties and furthermore is counterbalanced by the *Reichsrat*, the majority of whose members are appointed by the Regent. Thus the disadvantage of the presidential system which became plainly apparent at the fall of Brüning's cabinet, namely the government's virtual dependence on the head of state, is reinforced rather than weakened. The parliamentary principle is upheld only by the clause stipulating that the Chancellor be appointed with the assent of parliament; but the government's parliamentary dependence on the confidence of the majority is more or less illusory, since parliament is only able to effect a change of Chancellor with a qualified, presumably a two-thirds, majority. This constitutional construct, too, cannot be equated with the 'constructive vote of no confidence' whose only real intent is the avoidance of negative oppositional majorities.[123]

Goerdeler's plan restricts parliament to a purely controlling function as understood in liberal constitutionalism. With the *Reichsständehaus*, itself largely appointed by the Regent, it shares legislative powers in competition with the government, yet here too laws involving expenditure can only be passed with the assent of the latter. In this connection Goerdeler maintained that he was seeking ' a repetition neither of the Bismarckian Reich, nor of Weimar, nor of the Third Reich ', his aim being rather to combine the advantages of all three. This comment, written while he was under arrest in 1944, is an answer to the strong criticism to which his constitutional plan had been subjected from many quarters before the attempted *coup*. Right up to the eve of the attempt Popitz, through Hassell and Jessen, had made known his misgivings about Beck's and Goerdeler's plans, thus arousing in Stauffenberg the fear that these involved a return to the Weimar régime. Although Wirmer had transmitted and stressed the ' originality and constructiveness ' of Goerdeler's ideas and had stated expressly that these ' in no way represented a proposal for a rehash of old conditions '[124] there was still evidence of some mistrust towards Goerdeler. Leber and the Kreisau Circle were even more ruthless in their criticism. Yorck bluntly declared that a revolution under Beck and Goerdeler would bring into being an extremely reactionary régime, involving the resurgence of the old parties and trade unions, thus restoring the situation of 1932. The ominous expression ' Kerencky solution ' was also used, evidence of the great fear that Germany would experience ' Bolshevisation ' after her defeat.[125] Nor was Yorck's prognosis wholly unjustified, as the outline of Goerdeler's constitutional plan has shown. Goerdeler was still too much under the spell of political events during the era of Brüning and Papen, and until his death he continued to believe that he could have averted the fate of Germany by joining Papen's cabinet.[126]

Yet did Goerdeler really desire an authoritarian system, as near possible along the lines of Bulgaria or Hungary? In spite of the high esteem in which he held Bismarck's personality and historical achievement, his constitutional plans went back even further, for their prototype was the thought of the Prussian reformers, as interpreted by predominantly nationalist historians. The return to Steinian reforms and the German tradition of self-government found in Goerdeler an ardent advocate, and he was by no means the only one. The endeavour of the German Opposition to evolve constitutional reform that would be in keeping with the nature of Germany's development – with ' the essential

K

Germany' – together with their rejection of the Western constitutional models, a rejection for which the thinking of the
twenties had been a preparation, inevitably led to an attempt to
follow up the ideas on reform of Stein and his colleagues. The
psychological conditions under which the Opposition was working, especially in view of 'the absence of contact with what the
outside world was thinking and feeling ',[127] led to the belief that
the democratic parliamentary system was now completely obso-
lete. Thus Bonhoeffer, in a memorandum intended for external
consumption, was able to put forward the view that it would be
impossible for many European countries, including France and
Italy, to revert to a fully evolved system of parliamentary democracy.[128] The memory of the Prussian revolution was, for the
conspirators, a living, dynamic impulse. Their strength to rebel
came from an unbroken historical continuity, and their chief
concern, as Trott expressed it, was not to save the German Army
and German power but above all 'to safeguard Germany's historical continuity '.[129]

The recourse to Stein is a very real factor in the thinking of
the Opposition. Whereas Popitz and Hassell turned to the conservative elements in Stein's concept of state and Goerdeler
stressed his liberalism, Steltzer, Delp, Moltke, Trott, Haubach
and Mierendorff looked to the earlier statesman rather for what
his reformative plans contained of ideas on partnership. Leuschner demanded 'autonomy in all spheres of social and economic
life ', and when they were in prison both he and Leber studied
the works of Freiherr von Stein. In Bergstraesser's memorandum
mentioned earlier, we also find an affirmation of the tradition of
self-government which derives from Stein.[130] Yet while this may
have been the common origin of the plans for reform, each of
the latter was to have its own particular slant. Steltzer believed
that what Stein had in mind in thinking of municipal order –
'the urban society as a moral and spiritual community of free
and honourable men ' – had been lost in the course of industrialisation and 'stereotyping '; he therefore regarded as essential a
deliberate reconstruction of the sense of community, and cited
Stein's view that what is important is not the 'organisation of
the constitution' but the 'perfecting of man ': 'The charac-

ter of volition must be formed, not knowledge alone.' Steltzer defined self-government as ' democracy in the structures upon which political life is built '.[131]

Goerdeler, on the other hand, was of the opinion that self-government had continued unimpaired, that it had manifested itself even in Wilhelmian Germany ' so clearly as to arouse universal admiration ', and that throughout the Weimar Republic ' in spite of the extreme democratisation of the franchise ' and of ' widespread demoralisation among the political parties ', it had successfully survived. He did not regard self-government as the product of Prussian reform but, like Stein, related it to ' the ancient Teuton autonomy '. In Goerdeler's view, self-government was the state-forming principle *sui generis* and was in total opposition to the democratic (to him, plebiscitary) idea.[132] ' Self-government and democracy are thus independent forms of organisation and operation ', he wrote in his unfinished *Gedanken zur Neuordnung und Selbstverwaltung* (' Thoughts on a New Order and Self-Government '). ' Self-awareness and a sense of responsibility ', as also tradition, were the foundations of all self-government, but these had been considered by Weimar as a stumbling-block to political democracy : ' Democracies endeavour to suppress self-government because the stabilising effect of self-government on practical work is intolerable to party headquarters engaged in struggling against each other.' Hence, in his memorandum intended for Hitler, Goerdeler was able to put forward the view that healthy self-government was essential in the ' Führer state ' if it were not to succumb to spiritual decay as a result of the hypertrophy of purely bureaucratic elements, or fall victim to the subversive influence of individual group interests under cover of the NSDAP. Later he was to suggest that countries without self-government, like the USA and the USSR would succumb to internal subversion or, as could be seen in France, to inner stagnation.[133]

In spite of the *dirigiste* tone of Goerdeler's terminology and his view of self-government as the panacea for all political systems, these also served the Kreisau Circle for the same ideological purpose, which was to deflect the egalitarian and plebiscitary tendencies in modern society and to substitute a sense of community for a prevalence of private interests. By comparison with this, Moltke regarded the nature of the state as being of secondary importance, though, with good reason, he believed a monarchy to be impossible. The arguments brought forward by Kreisau in support of self-government were the same as Goerdeler's, but here self-government meant partnership in the form of collaboration in a political community, and not merely a controlling and counselling factor for the executive; nor were the elected officials regarded as magistrates in the traditional sense, but rather as executors of communal decisions. Both conceptions agree, however, in their endeavour to restrict political policy-making to the field of rational, practical decision, to eliminate in so far as possible the struggle for power between groups, and to replace proportional representation by a principle reminiscent of the block voting system. The self-government of trade groups planned by both Goerdeler and Kreisau, leading to a state economy dependent on the indirect vote such as Moellendorf had aimed at in the 1920s, was in accordance with this idea. Both envisaged the equal representation in trade associations of employers and employees from the relevant occupational groups. By thus creating a twofold structure of political and occupational self-government, which in turn would be represented in the second chamber, a harmonious settlement at regional level of divergent social interests seemed to be assured.[134]

The prevailing mentality of the Opposition, which regarded political policy-making as the layman's participation in public administration, is plainly apparent in the identification of the principle of self-government with federalism. Neither Goerdeler nor Kreisau enlarge on the question as to how far the *Länder*, which are described as ' self-governing bodies ', are to have an independent political character. This is particularly the case with Kreisau, in spite of the federal nature of the proposed institutions of *Land* ' Administrator ' and *Land* ' Lord-Lieutenant '. Paradoxically, Goerdeler was inclined to give greater powers than did the Kreisau plans to the *Land*, which he regarded as a self-governing entity. Besides the ' Lord-Lieutenant ' there was to be the Supreme *Land* President whose office with respect to the lower authorities was purely supervisory and not executive. As opposed to this, the Kreisau plan provided for considerable powers of intervention on the part of the central government in economic, social and political matters, as also in questions of regional planning. In practice this would have meant lasting restrictions on the independence of communal and district self-government. This was not consistent with the basic intention of Kreisau thought; obviously their original idea had been to eliminate the financial supremacy of the Reich, but this had been given up largely at Schulenburg's instigation.[135]

Goerdeler's conception of a strong administration with extensive self-government unhampered by competing authorities meant that the representatives of the autonomous bodies, particularly the supreme *Land* executives, would become a powerful intermediate leading class within the state. This was not so with Kreisau. The *Land* Administrator, elected by the *Landtag* for a term of 12 years, who was at the same time a member of the *Reichsrat*, was empowered to put up a ' Lord-Lieutenant ' for election; the former had supervisory powers over the *Land* administration and was also responsible for the implementation of Reich policy. His appointment had to be ratified by the Reich Regent. Thus the position of the *Land* ' Lord-Lieutenant ' was in practice much weaker than in Goerdeler's plan, while the *Land* Administrator necessarily became the representative of national interests. This unintentional fault in the Kreisau construct derived from the partnership principle which in no way corresponded to the demands of modern political administration. This prevented Kreisau from conceiving a federal structure within a federal state, so that they too regarded the National Socialist coordination of the *Länder* as a *fait accompli*, and envisaged, in contrast to Goerdeler, complete territorial reorganisation involving the abolition of the older *Land* divisions.[136]

## *The Party System, Trade Unions and the Democratic Collective Movement*

The German Opposition's proposals for a new order follow the Nazi system in rejecting the responsible political rôle of the parties which is an inherent feature of the modern parliamentary system. Bergstraesser's constitutional plan was an exception to this; it did not, however, advocate an immediate return to the parliamentary system, or early elections which would be premature, but sought, as did the others, the revival of political life by the introduction of local self-government with the help of the churches and the trade unions. Here again we find the proposal to form a second chamber, by indirect election, out of the self-governing bodies which was intended to counterbalance the parliamentary rule of the parties.[137] All the other plans looked upon political parties as predominantly separatist forces, having no inner bond with the people and without democratic legitimation and therefore a menace to the unity of state and 'community'.

The repudiation of the party system, which was the fruit of organisational and *étatiste* thinking, throws light on Steltzer's remark, made in 1949, that the parties had not succeeded in getting beyond their ideological origins and the limitations of narrow perspectives. Before the Parliamentary Council met, he had recommended the adoption of the Kreisau system on the grounds that only a structure of that nature could safeguard democracy against the claims to power of centralist parties 'which demand supremacy over the state and thus render impossible the construction of a healthy polity'. German democracy, as it was evolving after the war, he described as 'a disguised form of new party totalitarianism'.[138] Ideas of this kind were typical of the Opposition generally, none of whom, remarkably enough, appeared to notice the qualitative difference between the NSDAP and the Weimar democratic parties. Goerdeler, too, was strongly opposed to the 'party state' and in a conversation with Kluge said of his plans that they were concerned with 'a balanced synthesis without a party structure'.[139]

Yet it was a question about which he could not make up his mind. In the party fragmentation of Weimar he rightly saw a prime cause of the crisis. The demand for the majority franchise was, for Leuschner, Leber and Kaiser, a consequence of their experiences in the Republic. Goerdeler thought the British two-party system – which he knew no longer existed – to be ideal, but he doubted if it could be applied to German conditions and hence continued to explore all kinds of possibilities. Towards the end of 1944 he proposed that only the three strongest parties should be admitted, and that the mandates of the weaker groups should be cancelled. He had in mind the formation of conservative, liberal and socialist parties along English lines, while utterly rejecting any possibility of a new Communist party, or of parties with a denominational-Christian basis. It was only with reluctance that he reached this conclusion, but his travels in Bulgaria in 1938 had made him realise that the formal proscription of parties was ineffectual and that only a franchise carefully constructed in accordance with the people's educational standards could avert party fragmentation.[140]

Hans Peters declares that the Kreisau Circle, too, 'had not contemplated any immediate restriction of the party system';[141] but there can be no doubt that, at least to begin with, all forms of political policy-making were quite consistently rejected except for those based upon the autonomous system of the 'small communities'. This also explains the tension between Kreisau on the one hand and Goerdeler and the trade union group working with him on the other. The proposed restoration of the earlier associations with their ideological outlook seemed to the Kreisauites a retrograde step. This caused Delp to warn Letterhaus and Gross against Hermann Kaiser, Goerdeler's collaborator, as the advocate of a 'reactionary' programme recommending that they ally themselves instead with Schulenburg and Moltke.[142] At that time – the summer of 1942 – it was still hoped that a fundamental reconstruction of political life might be achieved.

The main bone of contention between the two groups was the trade union question. Leuschner's endeavour to transform the *Deutsche Arbeitsfront* into a unified socialist union was in opposition to the Kreisau policy of extreme decentralisation. Moltke and his friends were not inimical to trade unions; their object was the formation of factory unions. These were not, however, to assume the character of mere representative bodies for the employees, but rather of a works 'economic community', to which both factory owners and the whole of the labour force would belong. It was hoped in this way to establish contractually the rights and duties of the factory union, including co-decision by the workers' representatives in the running of the business, the provision of the workers with reliable information on the financial position, and their participation in profits and growth; all this was to be the responsibility of the industrial self-governing bodies. Here was a practical application of the idea of ' small communities '. There were to be no class differences in the factory union, which was to be a true ' works community ' on a comradely basis. It was a Utopian project that would have considerably hampered the workers' freedom of movement, and it bore a certain ideological similarity to the National Socialist labour system. Among the socialists, it found favour only with Mierendorff, being rejected out of hand by Haubach and Maass, and more especially by Leuschner. But since the trade unions were regarded as an essential element, a compromise was reached; the ' German Trade Union ', as a ' necessary means ' to the realisation of the economic programme and to the construction of the state this presupposed, was to exist only temporarily. ' Its purpose will be fulfilled in the execution of this programme and the transfer of its duties to the state authorities and industrial self-governing body ', declared the memorandum *Grundsätze für die Neuordnung*. It is noteworthy, as van Roon has shown,[143] that Moltke never gave up hope of being able to go back on that compromise. To avoid the rise of a class of functionaries distinct from the workers, Yorck and Moltke demanded that workers' representatives should spend at least half the day doing their accustomed jobs. Even Mierendorff opposed this suggestion which was typical of their social Utopian thinking, and Trott aligned himself here with the socialists.[144]

There is no doubt that Goerdeler's and Leuschner's views in this respect were a good deal more realistic, and it is not surprising that Leuschner was blamed by some of the Kreisau group, with whom he retained contact through Hermann Maass although no longer attending their deliberations, for remaining too much under the influence of the ideas of the ' old ' organisations. Leuschner had early begun to plan, in collaboration with Kaiser, a unified trade union as a rallying-point when the collapse came. He succeeded in persuading Goerdeler that it would be inadvisable to incorporate the *Deutsche Arbeitsfront* in the reconstructed state; its funds must be transferred to the 'German Trade Union' which would act as the workers' only representative body, membership being compulsory; further, it would have parity of representation with the trade associations in the *Reichsständehaus* proposed by Goerdeler. Under the influence of Goerdeler, but also because of his reiterated belief that German labour was satisfied with the institution of the *Deutsche Arbeitsfront*, Leuschner would appear seriously to have considered giving the union a vital position in the new political order, while renouncing the formation of political parties. The 'German Trade Union', as Goerdeler explained, was to be 'an organic continuation of the equally comprehensive *Arbeitsfront*'. Undoubtedly the principle of the *Deutsche Arbeitsfront* was seen by the trade unionists as a possible solution to the social problem, and the decision to avoid politically orientated unions in the future belongs within the context of the universal criticism of the political party system. Leuschner admitted the principle that the unions must be free of all influence from political groups. He adopted Goerdeler's plan whereby the union would be responsible for social insurance and would take over the work of the labour exchanges; in addition he aimed at the socialisation of basic and key industries, as well as an independent economic existence for the trade unions which would enable them to 'exert considerable influence, in their capacity as producers, upon the shaping of the economy'.[145]

It was inevitable that Popitz should object to the exceptional power that would accrue to the unions through Goerdeler's plans. Leuschner, on the other hand, would seem to have overrated the political opportunities he believed the unions would afford him. He declined the offer of the Chancellorship after the revolution on the grounds that it would hinder his work of building up the 'German Trade Union'; nor was he at all anxious to assume the post of Vice-Chancellor. Leuschner was a practical politician, and for that reason it is difficult to pin down the social order he had in mind. He appeared much impressed by Ludwig Reichhold's ideas, which were debated in the Jakob Kaiser/Elfriede Nebgen circle. From some surviving notes he made in 1942, it would seem that he held Reichhold's obscure conception of a new class order to be viable. 'The labour movement' he wrote, 'represents the political class of the workers as a class of the European community equal in rank, deriving from the same roots, subject to the same laws and enjoying the same rights as the peasant and the middle classes.'[146] These formulations which incorporate part of Reichhold's theses, show a tendency towards a democratic class state.

It is of significance for the assessment of the socio-political ideas of the Opposition that the desire to leave behind the parliamentary party state was not confined to conservative groups in the narrower sense. Not only Leuschner, but also Habermann, Wirmer, and perhaps too Jakob Kaiser, whom Delp criticised for his trade-union orientation, all contemplated the synthesis of professional and democratic elements. Habermann suggested to Schulenburg that he should take over the leadership of a proposed peasants' party. There would also be corresponding middle-class and workers' parties; the latter, after the pattern of the British Labour Party, would not be Marxist-orientated and would probably be the responsibility of the trade-union organisations. The Christian trade unionists, for their part, rejected the idea of restarting the SPD, as also the possible revival of a socialist class party. The Cologne Opposition proposed the creation of a ' party ' consisting of all 'working men', while Hermes postulated a broad, Christian-orientated people's party, but as the war went on these plans began to crystallise into a conception common to all the Opposition groups of a democratic collective movement comprehending all sectors of the community.[147]

By his emphasis on the trade union idea, the more so in that this involved consideration for his Christian-minded partners, Leuschner was brought into some degree of controversy with the representatives of Social Democracy, albeit mitigated by their mutually friendly relations. This applied particularly to Leber and Mierendorff, the latter having collaborated in drafting the programme for the unified trade union. Of the situation at the end of 1942, Maass wrote :

The question as to whether there is to be a special political organisation besides the trade union has not yet been settled.

Some measure of agreement was reached in that it was decided not to restore the former multi-party system, *one* party at the most being contemplated, which should consist of a careful selection of politically conscious elements.[148]

The reserve which, as a result, Leuschner felt towards the idea of founding a popular party independent of the trade unions is confirmed by Bergstraesser's memorandum in which the leading rôle after the collapse is assigned to the churches and to the trade union.[149]

In the concept of a wide democratic popular movement which would support the government formed after the revolution, the plans of the Opposition coincided with those of the European *Résistance*, but with the distinction that a popular movement could not be formed until the revolution had taken place. In this we see a reflection of the ideological dilemma : on the one hand it was thought undesirable to erect a new order on a plebiscitary basis, and on the other (though this did not apply to Popitz, Hassell and Jessen) the cooperation of the population was felt to be indispensable. Hence this question stirred up bitter disputes among the different groups of the Opposition, which at times was on the verge of disruption. The idea of replacing the former major parties by a single integrated democratic party comprising all the available politically constructive elements was not inapposite in view of the social disintegration then in progress in the Third Reich yet neither was it devoid of fascist characteristics. Maass introduced into Jakob Kaiser's circle a paper by Mihail Manoïlescu, a Rumanian and supporter of the ' Iron Guard ', on ' the single party as a political institution in the new régime ', in which the one-party system was put forward as the solution of the future, when the state party would be responsible for the formation of the élite essential to the modern mass society. Maass' propositions, however, met with little response except by way of opposition.[150] Moltke's suggestion that a new political élite should be drawn from all social strata, while based on a totally different premise, was perhaps not wholly foreign to such ideas. Schulenburg's views were doubtless of a similar nature, since he had originally wished to transform the NSDAP into a political order whose function it would be to select and educate potential leaders in a special community though itself not seeking political power.[151] There were other schemes of the same kind; Stauffenberg's so-called ' oath ', for instance, though little is known of its origins.[152]

These conceptions, which bore the imprint of the irrationalism of the twenties, retreated in face of the plan for a ' popular movement above all party ', a collective movement, that is, which incorporated the vision of the ' people's community '. In the early summer of 1943, Mierendorff and Haubach were elaborating a programme for ' Socialist Action ' which, as a ' popular movement above all party ', was to unite Christian, socialist, Communist and liberal forces to save Germany. The programme's objectives were moderate and socialist in the Kreisau manner; emphasis was laid on the Christian foundations of European culture, a settlement was demanded both with the West and with Soviet Russia, and ' all enemies of National Socialism ' were called upon to create ' a united front ' – as opposed to ' party strife '. The programme, which had originated from the deliberations of Moltke and Yorck, reflected Mierendorff's conviction that the future must bring an alliance of the two forces which alone had resisted the chaos of National Socialism – Christianity and Socialism. Yorck, as opposed to Beck and Goerdeler, demanded a broader basis for the proposed revolution ' to include Social Democracy, even its most extreme left wing '.[153]

The determining factor in this plan was the necessity to oppose Communist agitation with an effective political power, a consideration which led Kreisau to proceed beyond mere ' emergency and rallying measures ' to the reshaping of political reality, thus assuming an active rôle in the conspiracy. In a memorandum commissioned by Moltke and written in Turkey towards the end of 1943,[154] which was intended to convey the conspiracy's aims to the Americans, stress was laid on the danger a Communist-Bolshevist Germany and German national Bolshevism would present. It could happen that ' a democratically inclined German government would meet with opposition from the working masses '; an attempt must therefore be made to win over hitherto pro-Russian circles. ' In order to secure a position in which

it was not altogether helpless in face of the workers and their
Communist tendencies, such a government must, for the purposes
of domestic policy, be possessed of a very strong left wing and
must emphasise its reliance on democratic and trade union circles.'
Further, it would be desirable to incorporate Communists whose
outlook was known to be reasonable and not dictated by Moscow.
This was an expression of Reichwein's views, in particular; he
was loosely connected with Communist groups, being acquainted
more especially with Arvid von Harnack and Schultze-Boysen.

Anxiety about the possibility of Communist revolution, already
intensified by the course the war was taking, was now confirmed
by the activities of the *Nationalkomitee Freies Deutschland*
(National Committee for a Free Germany), whose psychological effect upon the conspiracy would be difficult to overestimate.
This can be plainly deduced from the communications conveyed
by Trott to Allen Dulles in the spring of 1944. The shift to the
extreme left assumed astonishing proportions and was to become
increasingly significant. In this situation, Trott was mainly concerned with securing Allied assurances that would support the
socialist position in regard to domestic policy – hence the demand
that the West should encourage the workers ' to shape the German labour movement along their own lines, without interference
from Western capitalist groups with anti-labour tendencies '.[155]
This pursued the same train of thought as the tactical memorandum from Turkey and was in keeping with Trott's strongly anti-
capitalist outlook; a year earlier he had told Dulles, in justification of a possible turning towards the East, that both Germans and
Russians had broken with ' *bourgeois* ideology ' and were seeking
a radical solution to social problems that ' would transcend
national frontiers '. By 1944 the hopes Trott had cherished of an
internal dissolution of Bolshevism and the return of both peoples
to the spiritual traditions of Christianity had given way to the
full realisation of the extent of the Communist threat.[156]

Goerdeler now adopted the idea of a ' Popular Movement '.
This was to ' unite all classes, levels and regions ' and ' all Germans, from Social Democrats, via the Centre, to German Nationalists '. To begin with this ' Popular Movement with the broadest
possible basis ' would be directed by the government, of which

it would later become independent; the movement would admit oppositional groups, the nuclei of future parties. The concept aroused so much interest among the various groups of the Opposition that it became necessary to set it down in more precise terms. The endeavour in the spring of 1944 to lay down the principles upon which the ' Popular Movement ' would be based, led to serious conflict. From Trott's communications with Dulles it is evident that the socialist groups had gained considerable political impetus and had succeeded in imposing definite demands. Otto John reported that Leber planned ' a new kind of popular front based upon all surviving and viable socialist and democratic elements '. He was not prepared to admit Christian principles into the programme for the ' Popular Movement ', and objected strongly to Mierendorff's and Reichwein's proposed formulation : ' The Popular Movement confesses to German culture and to the Christian past of the German nation '. As opposed to Leuschner and Jakob Kaiser, Leber maintained that ' even at the cost of the unity they desired ', he would ' not allow former Social Democratic principles simply to be jettisoned ', and he opposed the imposition of a Christian character on the future state, a character that was particularly desired by the Christian trade unionists.[157]

## Military Coup d'Etat and 'Democratic' Popular Rising

The conflicts that flared up after the spring of 1944 were due partly to the nervous irritability of the conspirators, which was related to the realisation that the attempt was long overdue and that perhaps the opportunity had been missed altogether. It was such considerations that led both Leber and Leuschner to conclude independently that they must not commit themselves politically by taking part in a Beck-Goerdeler government. The generals' passivity, unanimously condemned by the civilian conspirators, led Leber and Leuschner to doubt whether there ever would be a revolution, and also gave rise to widespread opposition to Goerdeler, from Leber, Moltke, Yorck, Gerstenmaier, Delp and Haubach on the left, and Hassell, Jessen and Popitz on the right. Though their views differed their motives were the same. The extreme Conservatives believed that ' in view of the completely proletarianised millions now inhabiting Central Europe ', a Bolshevist insurrection could only be averted by a strongly authoritarian leadership; of this they believed Goerdeler, with his tendency for compromise, to be incapable, aside from the fact that they mistrusted his trade union proposals. Leber, Yorck, Moltke and Trott (the latter had already declared that ' all taint of reaction ' must be avoided in the event of revolution), believed that Goerdeler's domestic policy was no longer viable, a contributory factor being their not altogether correct assumption that Goerdeler represented ' big business '. They reproached him with harbouring illusions in regard to foreign affairs; here they were unfortunately justified, for until the summer of 1944 Goerdeler continued to think it perfectly possible for Germany to emerge from military defeat virtually without loss of territory. While Yorck and Moltke were already thinking in terms of a complete occupation of Germany and had resigned themselves to the surrender of territory well within the frontiers of 1937, Goerdeler – like the Nazi goverment – still gambled on the likelihood of being able to exploit the aversion of the Western powers for Bolshevism. Leber toyed with the idea that when the collapse came the socialist forces might act independently, and he agreed with Yorck that any government set up after the revolution must be extended as far to the left as possible.[158]

Stauffenberg, who was increasingly coming to be recognised as the centre of the conspiracy – thus incurring Goerdeler's mistrust, as also at first that of Leuschner, both of whom wanted to ' keep the generals out of politics ' – had at one time repeatedly stressed that the National Socialist government must be replaced by a ' more central, middle-class administration '. His fundamental outlook was of strongly conservative stamp – the ' oath ', of somewhat doubtful provenance, contains a reference to ' the lie of equality ' – and was strongly influenced by military views. In justifying his revolutionary plans to Hösslin, he declared that in case of military defeat the officers' corps must not again hold back and allow others to take the initiative, as had happened in 1918.[159] This conclusion, deduced from the events of the November Revolution, clearly reveals the difference between his

views and the conventional outlook of the officers' corps, for it
implied the conviction that the army had political responsibilities.
In the same context Stauffenberg remarked that ' in our country
the army is a conservative institution, yet it is also rooted in the
people '. It is a characteristic statement, showing that his views
resembled the conservative-socialist views of Trott; it also reveals
that he did not seek to preserve the army merely on nationalist
grounds or for reasons of power politics, and explains why he
should have decided to work alongside the socialists. Stauffenberg's own proposals, like all the other material relating to future
domestic policy produced during this final phase, do not appear
to have survived; they aroused the mistrust of Maass, the more so
in that they were couched in very general terms. Stauffenberg's
*exposé* was no doubt a highly emotional and idealistically tinged
synthesis of socialist and conservative ideas. He often attended the
Kreisau Circle's deliberations and his views were not unlike those
of Yorck. Yet he was indubitably pursuing a political line of his
own, if a somewhat nebulous one, and was therefore very reserved about his views.[160]

Originally Stauffenberg had opposed the reconstruction of the
trade unions and must, indeed, be regarded as altogether hostile
to any return to the conditions of 1932. Yet his intense awareness of the threat of Bolshevism both inside and outside Germany, as also the growing cordiality of his relations with Leber,
to which the latter's constructive view of military matters no
doubt conduced, allayed Stauffenberg's doubts on this point.
Another contributory factor was the memory of the alliance,
which he believed to have been belated, between Ebert and Groe-
ner, together with the realisation of the High Command's failure
during the First World War. Beck's suggestions are here in evidence, and that Stauffenberg continued to develop these is shown
by his remark to Fahrner that ' mere ' soldiers ' when they seize
power in a state are never capable of social solutions and this
precipitates their fall; they often fail to realise that they are
merely using up and living off the remains of traditional social
orders '.[161] It was considerations such as these that persuaded him
of the necessity to go along with the ' left '.

There is every reason to believe that Stauffenberg encouraged

Reichwein and Leber to make contact with the Saefkow group. This was clearly undertaken with the intention of discovering whether there was any chance of securing the cooperation of individual Communist groups. After the first contact, which led to his arrest, Leber was highly suspicious because the Communist demands – in accordance with the official line – seemed to him over-moderate. The feelers put out towards the Communists were the result of a tactical consideration that in this way agitation by the Russian-manipulated *Nationalkomitee* might be averted. Both Moltke and Trott feared that the tendency displayed by the *Nationalkomitee*'s programme to combine nationalist and Bolshevist elements might lead to ' German national Bolshevism '. The Turkish memorandum of late 1943 declares : ' At all costs a situation must be avoided in which a democratic German government could be branded as non-national or anti-national, thus finding itself in opposition to a combination of nationalist, Communist and pro-Russian elements.'[162] The fear of such a combination, which experience during the later phase of the Weimar Republic seemed to justify – a combination that was to prove one of the principal factors in Stalin's policy towards Germany after 1945 – also corresponded to the identification, mentioned earlier, of National Socialism with Bolshevism in the thinking of the Opposition. Hence the attempt to take up relations with Communist groups represented the very opposite of an eastward orientation; it was in fact an endeavour to persuade independent-minded Communists to abandon the political line laid down by the *Nationalkomitee*. Such a policy, however, postulated the avoidance of external conflict with Russia and this, indeed, had been demanded in Trott's memoranda, in the document produced at Moltke's behest in Turkey in 1943, and in Mierendorff's plan of action.[163] This explains Stauffenberg's ostensible turning to-wards Russia, by analogy with the Russo-German relations of the twenties, as a tactical decision and in no way an acceptance of the Soviet system.

Stauffenberg, some time before Leber's arrest, had proposed that Leuschner should be the new Chancellor and, on his refusing, had suggested Leber instead.[164] This led Goerdeler, even in prison, to inveigh strongly against Stauffenberg's ' uncertain

L

political line, based upon left wing socialists and Communists ', and caused Gisevius to pass on Dulles' highly misleading information about the plans arising from Stauffenberg's political manœuvring. Indeed, the spring of 1944 was to see considerable changes of front among the Opposition. While Beck and Goerdeler sought a change of government followed by reforms whose extent and nature were hotly disputed by the circle round Popitz, Jessen and Hassell, the aim of Stauffenberg, Leber and Trott, as also no doubt of Schulenburg and of such members of the Kreisau Circle as remained active, was a revolutionary uprising by the army and the people. This was planned to take place after the *Walküre* operation and the assumption of political power by the military in order to ensure the political success of the revolution. The coordination of the ' revolution from above ' with the ' revolution from below ' was most misleadingly described by Gisevius as a ' revolution of workers, peasants and soldiers ' in the Communist sense.[165] The creation of a democratic popular front made sense within the terms of this conception, whereas the realisation of Goerdeler's plans, according to which reforms were to proceed from a military dictatorship, would have resulted quite unintentionally in a somewhat dubious replica of the National Socialist state party.

It was typical of the distinct mentalities underlying these two tendencies that Goerdeler and Beck should have sought their historical prototype of Prussian reform, whereas Leber and Stauffenberg invoked the German uprising of 1813. This did not run counter to Stauffenberg's opinion, reported by Fahrner, that Gneisenau's handling of the popular rising could not serve as a model for modern politics, since it was only permissible to unleash such forces when ' the state and society possessed a moral fabric strong enough to counterbalance them '.[166] In 1944, with the imminent collapse of the Third Reich and the resulting threat of Bolshevist dictatorship in Central Europe, such reservations were no longer justified. Hence Stauffenberg was determined to rally those forces which had fought each other so bitterly after the 1918 defeat (thereby depriving Germany of freedom of action abroad), and to lead them to victory. The extent to which his thinking was determined by the events of 1918 is shown by his disputes at this time with Trott on the subject of the chances of negotiation abroad, and his insistence that an attempt should be made to avert military disaster by diplomatic moves.[167]

During the final phase the inner leading group of the conspiracy consisted of Stauffenberg, Leber, Trott and Schulenburg. They were united by a marked sense of national responsibility, the desire for unequivocal political leadership and authority, and the realisation that in history the clock cannot be turned back; their actions concerned an uncommitted future, a future that would lead to new political forms. Leber spoke of the new state ' for which we must seek a new, constructive content and a convincing formulation ', and then conceded that he himself was unable to formulate the ' constructive goal ' with which to confront National Socialism. Trott was similarly feeling his way towards a basically new social solution that would go beyond the political models so far put forward by different schools of opinion.

He wrote in February 1944 :

> The recognition of one's true and particular task is liberating, gives purpose to life, and makes it possible to choose unerringly among the multitude of principles and values which blur the horizons of the present-day citizen of the world. In the twentieth century we must throw off the burden and the soul-destroying restrictions imposed by the nineteenth and, by our own toil and sweat, erect a new living structure. This we have only just begun to do, but the nature of our task is clearly written in the black outlines of the ruins.[168]

These conceptions which Stauffenberg, as a close friend of Trott's, probably shared, evince the hope of a future organic society that would be a lasting synthesis combining naturalness and immediacy with the actuality of modern technological, industrial civilisation, national tradition and European awareness.

## The 'German Way'

The social and political ideas of the Opposition must be assessed in the light of a period which saw itself as a time of transition and of the destruction of organic historical forms, a period seeking new and universal solutions that would not entail the severing of ties with historical continuity. ' January 1933 ', wrote Trott in that same year, ' has witnessed a *European* revolution, a revolution which has not destroyed our goals but which has undoubtedly blocked the approach-routes by which we had hoped to reach them. We must now think again.'[169] In National Socialism's seizure of power Trott and his friends saw a manifestation of the decline since Versailles of the European community of nations. To them, the National Socialist régime seemed the culmination of a development determined by the rise of the mass society and the loss both of personal values and of the moral and Christian tradition of Western Europe.

The thinking of the Opposition turned on the means of resolving what, in the final analysis, was an anthropological and religious crisis in European society, and they sought a solution that would unite the former social and political fronts in a qualitatively higher synthesis, and would restore Western man's relationship to his historical tradition and his transcendental destiny. This conception was set down by Alfred Delp in a comprehensive memorandum, *Die dritte Idee* (' The Third Idea '), which has not survived. As opposed to capitalism and Communism which, from ' too narrow a premise ', played off the individual against society or society against the individual, he looked for a social order that would restore the unity of person and society.[170] Trott's memorandum, *Deutschland zwischen Ost und West* (' Germany between East and West ') which is also lost, departs from much the same premise, and seeks a middle way between the ' reality principle of the East ' and the ' personality principle of the West '. The romantic view of Russia that prevailed during the twenties was unconsciously at work in these ideas. Hence the simple, personal, communally centred existence of the Russian Orthodox peasantry, untouched as it seemed by Bolshevism or by technological civilisation, was seen as one pole, the other being the West with its emphasis on the freedom of the individual and on rationality; both these were to be brought into relation. Trott spoke of ' the mission of the German spirit as material mediator between East and West ', and deduced from this the indispensability of a German presence in any future European peace settlement.[171]

These tentative efforts to attain a new synthesis are typical of the Opposition's view of society, except in the case of some of the officers, such as Oster, who still remained tied to the unbroken tradition of imperial Germany.[172] Goerdeler spoke of a solution halfway between ' Russian Bolshevism and Anglo-Saxon capitalism ', Schulenburg sought a new ' communal order ' that would eliminate ' parasitic capitalism and collective Bolshevism ', and Leuschner postulated the synthesis of individualism and collectivism in the concept of the ' person '. The attempts, as Gerstenmaier expressed it, to create a new social and economic order that would transcend the old party doctrines, ranged between Western formal democracy and Eastern totalitarianism, between the subjective concept of state and the objective concept of people, between private economic initiative and socialist planned economy.[173]

The social and political thinking of the Opposition exhibits features that are distinctly Utopian and irrational, in exact analogy to the forms manifested by the spiritual and intellectual life of the Weimar period. Many of the problems discussed at that time never reached foreign ears, for they were blanketed off by the Nazi régime; conversely, the Opposition was increasingly cut off from outside influences, a psychological factor which led to some degree of introversion in political and social thinking even among those who succeeded in maintaining contacts. An attempt to get an overall picture of the social model envisaged by the Opposition reveals considerably divergent views. These were variously expressed : a considered realisation, for example, of principles annexed – and morally and politically perverted – by National Socialism; an up-to-date version of the ideas of the Prussian reformers; an altogether ' revolutionary ' reversion to an image of man, but one which had, in fact, been slowly decomposing ever since secularisation; or the realisation of conservative-romantic visions of a ' Christian state '. Yet there is a certain unity in the basic features of this image, for it derived from the rejection of the plebiscitary and egalitarian tendencies in modern society and from the endeavour to concentrate the pluralism of political interests and social forces within an organic communal order. The concept of a society devoid of conflict was one the Opposition shared with National Socialist ideology, and its idea of a ' people's community ' itself related to the tautological entity of ' people and leaders ', ' community and state ', ' individual and community '. This was also true of the agrarian and middle-class programme; again, views on the formation of an élite which would to some extent be institutionalised, exhibited certain superficial similarities.

Everyone, including the majority of socialists, was convinced that parliamentary democracy had proved itself to be unviable. Even those who still defended it – Leber, Bergstraesser and to a certain extent Jakob Kaiser – deemed it essential that the party state should be under the control of a strong leadership. The new forms of democracy envisaged by the Opposition restricted in varying degrees the part played by political parties, as also the rôle of public opinion. The realisation, induced by the failure of the Weimar Republic, that a minimum basic consensus is necessary if a modern democracy is to function at all, assumed the form of a Utopian demand for an organic, communal unity in which political policy-making would be restricted to the field of practical decisions and become the responsibility of representative assemblies elected by indirect vote. These would come into being, not after a widely publicised conflict of political opinions, but on the basis of a selection of the local communities' most worthy and respected citizens. This revealed a strong tendency to ' depoliticise ' which is understandable in view of the thoroughgoing political permeation of all spheres of life under National Socialism, but which also derives from the traditionally unpolitical nature of the German mind; it highlights, too, the lack during the Weimar period of a theory of politics and of any political and social policy.

Ranke himself had rejected the idea that Western constitutions should be copied, on the grounds that they were unsuited to the German character. This view, based upon the particular nature of German history, was one which made it extremely difficult for democratic parliamentary forms to take root in Germany, contributed materially to their alienation in Weimar, and was central to the social and political thinking of the Opposition of 20 July. It is found in Popitz, Hassell, Goerdeler, Bonhoeffer, Schulenburg, Trott, Delp, Moltke, Leber and Stauffenberg, and reveals the strong traditional ties of the Opposition, as also German society's failure to break away from the idea of a *bourgeois-* 'notable' social constitution. The Allies' unwillingness to enter into contact with the Opposition only served to strengthen the latter's trauma in regard to the West, a trauma which Plessner, Fraenkel and Dahrendorf consider to be one of the causes of German crisis in the twentieth century.[174] Individual democratic groups within the Opposition deliberately detached themselves from the mainstream of oppositional thinking, and this even when Germany was hermetically sealed against outside influences; as early as 1937 Brill, the founder of the 'German Popular Front' and joint author of the 'Buchenwald Manifesto', was analysing, under the concept 'German ideology', the sequence of ideas evolved by the Nazis as a basis for the 'concept of the people's community' (*Volksgemeinschaftsgedanke*).[175]

Trott and Moltke enlarged the idea of the 'German way' to make it into a deliberately European programme, but it was one that necessarily encountered misunderstanding abroad. In their view of society the Opposition specifically emphasised unity as opposed to 'pluralistic fragmentation'. This was in accordance with the 'sideways-facing front', as Dahrendorf succinctly described the Opposition's position; the régime they were fighting was one in which, under cover of unity and community, the substance of the state was being corroded by the internecine strife of a multitude of rival organisations and cliques, while at the same time a radical levelling was taking place under the domination of an ideology which was clearly opposed to it. Hence the régime was regarded by the Conservative elements of the Opposition as revolutionary and, indeed, Bolshevist; it was only a minority that was determined to oppose the régime, not by 'counter-revolutionary' measures alone, but by deliberately democratic revolutionary methods.

It was the Opposition's anti-pluralist and not, as Dahrendorf supposes, its anti-liberal outlook, which prevented it shaking off, either in its political thinking or in its own idea of itself, its social origins as a legitimate élite. Thus it was unable to progress towards a democratically constituted, open society free of the rigidity in political planning induced by the excessive institutional canalisation of diverging social and political conflicts. The constitutional thinking of the German Resistance was not adopted in all its essentials when the German polity was restored in 1945. Such of its representatives as remained, although some occupied leading administrative positions, found themselves increasingly isolated politically; events had left them behind. The German Opposition's view of society and their constitutional plans, which were so much in thrall to the German tradition of state and to its specifically apragmatic understanding of ' politics ', still remained representative of a certain characteristic type of political thinking in postwar Germany, although beating a gradual retreat before the newly founded Federal Republic. But the influence of similar concepts, deriving from the ' German way ' model – for instance Erhard's proposal for the ' Formed Society ' as a means towards the execution of ' communal tasks ' – is still at work today. These ideas are as indistinct, and give evidence of the same mistrust, if not open hostility, towards the pluralism of social forces, as is shown by this particular aspect of the Opposition's social and political programme. They overtax the political opportunities possessed by parliamentary democracy in conditions imposed by a world of technological and industrial labour. Integration as a continually renewed process, more especially in the democratic state, postulates the free growth of pluralistic, perhaps even antagonistically orientated, groups, if it is not to become rigidly ensconced in a system of vested power interests.

The question of the German Opposition's concept of society is without doubt closely linked to the question of the motives which impelled the conspirators to make a radical break with the National Socialist state or, in Stauffenberg's words, ' to commit high treason with all the means at our disposal '. These motives are discernible in the plans for the new order, but not in their entirety, and it would be incorrect to assess the extent of the Opposition's legitimation only in terms of social and constitutional ideas determined by one particular historical situation. The German Opposition was fighting for human dignity and the Christian destiny of man, for justice and decency, for the individual's freedom from political force and social compulsion. The circumstances, both historical and ideological, in which that struggle was conducted appeared to herald the death throes – not only in Germany – of parliamentary democracy, whose subsequent revival therefore seemed questionable. Hence, in elaborating their proposals, the Opposition turned to the experience of history and, though not unaware of the social problems posed by modern existence, they never shook off the trammels of German idealist philosophy, and thus found it difficult, as Reichwein[176] repeatedly pointed out, to form any immediate relationship with politics. It is easier to understand the German situation during those years if we realise that even Hitler's opponents, much as they desired to do so, were not able to break out of the isolation of German political thinking. The abortive attempt at revolution of 20 July 1944 not only marked the tragic failure of a heroic undertaking; it also meant that Germany was now heading for unavoidable and total disaster. It spelt, fundamentally, the end of ' the German way '. More concisely, it might be said that German society, because of its traditional political stance and the narrowness of German political thinking, itself a reflection of retarded emancipation in social matters, was incapable of countering Hitler's dictatorship – reactionary in the profoundest sense of the word – with an alternative that would be in keeping with the circumstances of modern industrial society. To realise this helps to explain how it came about that in 1933 National Socialism was able, without serious opposition, to take possession of the machinery of state. Again, this insight is essential if Germany is to find, or so much as begin to find, her true affinity with the Western political and constitutional tradition.

# Resistance in the Labour Movement

HANS-JOACHIM REICHHARDT

Resistance to the National Socialist régime had its beginnings in the labour organisations, for they were the first to experience the full terror of a system which regarded them as its most dangerous adversaries. Literature on the subject has hitherto mainly emphasised the history, work and development of the émigré organisations, while a number of shorter publications are devoted to descriptions of the activities of individual resistance groups. Others, again, attempt to convey the many layers of the Resistance by a random juxtaposition of accounts of their activities and experiences. But up till now there has been no comprehensive and systematic examination of the subject. Unfortunately this gap in contemporary history is unlikely ever to be filled, since the necessary material is largely unobtainable.

It is virtually impossible to give a factual and wholly accurate account of this aspect of the Resistance or of its underlying motives and outer forms, because these were necessarily determined by the secretive conditions of the underground which, for reasons of mutual security, precluded written communications.

Another approach to the Resistance may be made as it were from the opposite direction, through an examination of court records and the official reports of departments concerned with underground activities. But it is precisely these sources that must be treated with the greatest reserve, for it was obviously of the utmost importance to anyone arrested to divulge as little as possible, and even then to confess only to what could clearly no longer be contested. The only documents available from the Resistance itself are a few pamphlets; on the official side large numbers of files were destroyed through the hazards of war or by various agencies before they were dissolved, while others are in

East Germany where, at least for the time being, they are beyond our reach.

This lack of source-material can only partially be made good by interviewing those who were involved. For the purposes of a learned enquiry, it is a difficult task to extract the necessary details from the memories of those who, spontaneously and with little reflection, were active participants in these events. Some still suffer from the after-effects of violent ill-treatment under Gestapo interrogation or in concentration camps. Others, some 30 years later, find it almost impossible to recall what they believed at the time was the right course for the Resistance. And with advancing years memories of dates and facts have inevitably become hazy. Again, there were many in the movement, particularly the leaders, who paid with their lives or who have since died; others live beyond the zone and sector boundaries and cannot be approached. All these circumstances will give an indication of the difficulties facing the student.

In giving an account of the Resistance within the labour movement, the historian must resign himself to more approximations and even larger gaps than those which usually face the student of other complexes of contemporary history. We may be almost certain that it will be impossible to satisfy Erich Matthias's perfectly reasonable demand for a carefully documented and systematically presented survey of the Resistance within the labour movement – the different types of group ranging from a meeting round an inn table to a rigidly indoctrinated cadre organisation, the communications between individual groups, the contacts with émigré organisations, and so on.[1] Therefore, despite certain misgivings, we shall not attempt to give more than a brief account of events in one region, namely Berlin; indeed under existing circumstances it would not be possible to do otherwise.

## The Social Democratic Party (SPD)

There is no doubt that the decline of the Weimar Republic was in large part due to the breakdown of politically organised labour in the face of the National Socialist movement.[2] It is true that, right up to its demise, organised labour's attitude was one of un-equivocal and uncompromising opposition to National Socialism, but the schism that had existed since the First World War con-stituted a disastrous handicap. The Communists failed utterly to understand the situation and the approaching danger, regard-ing as their main enemies not the National Socialists but the Social Democrats whom for years they had calumniated as ' social fascists '. Despite their carefully reiterated slogan, ' Creation of a united working-class front ', they were hindered by tactical and purely party considerations from genuinely aspiring to this aim and from making any real effort to realise it. Indeed, so in-tense was their blind hatred of the SPD and the Weimar demo-cracy that they sometimes went so far as to make common cause with the National Socialists. One such occasion was the strike of the Berlin transport service (BVG) in the autumn of 1932, which in turn led to increasing bitterness on the part of the Social Democrats. Nevertheless, there were certain features of Social Democratic policy during the last Weimar phase that materially contributed to the general decline.

After the lapsing of the Anti-Socialist Law, the SPD had grown into a legal democratic opposition party and had, by 1912, become the largest party in Germany. When it assumed responsibility in 1918, the solution of day-to-day political prob-lems absorbed its energies to such an extent that the achieve-ment of socialist objectives was barely considered. Even if most Social Democrats preferred not to identify themselves with the Weimar state, which had done little to change prewar social conditions, they were nevertheless determined to uphold the Republic and what it had so far achieved. But in the final analysis neither the leaders of the trade unions nor those of the SPD felt that they could take responsibility for exploiting this deter-mination among the overwhelming majority of their members on occasions when it could have been decisive.

After the resignation of Müller, the Social Democratic Chan-cellor, in 1930 the Party, finding itself on the defensive, adopted a policy of toleration towards Brüning's emergency decrees. But the Social Democratic workers continued to maintain an unswerv-ing allegiance to their Party and remained convinced, despite noisy agitation from Right and Left, that one day they would be called upon to fight. Not until 20 July 1932, when the Prussian government under the Social Democrats Otto Braun and Carl Severing yielded without a struggle to Papen's *coup d'état*, did ' lightning shatter these foundations '.[3]

Although the reasons put forward then and later by the leaders of the SPD and the trade unions for their failure to resist effectively must carry weight, they cannot be wholly convincing from the political aspect; a show of protest, a vigorous demonstration of democracy's unbroken will to assert itself even in the face of violent reprisals, might have been of crucial importance to future developments.[4] A struggle for power outside the customary parliamentary sphere was, however, unthinkable to the leaders of the Social Democratic Party who, over the years, had been brought up to believe in the workings of constitutional order. Only this can explain why they underestimated so gravely the extent to which the *Reichsbanner* and the *Eiserne Front* were prepared for the fight. During the vital hours both these organisations gathered at their assembly points to await their leaders' call.[5] The manifestation of sluggishness and indecision combined with a lack of a clear-cut political concept proved disastrous, particularly from a psychological viewpoint, because they seriously impaired the confidence of the masses in the leadership.[6]

A rousing appeal by the leaders of Party and trade unions, on or immediately after 30 January 1933, for concerted countermeasures might have met with vigorous response, since the will to resist had not, despite much disillusionment, been wholly extinguished – as was shown by the mass demonstrations in the larger German cities after Hitler's appointment as Chancellor. These powerful demonstrations obviously made an impression on the various SPD headquarters, and many regional leaders returned from meetings of the highest Party and trade union bodies in Berlin on 30 and 31 January convinced that from there would come, at a suitable moment, the signal for action.[7]

But when, after the first show of force, there was still no word from above, the will to resist slowly languished. The measures that followed the *Reichstag* fire and the decree ' For the protection of People and State' almost wholly removed the psychological prerequisite for mass action.

The Party and trade union leaders were deluded by the belief – a belief which the solidity of the Social Democrats' majority in the *Reichstag* elections on 5 March seemed to confirm – that Hitler's government would be merely one more in a long string of coalition cabinets.[8] Wholly ignorant of the dynamics of a totalitarian mass movement, they dreamed of tension among the members of the government, rivalry between SA and *Stahlhelm*, insuperable economic difficulties, intervention by the *Reichswehr*, or moral indignation on the part of the educated middle classes, and although these day-dreams were shattered, they continued to be cherished by some of the SPD leaders right up to the proscription of the Party in June. Nevertheless the attitude of the leaders in general – exemplified in the brave and dignified speech by Otto Wels, the Party leader, on the subject of the Enabling Act – showed a high degree of integrity and staunchness.[9] By contrast, the leaders of the General Trades Union Federation (ADGB) hoped to save their organisation by severing connections with the Party and thus becoming 'unpolitical'. Their appeasement policy reached its peak with the decision on 19 April to participate in the National Labour Day celebrations that had been proclaimed for 1 May. A call to take part went out to all members. For the National Socialists, of course, this provided an excellent opportunity to exploit the trade union leaders' feelings of insecurity and resignation for the purpose of bringing about their carefully planned downfall, and, on 2 May, the complete destruction of their organisation.[10] The abolition of the trade unions did not fail to have its effect on the Party and sapped even further its powers of resistance.

On 10 May a pretext was found to confiscate the Party's funds and the last Social Democratic newspapers went out of circulation. Since the Social Democrats were now deprived of almost all opportunity for legal activity, the Executive decided to send some of its members abroad where they could continue their work. Those at the head of the Party who advocated the way of legality, however, especially Paul Löbe and Max Westphal, sought to keep the remains of the organisation together by the cessation of

M

all activities. In the hope of pacifying the National Socialists and above all of alleviating the lot of the many Party members in concentration camps, they decided to endorse a Peace Resolution in the *Reichstag* on 17 May, a resolution that was, in fact, a vote of confidence in Hitler's policies. Two members of the Executive, Hans Vogel and Friedrich Stampfer, who had hastened back to Berlin from Saarbrücken, sought in vain to dissuade the residual group in the SPD from attending the *Reichstag* session and to convince them of the uselessness of further important concessions, since nothing could be done to save the Party from the fate that lay in store for it.

At two Party meetings of the Executive in Saarbrücken and Prague during the second half of May, conflicting opinions as to what should be the future tactics of the SPD again led to heated discussion. Those who had already emigrated expressed the view that, since Party activities were no longer possible, the Executive should continue its work abroad and that there should be a public announcement to this effect. Only in this way could German Social Democracy uphold its credit in labour circles and prevent the Communists from taking the lead in the struggle against National Socialism.

The members of the Berlin Executive too, were convinced that the National Socialist régime would attempt to suppress all activities on the part of the Opposition, but doubted whether such attempts could really succeed in Germany. They did not think that there was any hope of ending National Socialist supremacy by action from abroad so long as there was little sign of internal unrest, for history had proved that émigré policies seldom exerted any influence on absolute and fascist systems.

Open conflict between the two schools of thought in the Executive was not long in coming. It reached its peak on 18 June 1933 with the call ' Break the Chains ', in the first number of *Neuer Vorwärts*, now appearing in Prague. This challenge had grave consequences. Four days later every leader still accessible was either murdered or arrested, and the SPD proscribed.[11]

Already during the period of Franz von Papen's Chancellorship in the summer of 1932 the SPD leader, Otto Wels, had suggested the formation of an illegal organisation alongside the official one for the day when the Party might be proscribed or seriously curtailed. It is still not clear what shape this proposal took, for the matter was not discussed by the Party Executive. Possibly Wels approached reliable Party Officials in the regions after confidential discussions with some of the members of the Executive. Who his individual proposals were directed to and what kind of response they met with is difficult to ascertain : there is evidence of preparations for underground activities in Hanover, Leipzig, Hamburg, Magdeburg and in the Socialist Labour Youth Organisation (SAJ) in Berlin.[12] They had little effect on the fate of the Party, however, the more so as its leaders did everything possible at the beginning of 1933 to suppress all traces of an illegal organisation so as not to prejudice their policy of nonactivity. The leaders' illusions concerning questions of legality were largely incomprehensible to the younger, activist members of the Party; in Berlin, particularly, there were violent disputes on the subject between the two schools of opinion during March and April 1933.[13]

The Social Democratic Resistance groups which developed in May and the following months did not do so as a unified whole. In Saxony and Thuringia, particularly, where the left-wing opposition was highly critical of the Party leaders, the attempt was made to place the regional Party cadres in their entirety on an illegal basis and to use the period up to the time of the Party's proscription, an event that was assumed to be inevitable, in planning the development of underground activities.[14] Both at the session of the SPD *Reichstag* group on 10 June and at the Social Democratic Reich Conference on 19 June, the most influential members of the Party Executive still refused to countenance illegal activities. Those among the participants of the Reich Conference who supported illegality thereupon held a special meeting in order to set up a central committee devoted to underground activities in Germany; its members were Erich Rinner, Curt Geyer, Kurt Schumacher, Herbert Friedemann and Paul Siebold. Following Schumacher's arrest, however, in the summer of 1933, and the emigration of Rinner and Geyer, the group dispersed.[15]

The committee was unable to play a rôle of any importance.

On the instructions of the émigré Party Executive in Prague it attempted to establish contact by courier with underground groups throughout the territories of the Reich. Originally all communications between the latter and Prague had been channelled through Berlin, but individual groups in the regions later maintained direct contact for security reasons. The Prague Executive felt it to be its task to keep the Socialist International and the world at large informed of the true state of affairs inside National Socialist Germany and, conversely, to support the underground activities of its members in the Reich and supply them with information.

By the end of January the National Socialists had gained control of all the powers of the state and could count on a large measure of public support. Thus they were able to initiate the terror which, during the ensuing weeks and months, was to gain such impetus that to the majority of the SPD, though at heart they might never submit to 'coordination', resistance appeared both senseless and too dangerous : 'Only small bands of the bravest and most faithful . . . dared to give battle.'[16] Most of these did not feel that underground activities required any special decision : to them, despite their severe reverse and the increasingly difficult circumstances, it was a matter of course to continue the struggle against the National Socialists whose victory, they were convinced, could lead only to dictatorship and later to war.[17] In any case they were not prepared just to capitulate, for they were convinced that in one form or another 'something must happen and something be done'. Thus from the various sections of the Party such as the *Reichsbanner* and the SAJ, there sprang up underground groups, little versed in the ways of conspiracy and often amateurish, which sought to adapt their activities to the new conditions.

At the outset, individual groups differed widely in their views on the aims, and to a certain extent, the methods of illegal work. Put briefly, one side thought that the National Socialist régime would be of short duration since internal difficulties would soon lead to a severe crisis; the other was convinced that a longer period had to be reckoned with. The first group thought that

Social Democracy would continue to exist, even with illegal status, as it had under Bismarck's Socialist Law. However many might leave the Party through fear of the dangers of underground activity, the SPD, supported by a core of activist members, would, they believed, be able to hold its own under a National Socialist dictatorship. It was an attitude, however, that did not preclude unconcealed hostility towards the Party Executive in Prague which, as the embodiment of the earlier reformative policy, appeared to have been mainly responsible for the defeat. The other group expressed the view that the leadership and its spokesman had failed at crucial moments in the immediate past and that under no circumstances were they equal to the tasks that fascism had set the labour movement. Consequently the Party would have to be disbanded and replaced by an entirely new Party with new leaders, a new ideology and a new structure.[18]

One example of the groups which were demanding ' something new ' was the *Roter Stosstrupp* (RS) in Berlin.[19] Its very name (' Red Shock Troop ') indicates that it had no wish to be regarded as a mere continuation of the old Party organisation. Its origins go back to the socialist student organisations at Berlin University when, unknown to the Party, a number of members attempted to set up a system based on teams of five during the autumn of 1932, so as to be able to continue their work underground in the event of a National Socialist assumption of power. Soon after 30 January 1933 a succession of young Social Democrats joined the students, so that by the end of 1933 the estimated membership had risen to about 3,000. The leaders of this group, who called themselves the ' Red Staff ', were Rudolf Küstermeier, Karl Zinn, Heinz Spliedt, Karl König,[20] Strinz, and Schwarz. From the early part of 1933, the RS built up its activities in the field of illegal publications. Its newspaper, *Der Rote Stosstrupp*, was first mimeographed in a succession of private homes and then in a commercial agent's office run by Heinz Spliedt and Karl König in the Börse office building, a place particularly suitable for meetings and as a centre of distribution. At other times the paper was produced on a motor-boat on the Wannsee. It appeared regularly at eight or ten-day intervals and towards the end was numbering 3,000 copies. Distribution was effected through a well-organised system of go-betweens to the teams of five and was not restricted to Berlin alone, for copies found their way to the Mark of Brandenburg and even further afield to Breslau, Bielefeld, Stettin, and the Palatinate.

Funds for the paper's production were provided at great personal sacrifice by contributions from RS members as well as by grants from the émigré Party Executive in Prague following the establishment of contact in the summer of 1933. The RS leaders, however, continued to remain independent of the Executive even after contact had been made.

So long as any uncertainty remained about the stability of National Socialist power, the RS never excluded the possibility that the régime could be overthrown from within. In the first issue of the paper on 9 April 1933 under the headline 'What is to be done?' there appeared the following :

> . . . A new movement must be forged in the fire of the times . . . no party book, no badges. Under terrible pressure only the best can hold out. These will find each other and pledge their lives to socialism . . . We no longer bear allegiance to any party dogma, any party banner : we know only one battle-flag : the red flag of socialism. We know only one goal : the proletarian revolution.[21]

Number 8 of 7 June 1933 declared :

> . . . The question is now one of revolutionary rather than reformative policies. These illegal revolutionary activities are now being taken over by the Red shock troops who are rallying what remains of the active fighters and putting them to work for the proletarian revolution. We need an entirely fresh appraisal based on revolution. It is the task of the Red shock troops to promote this reappraisal and to prepare the way into the future of socialist action . . .

In number 10 of 21 June 1933 we read :

> . . . Fascism can only be smashed by the coming proletarian revolution. The revolution must be planned and led by an illegal organisation built up with the strictest discipline. The

reasons for the failure of the SPD and KPD were political and organisational. Hence it is our task to create a new revolutionary workers' movement which has learnt from the mistakes of the past, and which is ready to struggle for a socialist republic and the life and freedom that goes with it . . .

The ' proletarian revolution ' and the ' socialist republic ' were, of course, no more than distant objectives. Had it lasted longer the RS would without doubt have gradually adopted a more realistic line. Its propaganda was primarily intended to rally the still active elements of the SPD and other organisations within the workers' movement, to pass information to its own members, and to build up a nucleus of tried, trustworthy officials which could be activated during a given phase of the revolutionary process. But in December 1933, probably through betrayal by a member or carelessness on the part of a distributor, the RS was destroyed by the Gestapo.[22]

The great wave of arrests at the end of 1933 which struck the RS as well as many other Social Democratic groups in Berlin shattered a number of illusions about the efficacy of illegal publications and about the imminent demise of the National Socialist régime. Although probably rigged,[23] the plebiscite on Germany's withdrawal from the League of Nations held on 12 November 1933 clearly showed that Hitler's policies had so far met with the approval of large sections of the population.

Nevertheless the illegal Berlin Regional Committee, under Alfred Markwitz and Walter Löffler, succeeded during 1934 in dispersing the atmosphere of depression and in building up an appreciable organisation that maintained contact with groups in almost all the Berlin administrative districts. The distribution of *Neuer Vorwärts* and *Sozialistische Aktion,* printed on thin paper in small format, as well as much other literature originating from Prague, gave an extra fillip to underground activities since ' being technically superior to pamphlets produced under illegal conditions, they provided clear and visible evidence that the Party lived on '.[24] At first these publications were supplied only to former Party members, but they later came to be distributed to the public at large through private letter-boxes, by being left in telephone booths, or direct through the post.

Along the German borders, predominantly on Czech soil but also in Northern and Western Europe, the Party Executive had established frontier secretariats in different towns to maintain contact with the old Party organisation. These were to some extent welfare agencies for members in the underground, where the latter could obtain help and advice while passing on to the Executive confidential reports on conditions inside Germany. In this fashion the Executive remained in uninterrupted communication with the most important officials inside the Reich whom it summoned to courses and to weekend meetings, where they could regularly exchange views and discuss the situation and possible future moves. Further, the Executive in exile, which saw itself primarily as a sort of Party trustee, avoided issuing instructions which it would have been the duty of the underground to obey. Rather it confined itself to financial support, to the distribution of literature, to helping the dependants of political prisoners, and to advice and encouragement for those in the field.[25]

Through its frontier secretariats, which were eventually responsible for 24 former Party regions, the Executive obtained a relatively good overall view of its organisation, whose strength in Germany varied widely from region to region;[26] and it was thus always able to make a realistic evaluation of the Resistance's prospects of success. During 1933 and 1934 the Executive in Prague was still under the influence of the widespread ' radical renaissance '[27] within the ranks of labour, and still entertained hopes that National Socialism might collapse or be overcome by a revolutionary counter-movement founded on the illegal groups. But by the winter of 1935/6 this view had changed appreciably.

Early in 1935 an informer enabled the Gestapo to penetrate the organisation of the underground Regional Committee in Berlin and to arrest the leaders and a number of their associates.[28] After further groups had been broken up during 1935, the last Berlin Regional Committee fell victim, at the beginning of 1936, to a Gestapo which was steadily becoming more efficient. Even though various groups managed to survive up to 1938, the event nevertheless marked the end of a distinct phase in illegal

activities. After the appalling losses brought about by these operations, both émigrés and underground came to the unanimous conclusion that illegal activities such as widespread propaganda,
subversion within hostile organisations and terrorism were no
longer possible. Mass propaganda through the dissemination of
illegal literature – in this particular instance drastically reduced by
the Prague Executive after the 1935/6 arrests[29] – could not then,
any more than it could now, be successful in the face of an unimpaired police and informer network operated by a totalitarian
system. Subversive 'Trojan horse' activities inside hostile organisations, such as were proposed from time to time by the
Communists,[30] seemed wholly inappropriate. Social Democrats
attempting something of the sort had merely earned the misplaced
suspicion of their own comrades who were either unaware of the
motives behind the move, or had been kept in ignorance of them
for security reasons. And had they declared their new where-
abouts, the Gestapo would soon have laid hands on them. Acts
of terrorism were excluded, since the Social Democrats believed
that at that period resistance in such form would in no way
affect National Socialist domination, but would only serve to consolidate it.

Thus the conclusion was reached that opportunities for concerted activity within the illegal movement were extraordinarily
limited. In existing circumstances the aim and object henceforth
must be to maintain communications and to continue resistance
in the shape of activities on the part of individuals and small
groups where and when opportunity arose, so as to outlast the
National Socialist régime with the minimum of loss.[31] In 1937
the Gestapo gave the following account of Social Democratic
procedure:

. . . the expected change will come from outside. But preparations have to be made for this event so that past activities can
be resumed in a prearranged form. This inner conviction and
the wish of the SPD leaders that there should be no rigid organisations is reflected in the behaviour and solidarity of the
country's illegal workers. After work they join each other over
a glass of beer, meet former kindred spirits near their homes,

or keep in touch by means of family visits; they avoid all forms of organisation, and seek in the manner described to help their friends remain steadfast. During these meetings there is, of course, talk about the political situation and news is exchanged. They promote energetically the so-called whispering campaign which, for the time being, represents the most effective illegal work against the state, against its institutions and activities, and against the Party. The main subjects of discussion are price increases, low wages, economic exploitation of the people, freedom, shortage of raw materials, corruption, nepotism, gifts at the nation's expense, and so on. Since many former SPD and trade union officials are now commercial representatives and travelling salesmen, such catchwords will spread comparatively quickly into the furthest parts of the Reich. In spite of the extent of these subversive activities it has not yet been possible to apprehend one of these persons in the act and to bring him before a court for trial.[32]

The Social Democratic Resistance remained in being although many contacts with groups and individuals were lost after the Party Executive moved from Prague to Paris at the end of November 1937.[33] Social Democratic politicians, among them the former Minister of the Interior for Hesse, Wilhelm Leuschner, the *Reichstag* deputies, Julius Leber and Carlo Mierendorff, as well as many others, some of whom had been held in concentration camps until 1937, came to the conclusion that the resistance methods employed since 1933 were inadequate and that the totalitarian system could only be overthrown with the support of the *Wehrmacht*. In their search throughout the Reich for men of like persuasion to help in the formation of an organisation capable of resuming political activities after the fall of the régime, they made contact with middle-class Resistance circles and with members of the Opposition in the armed forces, an association that culminated in the *putsch* of 20 July 1944.[34]

## The German Communist Party (KPD)

To everyone's surprise, and in contrast to its repeated pronouncements, the KPD offered no more than half-hearted resistance to the events leading up to the National Socialist assumption of power. True, there were bloody confrontations during the ensuing weeks, but it was always the Communists' opponents who assumed the active rôle. The beginnings of a revolutionary uprising against fascism, of which there had been so much talk, were detectable only in Communist propaganda, never in the field of practical politics. They may have been seriously hampered by the swift and arbitrary intervention in the affairs of their Party – arrests, searches, and the prohibition of Communist newspapers, assemblies, and processions. But far more relevant to an assessment of the KPD's attitude was its dependence on the Soviet Union's foreign policy.

Moscow's tactics towards National Socialism, which Communist Party doctrine saw as the last stage in the demise of German capitalism, were determined by considerations of *Realpolitik*. In the view of the Soviet press, Hitler's assumption of power was the start of an essential period of transition, to be suffered in patience, before final victory was won through the elimination of National Socialism by a Communist revolution. In fact Soviet official policy was characterised by a temporising, if not a positive, attitude, as is evident from the marked failure to break off the close economic and military relations then existing between the two countries.[35]

In Germany itself the KPD called repeatedly for the establishment of a united front composed of all anti-fascists.[36] The savage struggle with the Social Democrats, however, had a bitter aftermath, for the rift that had been created over the years could not be closed in a matter of days. A Party that had contributed in full measure to the undermining of democracy and which at times had almost gone so far as to come to terms with the National Socialists, could no longer be regarded as trustworthy. Certainly there were all sorts of contacts, even in the last months of 1932,[37] between Communists and Social Democrats but, after the sorry experiences of the past, none of the parties was at all inclined to contemplate the Communist alternative to National Socialist dictatorship as the basis of a united front in which the advocates of a democratic and constitutional state could agree. No one at that

time among the leaders of the KPD was thinking in terms of a
' Popular Front '.[38]

Although in the first weeks of February a section of the membership was prepared for struggles and sacrifices and was wait-
ing for orders from above, others went over to the NSDAP and
SA. The leaders themselves sought overtly to make use of what
remained of their propaganda machinery for the *Reichstag* elections of 5 March, but secretly were beginning to place the
organisation on an illegal basis. Even though the KPD had emphasised on a number of occasions that it expected and was prepared for proscription, the Party's cumbersome structure prevented
the change-over taking place as smoothly as might have been
expected. ' The whole was so over-centralised . . . that it seemed
impossible to do more with this apparatus than barely keep it
going.'[39]

Thus, in the weeks leading up to the *Reichstag* fire on 27 February 1933, the leaders of the KPD failed to make any realistic
evaluation of political events or of the conclusions to be drawn
from them. By their own admission, many Communists were sur-
prised at the extent of the persecution set in train by the *Reichstag* fire.[40] The success of this action was attributable not least to
the fact that since their prolonged search of the Karl Liebknecht
Haus following the murder of the Berlin police officers, Lenk
and Anlauf, in August 1931, the Prussian political police had at
their disposal much valuable material in the form of documents
and addresses and had, furthermore, through informers among
Party officials from the top downwards, kept themselves relatively
well informed on all matters inside the KPD.[41] Accordingly, the
police throughout the country could be continually notified of the
organisation's preparations for going underground and of the
particular districts where developments should be kept under
surveillance.[42]

The mass arrests, including that on 3 March of the Party leader,
Ernst Thälmann, and his close associates, Werner Hirsch, Erich
Birkenauer and Alfred Kattner on secret premises in Charlotten-
burg,[43] created grave confusion among the heads of the Party.
New security precautions were called for in order to avoid fur-
ther arrests. Uninterrupted communications would have to be

resumed with the Party districts and new officials appointed to replace those arrested.

The elimination of Thälmann, however, aggravated the incipient struggle for influence and leadership within the Party, a struggle conditioned by the structure of an organisation based on the ' leader principle '. The main protagonists, John Schehr, Thälmann's deputy since Heinz Neumann's dismissal in 1932, Hermann Schubert, District Secretary in Hamburg, and Walter Ulbricht, District Secretary in Berlin-Brandenburg, fought a veritable war of succession. The contest was finally won by Ulbricht, who by then had emigrated.[44] From the early part of 1933, more and more officials left Germany either on Party instructions or independently. Schubert left for Prague in the summer of 1933. After the Party had decided that the many arrests had made necessary the transfer of the Politburo and Secretariat abroad, Ulbricht moved to Paris at the beginning of October. Aided by Kattner, the Gestapo arrested Schehr[45] shortly before he was due to emigrate.[46]

Despite the fearful blows which the KPD had had to suffer from the National Socialist terror, it refused to acknowledge this severe defeat, and anyone who used the term was dismissed by Fritz Heckert, the permanent KPD representative with the Comintern, with an expression as blunt as it was coarse (*Klugscheisser*).[47] In a resolution on 1 April 1933, the Executive Committee of the Comintern (EKKI) declared :

. . . The present quiet after the victory of fascism is no more than a passing phase. In spite of the fascist terror, Germany's revolutionary upsurge will continue inexorably . . . The establishment of open fascist dictatorship, which destroys all the democratic illusions of the masses and frees them from the influence of Social Democracy, speeds up the process of Germany's evolution towards the proletarian revolution.

The task of the Communists must be to make the masses understand that Hitler's régime is driving the country to disaster . . . It is imperative to consolidate the Party and to strengthen the mass organisations of the proletariat, to prepare the masses for the crucial revolutionary battles, for the overthrow of capitalism, for the overthrow of the fascist dictatorship by armed revolt.[48]

This, then, was the Party line that largely determined underground tactics during the first phase which lasted perhaps until the autumn of 1935. The main aim was first to gather in as many former members as possible.[49]

Not all Party members, of course, went underground. Many turned their backs on politics, having no desire to stand up for a cause which they felt to be hopeless, while others went over to the NSDAP and its subsidiary organisations. Most of those Communists, however, who had decided to resist were impervious to doubt. In any case the paid officials, whose names were known to the Gestapo, had no choice; they were dependent on the apparatus and could only hope that one day the Party would transfer them abroad. Many others were so imbued with Party discipline that they obeyed every directive given by the KPD or its representatives. All this, however, does not explain why the Communists resisted National Socialism. Thousands upon thousands suffered unspeakable tortures under Gestapo interrogation in concentration camps convinced that they had been fighting for a great and noble cause. In taking up the unequal struggle they had acted according to their principles and their consciences; many died without even suspecting that they had been the victims of their own comrades' treachery and of the unrealistic policy and unbelievable irresponsibility of the Party machine.[50]

For the achievement of the KPD's revolutionary aims the illegal press was ' a powerful factor, of the utmost importance, not only from a political point of view, but also for the purposes of organisation and mobilisation '.[51] In the late autumn of 1932 the Central Committee instructed the ' Reich Technician ' to make the necessary preparations for the production of illegal literature. It was his responsibility to direct and supervise the entire production and distribution of printed matter, at first on behalf of the Central Committee and later the illegal National Committee. These supplied him with manuscripts in the desired lay-out and notified him of the number of copies required. He then passed the manuscripts to the ' printing apparatus ' which in turn sent the printed literature to the despatch department. The 'Reich Technician' (after 1933 Willi Reimers) was responsible for the supervisors of the two latter departments as well as the technicians in the various Party districts. Communication with these individuals, as well as with the National Committee, was normally by courier. In Berlin alone ten presses were at the disposal of the KPD, whose publications were also printed in Leipzig, Königsberg, Magdeburg and Düsseldorf, more especially after the requisition of all presses in Berlin and the break-up of the Central Administrative Committee in October 1933.

In addition to the central organ of the KPD, the *Rote Fahne*, whose Berlin edition is said to have increased its circulation from 70,000 to 300,000 after the *Reichstag* fire[52] but which, according to Reimers, did no more than retain its existing readership, a whole series of pamphlets and other publications appeared under the auspices of the National Committee.[53] Apart from the material produced centrally there appeared, even in the first weeks of illegality, a host of clandestine publications run off on duplicating machines by subordinate groups as prescribed by the leadership. All this activity, which was directed at the achievement of a mass impact by calling for demonstrations, strikes, and so on, led to severe and often immediate losses. According to legal records still in existence, the Berlin Supreme Court in 1933 alone passed sentences in what is estimated to be nearly 1,000 trials of KPD groups and individuals accused of illegal activities in the capital of the Reich.

On 2 May 1933, after the destruction of the trade unions, the Revolutionary Trade Union Opposition (RGO) was told to re-form as a 'broad opposition movement for the mass of trade union members' with the aim of swelling the Party's ranks. The RGO was to adapt itself to the structure of the trade unions 'so that the latter's erstwhile members, by a process of isolated struggle, might be led into mass and general strikes against fascist dictatorship . . .'[54] The KPD was speculating on a change of mood among the members of the trade unions and hence on 'most favourable objective opportunities for the conquest of the trade union masses'. In August 1933 the Central Committee decided to set up independent Class Trade Unions untouched by Social Democratic ideology and influence. The sole upshot of these tactical gymnastics and somewhat muddled ideas in the field of trade union politics was that the scattered remnants of the RGO still in existence simply renamed themselves Class Trade Unions.

Today, the Communists attribute the failure of this operation to the fact that later decisions on the formation of Class Trade Unions were not able to utilise fully what had been at first ' a wholly correct orientation towards mass activity among members of the coordinated trade unions ' and this virtually prevented the common struggle of the Communists and the Free Trade Unions. True, there were successful attempts in the winter of 1933/4 at reestablishing committees for the majority of the industrial and some of the factory groups in Berlin, all of which, as it happened, were destroyed again by 1935;[55] but basically it still remained an RGO operation as before, relying on its former members rather than on ' the vast masses of trade union members impressed into the DAF [German Labour Front] '.[56]

After the leading officials of the KPD had all gone into voluntary exile in the autumn of 1933, the decision was taken in Moscow to set up a National Committee in Berlin for the whole of the Reich. Ferlemann, Lambert Horn, and Hans Fladung were to be appointed District Secretaries of Saxony, Berlin and the Rhineland, respectively, but before they could take up full duties Fladung, in company with John Schehr, was arrested on 9 November 1933, Horn a few days later, and Ferlemann at the beginning of 1934.[57]

Wilhelm Kox, who had been sent to Berlin from the Lenin School in Moscow in December 1933, and Herbert Wehner now attempted to maintain and consolidate communications with the regions by means of couriers and instructors. Besides providing information and a press service, they sought to revive the *Rote Fahne*.[58] On the two occasions when copy and cash were sent to the appropriate offices abroad, since printing there would be both safer and quicker than in Germany, no newspapers were forthcoming and the cash was never seen again. Instead, printed matter came to be produced increasingly outside the country; channelled through the Comintern, it betrayed total ignorance of German domestic conditions. Indeed the officials abroad looked on the comrades in the underground as little more than a distribution machine for their material.

An illuminating instance of the indignation and bitterness stirred up by this attitude and by the publications arriving from abroad has been given by Gustav Regler in an account of a meeting in the Saar between an important Party official and members of the underground in 1934 :

> I came just in time to hear the final remarks of a young man who had been making a report on the Reich. He took a pamphlet from his pocket and threw it down at the official's feet. 'We've been distributing that for months', he said, almost revelling in his scorn. 'We've put up with a lot from you people, but this is too much. Who's that supposed to be for?' He indicated the despised booklet with his foot and, speaking with the utmost firmness, concluded : 'None of us is going to risk the chopper for that tripe!'[59]

Frequently changes among its officials disrupted the work of the National Committee during 1934. Early in 1935 a new Committee consisting of Adolf Rembte, Robert Stamm and Max Maddalena was sent to Berlin from Prague for the purpose of introducing the united front tactics laid down by the Party. The Committee was, however, destroyed within a matter of weeks. At a meeting with a number of district leaders on 27 March 1935 for the purpose of drafting common directives for illegal activities, all taking part were arrested by the Gestapo. After this no further National Committees were formed.[60]

Meanwhile, in the matter of communications and supervision, the districts within the Reich were becoming increasingly the responsibility of the leadership abroad and of the Party representatives under its direct control who were stationed on the borders of neighbouring countries.[61] No more than one-third of Party funds was used for the illegal groups, the remainder being spent outside the country. In fact the instructors sent into the regions by the frontier offices did no more than receive reports and issue

N

instructions, and were unable to investigate the problems and
circumstances of the organisation.[62]

The tactics to be adopted towards the Social Democrats in the
matter of the united front presented the KPD with one of its main
problems both before and after 1933. Even after the National
Socialist seizure of power, the KPD continued to pursue the aim
of alienating the Social Democrats from their leaders and of
winning their cooperation, if not their membership. But the
underground workers in a number of centres very soon ceased
to believe the absurd slogan that the SPD was the ' main prop
of the capitalist dictatorship '.[63] Some of the highest officials, too,
gradually came to have doubts about maintaining opposition to
the Social Democrats. The first signs of a change in policy regarding the united front became apparent at a meeting of the
Presidium of the EKKI in July 1934 and also in a resolution passed
by the Central Committee of the KPD on 1 August 1934. As representatives of the National Committee, Adolf Rembte and Otto
Wahls were informed of the new tactics at conferences in Paris
in August 1934 and in Saarbrücken in September 1934. But in
the Politburo itself there was still much disunity. While Pieck and
Ulbricht took the view that an agreement might be reached with
the SPD leadership, or at any rate its left wing, the group round
Schubert (Florin, Schulte, Dahlem, Kippenberger, and Creutz-
burg) refused to have anything to do with it. The Politburo, including Rembte and Stamm, was thereupon summoned to Moscow where, in January 1935, the political commission of the
EKKI ' settled ', as they put it, these differences after an exceptionally vehement discussion. In a resolution of 30 January 1935,
the Central Committee informed the KPD that the Party must
' effect a bold change in its mass policy for the organisation of
a proletarian united front so that the necessary conditions can
be created for increased revolutionary activity to mark the beginning of the fascist dictatorship '.[64]

For the émigré leadership of the KPD the main problem was
now to establish contact and open negotiations with the SPD
Executive in Prague. But first it was necessary publicly to repudi-
ate the tactics previously adopted. This was done at the 7th
Comintern Congress in Moscow from 25 July to 20 August 1935.

Shortly afterwards, in October 1935, the Fourth Party Conference of the KPD met near Moscow. (To mislead the Gestapo it was somewhat naïvely called the Brussels Conference.) After days of self-criticism over past mistakes a resolution was passed to establish unity of action with the Social Democrats and to set up a Popular Front.[65]

On the initiative of the KPD a discussion took place in Prague on 23 November 1935 between the Central Committee members, Walter Ulbricht and Franz Dahlem, and the representatives of the SPD Executive, Hans Vogel and Friedrich Stampfer, but the results were inconclusive. The KPD's change of tactics had come at least three years too late. What might earlier have been a sensible and successful venture was now devoid of all prospects. After the extensive losses suffered by the illegal Social Democratic and Communist groups since 1933, a mass basis for a united front had ceased to exist. Again, the Social Democrats were as yet unable to dispel their suspicions that this was no more than a routine tactical manœuvre on the part of Comintern — suspicions based on 17 years of bitter strife with the Communists, whose sole use of the 'united front' slogan had hitherto been as a stick to beat the SPD. Furthermore, it so happened that at the end of 1935 critical self-analysis had reasserted itself following the initial trend towards radical revolution. Once again it was realised that the values of personal freedom could have their place only in a true democracy, never in a dictatorship, nor yet in a 'dictatorship of the proletariat'. Any agreement with the Communists was therefore out of the question.[66]

Even if there were occasional instances of cooperation between Social Democrats and KPD and although the latter's instructors operating in the Reich were told to encourage it, it remained ineffectual. The Moscow trials that began in August 1936, with their shameful spectacle of the liquidation of the old revolutionaries, followed by the Russo-German non-aggression pact shortly before the outbreak of the Second World War, destroyed the last hopes for a united front of Social Democrats and Communists in Germany.

At the 'Brussels Conference' it was decided to move the main organising elements out of Germany and to initiate widespread decentralisation. KPD refused to fill the higher ranks of the underground controlling staffs, since these had already and all too frequently proved vulnerable to Gestapo attack. Their tasks were then assigned to Party representatives in neighbouring countries whose duty it was to locate, build up, and direct through the medium of instructors, the groups operating independently in the Reich. Following comprehensive changes among the leading officials, clandestine activities were carried on under this system until the outbreak of war. The only alteration to the plan took place after the Central Committee's resolutions in January 1937 to replace the Party representatives, who were individually responsible, by collectives, the so-called ' Sector Committees ' (*Abschnittsleitungen*).[67]

When illegal activities began, the existing system of organisation by districts was retained. The Berlin district was divided into three ' Sectors ' each under a ' Senior Adviser ', the sectors being subdivided into three or four areas each controlled by an ' Adviser '. As a rule an area comprised three Sub-Districts themselves subdivided into city quarters and, subordinate to these, the smallest illegal units, the street and works cells. Areas and Sub-Districts were identified by code numbers.

The ' Brussels Conference ' decided that wherever possible the old system of division by dormitory areas was to be discontinued. The main emphasis must henceforth be placed on the establishment of illegal cells in factories as well as in the National Socialist mass organisations whose planned subversion was deemed vitally important. To achieve the latter purpose, what the General Secretary of the Comintern, Georgi Dimitrov, described as ' Trojan horse tactics ' would have to be employed. Factory cells might communicate with one another, each through a specially appointed member, but to obviate the danger of police intervention, must communicate direct with their superiors in Prague.

Obviously the problems raised by an administrative upheaval of these dimensions could not be ironed out in a matter of hours, particularly under illegal conditions. In the beginning the Berlin organisation carried out the new directives only to the extent of breaking up the District Committee whose duties it delegated to the four sectors. The rest of the organisation remained provisionally unchanged. The middle of 1936 saw the completion of arrangements for bringing the factory cells in direct contact with the Sector Committee in Prague.[68]

But before the KPD could complete their reorganisation in Berlin, the Gestapo struck. At the end of 1936 it succeeded in rounding up a large proportion of the groups in the centre, north, north-east, north-west, east, and west of the city. According to surviving documents those affected were the Communist Party Sub-Districts of Prenzlauer Berg, Friedrichshain I and II, Weissensee, Lichtenberg, Stettiner Bahnhof, Charlottenburg, Zentrum, Wedding-Ost, Wedding-West, Köpenick, Pankow, Vineta (Pankow) as well as the Sub-Districts of Prenzlauer Berg, Friedrichshain, Weissensee, Stettiner Bahnhof, Pankow and the Land city district committee of the affiliated Communist organisation *Rote Hilfe*. During 1937 there followed the elimination of further Sub-Districts in Steglitz, Zehlendorf, Moabit, and Schöneberg. In a series of trials lasting in some cases until the first years of the war, several hundred members of these groups were convicted either by the People's Court or by the Berlin Supreme Court.[69] Unfortunately it is not apparent from the record of findings or other court documents how the Gestapo contrived to carry out the operation. Perhaps they had planted informers in particular groups, or perhaps the victims of random arrests had made statements, either voluntarily or under pressure, of 'severe interrogation', which in turn led to further arrests. There is every likelihood, however, that the distribution of Communist literature gave the police and other agencies repeated opportunities for intervention.

There is little or no sign in court records, at least in Berlin, of the employment of Trojan horse tactics by the underground. One man was held by the People's Court to have merited a severer sentence because he, a convinced Marxist, had had the temerity to join the DAF in July 1936, to have taken up an appointment in that organisation, and as one of its officials to have sworn an oath of allegiance to the Führer on 20 April 1937 at the Sports Palace. Had he thereafter 'continued to act on behalf of the KPD in any way that was significant or effective, there could have been, in the view of the No. 1 Court, no alternative to the death sentence, since it would have been a piece of unprecedented villainy had a compatriot [*Volksgenosse*] taken this oath with the intention of committing high treason'. From the foregoing it is obvious that anyone found guilty of such conduct in a National Socialist organisation would have been punished particularly severely and that the accused only escaped with his life because he had been arrested at an early stage. Another noteworthy aspect of the tenor of this judgment is the assertion by the People's Court that 'activity hostile to the State' becomes more serious the longer the period since the 'assumption of power' and the more 'the constructive work of National Socialism, particularly in the social field, becomes apparent to every sensible *Volksgenosse*'.[70]

Faced in January 1939 with the growing dangers of war, the leaders of the KPD carried out a review of their existing policies at a conference near Paris (the 'Berne Conference'). Along with their repeated demands for the creation of a united front of all workers and for the amalgamation of all anti-fascists in a Popular Front, the KPD declared as its aim the formation of a new democratic republic and a united party of the German working classes. It called on all Communists to draw hitherto non-activist comrades into this work, to establish contact with other anti-fascists and to set up Party groups and committees in the factories and the mass organisations.[71] The leaders of the Party, however, also admitted that the KPD's ability to mobilise the masses was in no way commensurate with the increasing gravity of the international political situation.[72]

In fact mobilisation was hardly feasible. In Berlin only a few elements of the illegal organisation had survived the mass arrests of 1936 and 1937. Through the medium of instructors, the Sector Committee, which in the meantime had moved from Prague to Copenhagen, sought to instil fresh life into its clandestine operations. Although Heinrich Schmeer met with little success in the Reinickendorf Sub-District,[73] in May 1939 Willi Gall found the organisation in that of Adlershof virtually intact. On his second visit to Berlin, Gall was overtaken by the outbreak of war and being unable to return to Copenhagen took over the leadership of this Sub-District. He gave a sharp impetus to illegal activities, holding regular discussions and explaining the Party's political line. Gall was a vigorous promoter of the work of the Party cells in a number of large Berlin undertakings. From these cells he requested written and verbal reports which were then used in the Party's illegal literature. By now Gall had become dissatisfied with these publications, produced as they were in small quantities on primitive duplicating machines. In October he decided to publish a newspaper, to be called the *Berliner Volkszeitung* (BVZ), which would appear at regular intervals and which would, he was sure, make a strong impression on the group. The first issue of the BVZ, numbering 200 copies, appeared in November. Before the next number came out on 14 December 1939, Gall was arrested as were, within the next few days, all the other members of the Sub-District.[74]

In January 1940, following discussions with officials of the Comintern, the members of the Central Committee resident in Moscow decided to issue a new directive which later came to be known as the January Resolution. The Party leaders decided to support Soviet policy towards Germany following the conclusion of the non-aggression pact,[75] but at the same time to continue the struggle against the National Socialist régime. Some in Moscow were convinced that the pact would lighten substantially the Party's illegal tasks in Germany. Philipp Dengel went so far as to declare that ' the comrades working in Berlin need no longer fear decapitation, since Stalin would make sure that Hitler kept the terror within certain bounds '.[76]

With regard to organisation, the existing decentralisation was to be abandoned and orders were given to build up a rigidly centralised Party system inside the Reich. The new committees in Germany were to be composed largely of ' legal ' persons who nevertheless would supervise ' illegal ' instructors under the direction of an illegal secretariat to be set up in Berlin. Herbert Wehner, who had been chosen to head this secretariat, travelled from Moscow to Stockholm as the first step towards taking up his post.

The infiltration of officials into Germany through Sweden was, however, proving extraordinarily difficult. The only line of contact of any importance was the one maintained with the aid of Swedish sailors to Wilhelm Knöchel (' Erasmus ') who, since 1935, had been the KPD's representative with sole responsibility for the Benelux countries. At the beginning of 1941 he was able to despatch the first instructors from Amsterdam to Western Germany. On arrival their task was to prepare accommodation for the officials who would be following later, and to send reports on morale which would be used as a basis for future political activities. Knöchel did not transfer his operations to Berlin until January 1942. His orders were to promote the growth of the organisation in Western Germany, to maintain contact with the Party offices in Moscow and Stockholm, to keep them informed of German internal affairs, to promote illegal activities and lastly, after the middle of 1942, to prepare for the arrival of the officials appointed to the secretariat.

The output of propaganda had hitherto been small and had been the responsibility of the instructors. Now, under Knöchel's leadership, it was appreciably increased and distributed by go-betweens ' to wider sections of the population '. He was also at pains to establish a radio link with Moscow and, about the end of 1942, an expert arrived from Holland with a secret code and parts of a transmitter. But at the end of January 1943, Knöchel's arrest prevented the initiation of transmissions. Up till then the results of the January Resolution to reconstruct a centrally directed illegal organisation had been disappointing. Apart from some progress in Western Germany, Knöchel and his associates were unable to muster a closely-knit following of any appreciable size.[77]

Nevertheless a large number of new illegal groups had arisen, working on their own initiative and wholly independent of those ' above '. The two most important were led by Robert Uhrig and Anton Saefkow. Uhrig, who had been sentenced by the Berlin People's Court to 21 months' imprisonment in November 1934 for ' preparing to commit high treason ', thought, after his release in 1938, that the time was ripe for the resumption of illegal activities in company with kindred spirits whom he had met in prison. At first Uhrig restricted his operations to propaganda among acquaintances and workmates, but at the beginning of 1940 he and his closer associates proceeded to form an organisation which in course of time increased its membership in Berlin to at least 100. Besides making contact with groups in the Tyrol, Vienna, Essen, Hanover, Hildesheim, Dortmund, and Hamburg, they also got in touch with the former *Freikorps* leader, Dr Joseph (Beppo) Römer, in the autumn of 1941. 'According to the reliable statements' of one of his fellow-accused, Römer's plans envisaged the creation of an organisation, modelled on the Soviet Union, that would assume power after the collapse of National Socialism. At the outset Uhrig and Römer arranged that the groups should cooperate, although retaining their separate identities. During later discussions plans were prepared for the establishment everywhere of district committees and, later, of a joint central national committee. Besides issuing a monthly *Informationsdienst* that made its first appearance in November 1941, Uhrig and Römer decided to set up 'activist groups' which, depending on the circumstances, were to be engaged in terrorist operations. Before these long-term objectives could be realised, the Gestapo, probably helped by an informer, arrested Uhrig and Römer, as well as most of the members of their groups.[78]

In 1939, having served a sentence in prison and concentration camp, Anton Saefkow, like Robert Uhrig, started making contacts in Berlin in order to resume illegal operations. There, by tireless and dogged spadework, he built up an extensive range of activities in company with Franz Jakob, who had fled from Hamburg after evading arrest in October 1942, and Bernhard Bästlein, who arrived in May 1944. At the same time they made contact with strong Communist organisations in other German cities as well as in Saxony and Thuringia.[79] In giving the reasons for its sentence, the People's Court declared that the case 'had conjured up the very gravest dangers to the Reich'.[80]

With the use of propaganda put out by the so-called *Nationalkomitee Freies Deutschland* (NKFD), the accused began to enlist into their organisation other circles hostile to the state, these being offered the prospect of participation in a 'popular democratic government' after the planned overthrow of the National Socialist government . . . The accused have directed and supervised the illegal activities of the organisation in all areas, have laid down political directives, have, above all, built up their subversive activities in the country's industries and participated in the production and distribution of inflammatory and subversive material both at home and at the front.[81]

These words, the first in the charge against Saefkow, Jakob and Bästlein, pay an indirect tribute to their work.

In an attempt to discover the aims of the Communist Resistance movement, the Social Democrats, Dr Julius Leber and Professor Adolf Reichwein, held a discussion on 22 June 1944 with Saefkow, Jakob and Ferdinand Thomas in a doctor's house in the Schönhauser Allee in Berlin. Immediately prior to the second meeting, arranged for 4 July, all were arrested. It has never been discovered who informed the Gestapo. Nor is it easy to explain the extent of the group's illegal activities and the many ramifications of its contacts. During the interrogations, Gestapo officials are said to have asserted that more than 1,000 people had been associated with the Saefkow-NKFD complex and that some 400 death sentences had been passed.[82] But even after the destruction of the Saefkow organisation in the summer of 1944, small, isolated Resistance groups managed to carry on, for illegal handbills and pamphlets, testifying to their activity, began to reappear in Berlin.[83]

## Neu Beginnen*

Over the years a number of smaller groups separated from the large workers' parties, the SPD and KPD, often because of minor differences in matters of ideology. Although the result was to aggravate the disunity inside the German labour movement, the groups themselves were generally of little account, since they did not succeed in winning over any appreciable number of SPD or KPD members. These groups continued with their work after 1933 and, since they were so tightly knit, managed passably well after

* This section is based on an article by Hans J. Reichhardt that appeared in the *Jahrbuch für die Geschichte Mittel-und Ostdeutschlands*, Vol. 12 (1963), pp.150 ff., entitled 'Neu Beginnen – Ein Beitrag zur Geschichte des Widerstandes der Arbeiterbewegung gegen den Nationalsozialismus'.

they had gone underground. As an example of them all it is proposed to give here a short account of the fortunes of the group that came to be known as *Neu Beginnen* ('New Beginning').

Its origins go back to 1929 when its founder, Miles,* once a member of the Free Socialist Youth – a group with Communist leanings – who had later gone into opposition against the KPD, foresaw that the consequences of the world economic crisis would be a succession of fascist revolutions and new wars. He thought that the main danger facing the Weimar Republic in the 1929 crisis was a fascist revolution which, in his view, could only be met by a united socialist party. His appraisal of the situation led Miles to suggest to a number of politically-minded friends, who almost exclusively were young, critical Communists and Social Democrats, that a new organisation should be formed for the purpose of reviving the German labour movement.

The organisation, which in the beginning lacked a name, saw as its first task a reconciliation of the two mutually hostile views within this movement. Since open criticism advocating amalgamation was impossible inside the two parties, it seemed that a more feasible plan would be to gain supporters among them by a surreptitious and unofficial policy of infiltration. This, would, of course, presuppose a measure of secrecy and conspiratorial tactics since the smallest deviation from the current party line often sufficed, particularly in the KPD, to bring expulsion. Another and more important reason for additional secrecy regarding the organisation's existence and activities was the danger of a National Socialist seizure of power. The leaders were convinced that the group would be exposed to lesser dangers if it managed to prevent its special character becoming known inside the workers' parties. For this reason Miles modelled the organisation largely on the ideas expressed by Lenin in his *What is to be done?* written at a time when Russian Social Democracy was banned. In particular he drew on Lenin for his operational doctrines, namely centralism, absolute authority of the leadership and conspiratorial concealment.[84]

The number of members gradually increased so that by the

* Pseudonym for Walter Löwenheim

summer of 1932 preparations could be put in hand for the build-ing-up of nuclei inside the SPD and KPD. Optimism as well as growing confidence in the organisation's powers were expressed at a conference at the beginning of January 1933, when the leaders explained their plans for expansion. In their situation report they declared that the first signs of recovery from the crisis were becoming evident and that a more favourable development of the organisation must allow for the extension and consolida-tion of its influence, particularly by the training of suitable leaders in both parties. But they also emphasised that the danger of a ' fascist solution ' of the crisis was not yet past.

When it became obvious after the *Reichstag* fire that National Socialism had carried the day, long-prepared plans for going underground were put into operation, with the result that the leaders and rank-and-file of the organisation, which maintained a number of now illegal offices in Berlin, managed to continue their work comparatively undisturbed. On going underground they were able to use their long-standing contacts with other cities as a means of extending their influence and their network. They also set up a special provincial office where a number of con-ferences were held with a view to founding new groups. The organisation made contact with the *Sozialistische Arbeitsinter-nationale* (SAI) and in 1933 established a foreign secretariat in Prague under Dr Karl Frank. His task was to obtain funds for the operations in Germany and to influence foreign opinion.

Aside from matters of organisation, the leaders felt it necessary to set out in a manifesto their fundamental attitude to the new situation. Right from the start they had been compiling quantities of political and theoretical material for the instruction of their members and as bases for discussion; much of it could be incor-porated without alteration. This document, edited by Miles, was issued by the Social Democratic Party publishers, Graphia, of Carlsbad, in 1933 and bore the title *Neu Beginnen*.[85] From then on the organisation went by this name. The booklet made a con-siderable impression on labour movements in Germany and abroad. The polished style, the convincing analysis of the state of affairs in the labour movement and the prediction of what future steps would be necessary in the struggle against National

Socialism met with much approval. Such was the rallying power of the copies smuggled into Germany that they formed the basis of discussion groups, many of which felt themselves part of *Neu Beginnen*.

Miles began with a sharp criticism of the failure of the workers' parties, which had fallen victim to the ' fascist offensive ' without serious resistance and which had failed to adapt themselves to the new circumstances of a clandestine struggle against National Socialism. Even more serious in his view was their inability to grasp the essence of National Socialism, their illusory hope that the régime was no more than transitory and that sooner or later a return to democratic rule was inevitable. He pointed out that the régime would not collapse of itself but must be overthrown by a strong socialist movement, although that would in fact only be possible in the event of an internal or external crisis. For this reason *Neu Beginnen* was to become a pool for the ' best, bravest, most critical, and most devoted people ' in the labour movement irrespective of their particular affiliations. As a beginning Miles envisaged a free and critical discussion by all who thought regeneration necessary and who wished to work for this goal. He hoped that under ' pressure of the fascist terror ' the prospects for a collective organisation would be far more promising than any of the previous attempts that had been made by smaller groups.

Next to the regeneration of the labour movement, Miles thought it essential to win over ' all forces directed against the Fascist Party leadership ' for the abolition of the National Socialist system. Here he was expressing a requirement that only began to be realised by degrees during the late 1930s and was to lead to the plot of 20 July 1944.

At first *Neu Beginnen*'s underground activities were carried out in teams of three or five. Each was led by a representative of the committee with which only he maintained contact. The groups discussed general political questions as well as summaries of the committee's talks with representatives of the international labour movement. An analysis of important events was also a part of the internal programme of instruction and information. The groups compiled reports on activities both in industry and in the NSDAP and its subsidiary organisations which were passed to an editorial board appointed by the committee. From these many individual reports a full survey of the situation in Germany was prepared each month for internal and foreign distribution by courier under conditions of the utmost secrecy.

Long before 1933, *Neu Beginnen* had been paying much attention to the political technique of conspiratorial self-protection. On going underground it reaped the benefits of continuous training in these methods, for the Gestapo, in spite of having set up a special *Neu Beginnen* department after the appearance of Miles' booklet, had been unable to place an informer in the organisation. Nevertheless some wholly incomprehensible mishaps occurred which were to lead to the arrest of a large number of members in 1935.

*Neu Beginnen* began to experience increasing problems of organisation as it became apparent that there was also a negative side to effective conspiratorial techniques. True, it had managed to operate illegally for two or three years without losses, but these often irksome and complicated procedures, essential though they were and far superior to those of other groups, seriously inhibited the dynamics of the organisation. In addition to this, it had not been possible to gain control of other underground groups, nor were there yet any active anti-Nazi, middle-class elements with whom forces might be joined. Its work thus lacked the inspiring stimulus of visible success. Accordingly, the committee slowly came round to the view that there was now no longer any sense in continuing with the group's activities inside Germany. It had, moreover, become increasingly evident how slight was the influence the underground could exert on the population by comparison with the National Socialists and their monopoly of publicity media. One further event sapped their will to continue. At the end of 1934 the SPD Executive in Prague which, with a rare measure of democratic tolerance, had hitherto supported *Neu Beginnen* despite intensive criticism from the group, ceased contributions to the foreign secretariat because its head, Dr Karl Frank, had been actively concerned in the formation of a special organisation composed of opposition groups inside the SPD. *Neu Beginnen* was, of course, sorely hit by the stoppage of payments.

Every effort was made from Berlin to get the decision reversed by the SPD Executive in Prague or by the SAI, but without success.

Confronted by these many difficulties, the committee expressed the opinion that it would be impossible to continue the organisation under the National Socialist régime, since the vital revolutionary incentives were lacking. The few Marxists still active would have to close down the organisation in the Reich and seek new fields in countries where revolutionary opportunities continued to exist. After October 1934 strong opposition to this attitude arose in Berlin, supported by the head of the foreign secretariat, Dr Frank. The opposition, like the committee, was aware of the enormous difficulties presented by the continuation of illegal activities, but unlike the latter held firmly to the view expressed by Miles himself in his manifesto – the struggle against the régime must be waged primarily from within. They also believed in the maintenance of stable political cadres, however modest in size, during the period of National Socialist power, for the opposition believed that only those members of the underground who were intimately acquainted with domestic conditions would enjoy sufficient authority among the people to undertake the task of evolving a new political structure when the time came. After a number of bitter disputes the two schools of opinion remained irreconcilable; the opposition, led by Richard Löwenthal and Werner Peuke, declared the committee dissolved on the grounds of defeatism and proceeded to elect a new provisional committee. While the latter informed the SAI and its general secretary, Friedrich Adler, of these developments, in September 1935 Miles and some of his closest associates decided to leave the country. Miles also gave the SPD Executive in Prague his own account of events in Berlin and announced the dissolution there of *Neu Beginnen*. Thus the breach between the two schools of opinion was complete, not only in terms of the organisation but also its members. Even today, the latter refer to these events as ' the split ', although it was more a change of committee. As it turned out, the group did not continue as two independent units, for Miles' supporters ceased to operate as an organised body following his announcement that *Neu Beginnen* no longer existed.

For reasons that have never been explained, the Gestapo contrived to arrest a number of members in the winter of 1935/6[86] with the result that *Neu Beginnen*'s work suffered an appreciable, though only temporary, setback. Although the interrogators and the Berlin Supreme Court were able to form a very accurate impression of the group's development and aims, the 1936 trials and particularly the comparatively mild sentences that followed are evidence that the accused managed to play down or to conceal their illegal activities and their contacts with others who were still at large.[87]

The foreign secretariat recommended that efforts be made to form a united front of all groups within the labour movement, but failed to provide any practical help from abroad. This cautious attitude aroused the sharp criticism of the Berlin committee, which declared that conditions inside Germany demanded a ' national and international united front ' and the ' united organisation of the labour movement at any price '. It complained bitterly that the ' demoralising squabbles ' of various émigré groups were distracting them from their real task of unifying the working classes. This was a view no doubt prevalent in the underground, but it was rare for it to be made so explicit.

Not that *Neu Beginnen* in any way envisaged an immediate combination of all illegal groups – the danger of discovery would have been too great. It was far more concerned that the émigrés should coordinate their activities while, in Germany, contacts should be formed only very gradually and in accordance with circumstances, every known precaution being taken against endangering the organisation's members.

At a conference in February 1936 between the foreign secretariat and representatives from Berlin, Werner Peuke repeated these arguments, pointing out that the formation of a united émigré labour party would considerably bolster up the underground's morale and would help to reinforce the workers' resistance against National Socialism. A discussion of Peuke's ideas, however, failed to produce any clear-cut views on the formation of a united front. After a visit to Prague, where he also met members of the KPD,[88] Peuke was arrested early in 1936, not as a member of *Neu Beginnen*, but as a former KPD official with false papers.

During 1936 *Neu Beginnen* managed to recommence opera-
ions after the inactivity that followed the arrests and, early in
:937, to join up with the so-called Popular Front Group (*Volksfront-Gruppe*). This group, led by the former *Reichstag* deputy,
)tto Brass, and the Thuringian *Landtag* deputy, Dr Hermann L.
3rill, was made up of old SPD and trade union officials who had
net prior to the council elections in the summer of 1935 to dis-
:uss means of persuading industrial workers to oppose out-and-
)ut National Socialist candidates. After the victory of the French
Popular Front in May 1936 and the formation of a Popular Front
government in Spain, the group thought that the time had come
:o work clandestinely for a similar goal in Germany.

In explaining its ten-point programme, the group pointed out
that a German Popular Front would be quite different from
those in France or Spain, since the political, ideological, moral,
spiritual, economic and social elements which had contributed
to the Popular Front in those countries, were lacking in Germany.
Because the organisations within the labour movement now consisted only of a few remnants no longer concerned with the restoration of the old parties or a return to a bygone state of affairs,
there had arisen among the ' top, thoughtful layer of the proletariat a deep longing for unity '. A Popular Front would have
to be an entirely new departure where there would be no place
for the artificial preservation of the former parties or even splin-
ters of those parties. All who participated would have to undertake to suspend their own special party activities during the period
between the creation of the Popular Front and the overthrow of
Hitler. The Front must not come into being through the deliberations of a few residual organisations abroad, but would have to
live and grow in Germany according to the dictates of its own
programme.

In January 1937 Otto Brass sought to win over the SPD Party
leaders to this programme. The émigré Social Democrats took a
sceptical view of the prospects either of a united or a Popular
Front, and turned down any suggestion of cooperation with the
Communists on the grounds of wide differences in ideological
outlook. At a subsequent meeting with a member of the Central
Committee of the KPD, Anton Ackermann, Brass himself de-

o

clared his opposition to any form of association with the Com
munists. An event of some import during Brass' journey to
Prague was his encounter with Dr Frank, the head of *Neu Beginnen*'s foreign secretariat, who gave him an introduction to Kurt
Schmidt and Fritz Erler, the group's leaders in Berlin. The outcome was that *Neu Beginnen* and the *Volksfront-Gruppe*, although remaining independent of each other, jointly brought out
a series of papers in which they attempted to set out the fundamental principles of National Socialism and its methods of
domination, and to indicate means of effecting its defeat. Some
examples are *German Ideology, Of Dialectical Materialism, Anschluss and What Then?* and *Five Years of Fascism.*[89] In the
autumn of 1937 the *Volksfront-Gruppe* came to the conclusion
that the ten points were too exiguous and would have to be set
out more comprehensively. After deliberating various drafts for
months, the *Volksfront-Gruppe* and *Neu Beginnen* came to an
agreement on the wording in April 1938. The result was *German
Freedom, a Publication by the German Popular Front, 1938*
copies of which were run off on duplicating machines so that the
aims of the movement might become known in wider circles.

The argument for an enlarged version of the ten-point programme contains, among others, the following passage :

The Popular Front is the United Front of those who have retained their integrity and sanity under dictatorship. But the
growth within the German people of a purely moral form of
resistance to rule by dictatorship is not sufficient. Moral resistance must acquire a political shape . . . To this end the political organisation of the German Popular Front has been formed
to include past and present members of Germany's left wing
parties. This organisation leads the struggle against dictatorial
principles and, after the fall of Hitler, will be prepared to
take over the government of the German Republic with a
sound programme designed to rescue the German people from
the political and economic chaos created by Hitler . . .

An indication of the impression that this programme might have
made, had it managed to achieve wider circulation,[90] may perhaps

be found in the extracts from it quoted in the record of the judges' findings at the trial of Brass and Dr Brill in the People's Court. The judges obviously regarded as particularly objectionable points 1 (' Down with Dictatorship! '), 2 (' Right and Justice for All '), and 5 (' Peace '), although these were worded with the utmost clarity to show that the members of the *Volksfront-Gruppe* and *Neu Beginnen* felt bound by their consciences to resist National Socialism regardless of circumstances, in order to save the German people and the world from the unspeakable miseries of war.

Before either group was able to widen its field of activity, the leading officials were arrested in the autumn of 1938. Convicting them of ' infamous and underground subversion ' that had endangered the internal order of the German people which National Socialism had secured, the judges impressed on the chief accused that they would have been sentenced to death had the group been of greater consequence at the time of their arrest by the Gestapo.[91]

In Berlin, *Neu Beginnen* was virtually destroyed by the arrests in the autumn of 1938. Although former members kept in touch with each other after their release, organised illegal activities in the name of *Neu Beginnen* came to an end.

One of the tragedies of the German labour movement was that in the days when its survival stood in the balance, no means could be found to resolve its internal disunity so that concerted action could be taken against the common enemy. Thus each party and each group tried to continue the struggle on its own account. In the underground, too, plans for a united front came to nothing. Since the deep ideological rift between democratic Socialism and totalitarian Communism had already become too wide to be bridged, common political activity was largely precluded. But the formation of a united front would have had little effect on the labour movement's lack of success in resisting the overwhelming strength of the National Socialists; it is generally estimated that not more than ten per cent of former labour members were prepared to continue the struggle. Moreover, the creation of a revolutionary popular movement for this purpose was to prove impossible in the particular conditions of a totalitarian system.

Obviously both Social Democrats and Communists were anxious to build up a popular or mass movement, but even in the early stages when groups were establishing contact with each other, expanding their cells, carrying out illegal propaganda and so on, it became evident that circumstances set a limit to the size of formations. Where a small group consisted mainly of former acquaintances who trusted each other, the supervision of its members and activities was relatively easy, but the larger the intake of new members, the greater the risk of infiltration by informers and *agents provocateurs* with whose help the Gestapo often succeeded in rounding up a whole organisation. The distribution of illegal literature awoke little response in the people since its range was much too small to compete effectively with the National Socialist propaganda machine and its control of all the publicity media. In addition, any distribution outside the group's immediate circle involved too great a risk of discovery.

So it was that after several years the Social Democrats came round to the view that resistance of this kind would never be successful and would only claim an increasing number of victims. They abandoned any hope of being able to achieve a revolution with their own resources. Under the circumstances their object must be confined to the maintenance of contacts with fellow-sympathisers and to the stubborn prosecution of activities by individuals and small groups against National Socialism, whenever a safe opportunity arose.

By contrast the Communists, aside from changes of political line, generally held to their original views. Their organisation was better suited to underground conditions than that of the Social Democrats, whose activities had previously been confined to 'licit' politics in the field of mass labour, and who were now confronted by the laborious task of learning the rules of clandestine struggle. The KPD, drawing on traditional Bolshevist principles of organisation and method, adapted itself more readily to the underground although the first Communist groups were destroyed relatively quickly. Nevertheless the KPD did not change its methods of operation. In spite of severe losses new illegal groups were continually being formed for the distribution of literature produced by the Party within the country as well as by the leadership abroad.

Whereas the underground Social Democratic groups were at pains chiefly to preserve their members' loyalty as a valuable legacy of the old Party and to keep them immune from the blandishments of National Socialist propaganda, the Communists attached little importance to such aims. Their concern was to set the proletariat in motion and bring it into action; once it was on the move, indoctrinated cadres would be able to guide it along the desired course. In practice the Communists were concerned not so much with the preservation of loyalty as with the activities of their groups which, whenever they attempted to go outside their customary field of operations, were invariably destroyed.

The revival of the German labour movement by the healing of its breach, however rewarding in theory, inevitably presented *Neu Beginnen* with a virtually insoluble problem when the group sought to put this theory into practice. Before 1933 control of a party's apparatus might have been gained from within only by observing every rule of conspiratorial procedure: it would entail either the resignation of the former leading officials or their replacement with *Neu Beginnen* members elected by the party. While this might have been conceivable in the case of the SPD with its democratic structure – though not, indeed, within the short period between 1929 and the National Socialist seizure of power – there could be no hope of success in the case of the Communists, the KPD by that time having rid itself of almost every vestige of democracy.

Although the labour movement, by its collapse, had left its supporters more receptive than ever to new and changed ideas, *Neu Beginnen* was not prepared to admit an unlimited number of new members; its rules for selection had always been strict and the need for security precluded their relaxation now. Nevertheless the *Neu Beginnen* manifesto had an inspiring effect wherever it became known in Germany, not least by reason of its rousing title: it expressed the same dissatisfaction and discontent with the former party committees as was felt by many of the younger and more active sections of the labour movement.

The advantages and disadvantages of conspiratorial techniques to avoid detection are highlighted by illegal activity. Although *Neu Beginnen*, in contrast to the resistance groups of the two large worker's parties, remained in being for a comparatively long time thanks to its conspiratorial methods, it was able to do so only by virtually renouncing any effective or decisive expansion of its organisation. The creation of illegal cadres was, of course, essential to the development of a large revolutionary popular movement, but the moment these cadres moved out of isolation for the purpose of influencing the masses by the distribution of literature, they became exposed to the same dangers as those faced by other groups and, like them, they were destroyed.

Events since then have shown that there is no way of overthrowing from within a totalitarian régime which has at its command the whole modern paraphernalia of police and terror and which, like that of the National Socialists, enjoys the support of large sections of the public. It is only possible if the Opposition can win over the armed forces, or rather the army, and so bring off a *coup d'état* (' revolution from above '), or if an overwhelming majority of the population, stirred up by the Opposition, revolts against the régime and at a critical stage manages to bring a large part of the army over to its side.

But these sober observations do not represent an assessment of the Resistance inside the labour movement. Rather they are intended to make clear how much moral strength was needed in the face of a multitude of dangers and difficulties to follow the dictates of conscience and a better political judgment and, above all, to act.

However great their illusions and whatever their tactical mistakes the illegal groups of the Resistance are, when all is said and done, one of the few features of the history of Germany between 1933 and 1945 that redound to her credit.

# Political and Moral Motives behind the Resistance

ERNST WOLF

On 20 July 1944, when the Berlin *Wachbataillon* took part in the suppression of the attempted *coup*, its commanding officer was Otto Ernst Remer. At an election meeting of the Socialist Reich Party (SRP) in Brunswick on 3 May 1951, Major-General Remer was asked about his attitude at the time; he replied, not so much in his capacity as Vice-President of the SRP, but as one who had originally and quite by accident played a decisive rôle: 'Some of these conspirators were in large measure traitors paid from abroad', and again, 'The time will come when men will be ashamed to admit that they were part of the 20 July *putsch*. If a person is prepared to commit high treason against the state, it should further be asked whether such treason may not often be tantamount to the betrayal of his country abroad.'

It was not only Remer who held these opinions, for much the same views were expressed in certain circles both before and after he had made his statement. On 15 March 1952 the Brunswick High Court convicted him of slander and of defaming the memory of the dead, declaring unfounded his assertion that some of the men of 20 July 1944 had 'in large measure' been prepared to betray their country, and had received money from abroad to that end; hence his statements had been contrary to the law. Although the argument upon which the verdict was based did not – indeed could not – wholly remove the slur on the resistance fighters, the Remer trial, attended as it was by a large number of witnesses and experts, did entail a painstaking legal assessment of the attitudes of those who resisted. In this connection the court used the term 'unconstitutional state' (*Unrechtsstaat*) for certain aspects of the National Socialist state and declared that 'the situation had justified the struggle of the Resistance'. In like manner the Criminal Court declared that the resistance fighters of 20 July 1944, whether motivated by Christian, legal, military, political, or social considerations, strove to overthrow Hitler and his régime wholly in a spirit of fervent love of their fatherland, and with so great a sense of responsibility towards the nation that they were unhesitatingly prepared to sacrifice themselves. It was not their purpose to damage the Reich or the armed forces, but to help them.

Moreover it was for the same purpose that they had established connections abroad, thus incurring the reproach of having ' betrayed their country '.[1]

These legal decisions, whose arguments were the product of an already changed intellectual climate, are noteworthy because they represent in some ways the first departure from the Allies' endeavour to suppress or play down, on political grounds, the historical fact of the Opposition manifest in the disaster of 20 July, thereby upholding the official version promulgated by Hitler himself immediately after the event: ' A very small clique of ambitious officers, devoid of conscience and criminally stupid, hatched a plot to do away with me and at the same time to wipe out the directing staff of the German armed forces.' The speech was not only repeated but actually elaborated in a broadcast that followed immediately from Washington.[2] For the Allies it may be said that some of their misgivings were not entirely unjustified: a successful *coup* on the part of conspirators drawn exclusively from the military and the aristocracy would have meant the replacement of the National Socialist régime by one that was conservative, reactionary and nationalistic and would have been no guarantee that Germany would adopt a Western democratic system, even as represented by a reversion to the Weimar state. In postwar Germany, other motives were at work, deriving in part from the inherited corpus of nationalist military traditions – the very traditions from which the men of the 20 July had with difficulty succeeded in freeing themselves. Again, in the ambiance of the cold war, an attempt was made to obscure the picture by equating the Resistance with ' anti-Communism ', thus excluding from the movement such groups as the *Rote Kapelle* because they were Soviet-directed espionage organisations.[3]

Not until 1959 did the *Bundeswehr* pay a tribute, worded in very generalised terms, to the officers of the Resistance: 'The act of 20 July 1944 – an act directed against wrong and unfreedom – is a shining light in Germany's darkest hour' (order of the day by General Heusinger).[4] But it is, indeed, by no means certain that the following passage from Terence Prittie holds altogether true: 'Nearly 20 years after the war the German people had come in general to the conclusion that the actions of Hitler's opponents were justified, in that they followed the promptings of their individual consciences and their moral judgment.'[5] Abroad, there was a tendency summarily to dismiss the Resistance in the Third Reich either as the aftermath of Stalingrad – the conspiracy, that is, of a few disgruntled generals – or as an ineffectual counter-revolution. Indeed the movement was for a long time even regarded as taboo. A revision of these views, however, has since brought a willingness to treat the theme 'Germans against Hitler' more profoundly and with as much objectivity as possible.

The findings in the Remer trial were not the only reasons for a marked change of attitude towards the Resistance against Hitler and more especially towards the conspiracy of 20 July 1944. Of even greater importance was the action of the court in calling for and applying expert opinion to establish norms; not only did it hear opinion on historical matters such as the state of hostilities in the summer of 1944, the course of events on 20 July, the immediate motives of the resistance fighters, and the attitude of the officers' corps, but it also invited witnesses in the field of moral theology, Evangelical and Catholic theologians, who gave their views on the questions of the right to resist and the breaking of the oath. The fact that these latter aspects were exhaustively investigated does at least demonstrate an awareness that in order to explain and assess the Resistance, there must be an enquiry into the fundamental motives and the furthest antecedents of those who had resolved to take part. It was here, too, that progress was most difficult. In one particular synopsis, the Evangelical opinion (H. J. Iwand/E. Wolf), ends with the comment:

In the view of the Evangelical Church, the men of 20 July are to be reproached at most because they did not act until it was too late. No guilt, however, can attach to them for having seriously contemplated using force to effect a change in the control of the state by the removal of the highest political and military officials in the Third Reich, as soon as it had become evident that the leaders of the state under Adolf Hitler were making preparations for an unjust war. In explaining and excusing the late arrival of these men, it could be pointed out that the doctrine of the Reformed Church, which exhorts Christians to resist in accordance with the second table of the Commandments (for the benefit of his neighbour), had long since fallen into abeyance, and had been wholly superseded by the doctrine of patient obedience. But as soon as it had finally become clear that all was lost and that chaos threatened, the men of the Resistance movement formally broke the oath of allegiance and resolved to overthrow by force the incumbent of the highest office of state. This was an action symbolic of true Christian and political responsibility which might have initiated a reformulation both of justice and the limitations of political power. The fact that their attempt did not succeed in no way detracts from the spiritual significance of their action. It is, perhaps, a divine dispensation that their failure appears as sheer sacrifice and, probably for that very reason, of far greater moral and spiritual significance than success would have been. It is not our duty as Christians to assess the political, but rather the moral, importance of this manifestly public-spirited action in initiating a true reconstruction of our totally shattered polity.[6]

Two survivors of the Kreisau Circle have recently made some highly pertinent comments on the background to this summary which, though its tenor may derive from a standpoint determined by the church struggle, was written nearly ten years after 20 July 1944, at a time when the church was no longer the uncritical captive of the state and was therefore less emotional and more temperate in her attitude to social order. Harald Poelchau, the prison chaplain at Tegel where he had to attend many victims of political legislation during their last hours, expresses their common attitude to their self-imposed ordeal as follows: ' The course we have taken that has led us to death was not mistaken or false; on the contrary it was right and necessary, for the revival in Germany of justice and of esteem for man's dignity is more important than our lives.'[7] The writer then comments: ' Thus the churches of both confessions, through their members and through basic Christian insight, contributed materially to the Resistance in those years.' It is, however, incorrect to speak of the ' Resistance of the church under the National Socialist régime', since this was ' never voiced by the official institutions of the Evangelical Church or the Catholic Church, nor yet by the unofficial Confessing Church [*Bekennende Kirche*] '.[8]

This is no doubt true, notwithstanding the widespread popular belief that the churches were part of the Resistance movement in the Third Reich, but Poelchau's limits are rather too narrow. The struggle of the Confessing Church was at bottom a ' reluctant Resistance movement ', however disorganised her actions and emotions may have been. The same applies to many Catholic Christians, although neither church actually turned against the régime, and both, in their own fashion, were at pains not to keep their followers out of the conflict. As another member of the Kreisau Circle, Paul Graf Yorck von Wartenburg,[9] rightly put it, ' the church thus saw herself compelled to grapple with the phenomenon of an obedience which involved sabotage of the authorities as breakers of the law and, indeed, a determination to bring about their removal '.[10] By this task, the churches, the Evangelical Church especially, were faced with a peculiar and painful dilemma by reason of their inherited ties with the state and, to a certain extent, with a romantic sense of nationalism.

So much were the churches wrapped up in their own world of the nineteenth century, so greatly did they stand in awe of the state, that only by degrees were they able to rid themselves of these categories of thought. It needed the whole enormity of the national crime to set this process in motion. The agony experienced by the church in severing her ties with the state is revealed by the haste with which she sought to restore them after 1945. The lawful ecclesiastical Establishment had failed in its confrontation with the ways of ' the world ' which is described on every page of the Bible.[11]

Nevertheless this struggle with the past does represent one, if not the, impelling force in the ' revolt of conscience ' which, either unadulterated or combined with some degree of political motive, sustained the Resistance movement; ' and this conscience had been developing over two millennia of Christian history and was rooted in respect for the individual '.[12] The changes in the Kreisau Circle, the laborious self-examination leading to a guilt-ridden acceptance of the plans for the *coup* as the only solution, the conflict, too, in the minds of the soldiers when faced with the inevitability of breaking the oath of allegiance, had more to do with matters of conscience than did the more essentially national and political plans of Goerdeler and the military for a future German spiritual revival founded on her Christian heritage. Here moral and religious motives played a smaller part than was the case with the Kreisau Circle, but even so individual decisions were finally confirmed by an appeal to conscience.

The aims of the resistance against Hitler could not be achieved by a preponderant political opposition nor yet, in certain circumstances, by a concomitant revolution – the Röhm *putsch* was a poor precedent for either. Hence the only alternative was conspiracy, resulting in an action carefully planned and up to the end carefully camouflaged, carried out by small groups whose members, by reason of their background and education, found the methods to which they were committed wholly abhorrent. Under these conditions the all-important decision could only be reached after a profound conflict of conscience. They had to be prepared to stake their lives for their moral convictions and to see beyond the immediate interests of Germans *qua* Germans. A restoration of previous conditions would not suffice; they must press onwards even at the risk of being misunderstood by those whom eventual success was intended to benefit. Assuming that an attitude of conscious hostility to the National Socialist régime was by no means restricted to the groups whose full extent was revealed by more than 700 arrests made after 20 July, it is a depressing fact that this day barely raised an echo. An uncanny silence surrounded the men of the Bendlerstrasse; the risk that had been incurred became patent only when it was clearly too late to strike.

Major-General Henning von Tresckow, a few hours after the operation had failed, said:

> Now everyone will turn upon us and cover us with abuse. But my conviction remains unshaken – we have done the right thing. Hitler is not only the arch-enemy of Germany, he is the arch-enemy of the whole world. In a few hours' time I shall stand before God, answering for my actions and my omissions. I think I shall be able to uphold with a clear conscience all that I have done in the fight against Hitler . . . The worth of a man is certain only if he is prepared to sacrifice his life for his convictions.[13]

The final version of the radio statement that the conspirators had intended to make to the German people on 20 July, contains the same, if more generalised and hence attenuated, expression of a new sacrificial spirit of freedom and selflessness:

> Let us once again tread the path of justice, decency and mutual respect! In this spirit each of us will do his duty. Let us follow earnestly and in everything we do the commands of God which are engraved on our conscience, even when they seem hard to us: let us do everything to heal wounded souls and alleviate suffering. Only then can we create the basis for a sure future for our people within a family of nations filled with confidence, sound work and peaceful feelings.[14]

Some credit must be allowed to the resistance of the churches in the creation of this new climate, which enabled a forward-looking political spirit to cast aside conventional ties and entanglements. It was a heterogeneous movement, tentative perhaps and not wholly disinterested, but was all the more effective in that it provided moral stimulus and guidance for the political Resistance by accentuating what was human in a unique situation.

To this extent Hans Rothfels is right in his judgment that the churches' opposition had ' been the only one . . . that had achieved patent success ' for the very reason that the churches, ' by offering resistance within their own particular sphere ', had provided ' the active Resistance with a harder core and a sharper cutting edge than would have been possible by any external revolt '.[15] For the church felt compelled to attack the National Socialist system in its essentials and to oppose its totalitarianism with the total demand of Christ, proceeding thence, without any suggestion of opportunism, against every suppression or violation of man's rights or dignity. ' Only on this basis was it possible to preach an uncompromising attitude and to translate the churches' protest into underground activities and political resistance.'[16]

Why should this have been so? Because centuries of tutelage had led religious movements, particularly Protestantism but also to some extent Catholicism, to a subservience to the state so uncritical that it was tantamount to deification. Thus subservience must now be overcome step by step out of religious conviction and not without profound altercation within the church, in a process which unleashed forces that were too strong for tactical or other considerations. It was an atmosphere that permitted ' conversion ' from a nationalism authorised by the church to an acknowledgment of the primacy of justice and supranational humanity, to a sense of responsibility for the whole of mankind. This can be most clearly demonstrated by giving examples proffered by the Evangelical Church, in close alliance with her Catholic fellow-Christians and with liberal humanists, as she conducted a self-critical examination of her true nature and exact task.

The church resistance presents a very clear picture on a smaller scale of the general political situation – National Conservative prejudice; the failure of liberalism as a way of life and the rejection of democracy, seen confessionally as ' Western Calvinism '; acceptance of the ' Reich ' concept combined with the ideal concept of a ' second ' Protestant-Lutheran Reich based upon a synthesis of church and state, or church and throne; a distaste for republics in general and the Weimar Republic in particular; ideological anti-Marxism and the spectre of Communism; the Versailles trauma and, not least, the rejection of ' political catholicism '. There was, too, anti-Semitism, which was not only latent. Here also we find the beginnings of an opposition in the decisions made by individuals on the grounds of conscience.

To all appearances this opposition was not, as is generally agreed, directed against the state but ' only ' against external and internal intervention in the affairs of the church. As a result, quicker and more incisive decisions could be taken than was possible in the political field. Moreover, there already existed a certain community of interests among those who within the church formed a fundamental opposition; on the Evangelical side, at any rate, individuals were never wholly on their own. Tactical inhibitions were not everywhere felt but were confined to certain leaders of the church administration of which the emergent ' Confessing ' community was relatively independent. In addition there was the very important residue of the church's traditional moral authority to counterbalance the inherited reverence for the authority of the state.

The spirit that characterised the beginning of the church struggle over a wide front, and which has been termed ' clerical nationalism ', was dominated by the idea of a new synthesis of *Volkstum* (' nationhood ') and Christianity, of church and state, and thus constituted a purely negative opposition to ' Weimar '.[17] All this led to an understandable and sometimes rapturous acceptance of National Socialism's ' popular ' revolution.

This ' acceptance ', though often combined with criticism of extreme and ' un-Christian ' nationalism, was the result of a deep sense of insecurity in two respects: firstly as regards the actual historical circumstances leading up to the reluctantly tolerated Weimar Republic; and secondly as regards the ideology of National Socialism itself. Both these aspects were related to political wishful thinking, shot through with resignation. It was, indeed, a nostalgic ' Conservative-National ' dream of a new synthesis of church and state based on the glorification of the facts of war and of a national grandeur associated with Bismarck and Wilhelm ii but since sullied and debased by treason, the ' stab in the back ', Marxist materialism, and above all, the ' shameful ' treaty of Versailles. A symptom of this was the announcement by the ecclesiastical authorities in 1919 of a ' Sun-

P

day of mourning for Evangelical Christians' in commemoration of the treaty of Versailles and in protest against the 'war-guilt lie'. Ten years later this day was still being observed. Another symptom was the almost complete loss of sense of direction among the Evangelical clergy after the events of 1918, itself a consequence of illusions harboured at the outbreak of the First World War, and at the same time the consequence of their hope in the unification of the nation and the closure of the rift between clergy and labour, church and SPD. In 1929 these hopes revived with the appearance of the National Socialist movement. But in between came the Weimar period which was regarded as a period of decline, if only – to quote R. Seeberg, the Berlin theologian and specialist in systematic theology – because 'the alliance of materialistic enlightenment and democracy is usually . . . a typical form of decline among civilised nations'. This judgment, too, betrays the unhistorical character of such wishful thinking and the wholly unconstructive aspect of its opposition.[18] Central to that judgment was a new, or rather a revived, nationalism, in the shape of the concept of *Volkstum* for which, after the end of the monarchy, a conceptually ambiguous nation and one susceptible of many interpretations, superseded the throne in the traditional alliance between church and state. 'For that at least', wrote P. Althaus in 1919, 'we must thank the hard times that have been our lot for the last five years; since 1914 we have known what a nation is and we have known that we belong to a nation. Man's greatest possession is his nation. For the most serious-minded among us such attitudes as individualism divorced from the nation and supranational cosmopolitanism have now become impossible.'[19] In this context, *Volkstum* to some extent assumed the character of a revelation. The ' hour of the church' and the ' hour of the nation' were to be seen as a simultaneous event and for this reason the proponents of a ' Christian-German nationhood' feared, so far as 'national regeneration' was concerned, that the church might let her great moment pass. It was precisely this which accelerated the momentum of insecurity; contributory factors were the emergent myth of the German race (*Deutschtum*) together with the gradually deteriorating critical power of the Christian concept. Extreme groups of a racist-

Germanic, as opposed to Conservative-National complexion, further obscured the situation as also the exact part played by anti-Semitic motives.

The attitude to the rise of National Socialism varied between one of enthusiastic acceptance and one of vague distaste. A solution was sought in history and theology, and the defence of National Socialism was undertaken from what was ostensibly a predominantly Christian standpoint. Some striking comments were made in this connection by a Göttingen religious historian : [20]

Whoever sees affliction and finds it within his power to help, must help. If today there are good men who dare to take on the difficult work of liberating our people from bondage and affliction, they may regard themselves as being in the service of God. Thereby they need no other justification than their own conscience . . . The church has no right to restrict a task begun with holy zeal and passionate devotion. She must beware of obstructing God's work [a sign indeed of profound uncertainty] to . . . Our nation, which in 1918 sought to evade its duty [a national misconception of the 1914-18 disaster in typically condensed form] is once more confronted with the task to be accomplished. Must the church be wanting when the historical deed is to be done, when a body of young men prepare themselves with reverence and joy to go into battle? . . . The sole lawful justification of a movement lies in its ability to demand the lives of its members in sacrifice. On these sacrifices depends the progress of the movement . . . The blood of the martyrs also wipes out the stains and guilt that inevitably attach themselves to the raiment of those who struggle . . . Thus anyone, who in his heart has honestly come to the conviction that here is the path to the salvation of our people, is bound to play a part and may not stand aside. According to Luther, a Christian may aspire to powerful office for the sake of love [we are not given the context, but of course Luther must be brought in somewhere] if he deems this necessary.

Thoughts of this kind were typical of the clergy in the Conservative National camp who turned, filled with hope, to National Socialism. Unquestioningly they interpreted Point 24 of the

NSDAP programme, with its formula for 'positive Christianity', in the sense of the synthesis of church and nation. By their anti-liberal political attitude and their historical-theological way of thinking they encouraged not only more extreme expectations of a National Messiah, but also an eschatological vision of the Third Reich. Their dreams of a strong state, of an anti-socialist, nationally orientated social theory of a Christian-German *Volkstum* restored to health, stemmed from their interpretation of the many aspects of the National Socialist movement. They transferred to Adolf Hitler's state all those honours which, in accordance with the traditional Lutheran interpretation of *Romans* 13, were due to the temporal power.

It comes, therefore, as no surprise that in 1934 the organ of the Lutheran bishops was already announcing that the judgment passed on the Weimar Republic by the National Socialists must be preached by the church and put into effect by the state; and that, since the task was to be carried out by the National Socialists, ' the latter must therefore be welcomed by Lutheranism '.[21] Nor is it startling that a prominent Lutheran theologian should assert : ' Our Evangelical churches welcomed the change that came to Germany in 1933 as a divine gift and miracle ', or again, in the context of the ' national revolution ', that he should jettison Lutheran reservations towards revolution generally on the pretext of a newly discovered ' *gratia historica* '. Further, it is not surprising that even a pietist like Karl Heim should have written this altogether unguarded passage as late as 1937 : ' In every century the living Christ has pursued his mighty course through German history. It was from Christ that there came the great concept of the Reich, this age-old dream of the spirit of Germany, which has now been fulfilled once more.' Finally, we find in the Ansbach Advice, the Lutheran protest against the Barmen Theological Declaration (a decisive turning point in German Protestantism!), the following words : ' As Christians we honour every authority, with thanks to God, even a debased authority.' As a corollary to this the compilers, as ' believing Christians ', go on to thank ' the Lord God that He has presented to our people in their hour of need a " pious and trusty overlord " in the person of the Führer, thus preparing the way to

" good government " . . . within the National Socialist state.'

It would be impossible, particularly in view of its relative in-effectiveness at the outset, correctly to assess the importance of the moral and political motives of the *new* spirit emerging both in the church struggle and in the politico-military field – as com-pared with the multifariousness of the traditions involved – with-out taking into consideration the following historical premise : the deep and restrictive involvement of the two main confessions in the Third Reich as also of many from Christian-humanist circles in the chauvinistic myth of *Volk* and fatherland. This moral myopia, already strongly in evidence between 1914 and 1918 and later aggravated by anti-democratic resentment, prevented the churches and many other circles from perceiving the opportunity and challenge presented by the Weimar Republic, and was to prove an encumbrance which, under pretext of an anti-socialist, anti-Jewish ' national regeneration ', initially led to the sacrifice of all critical awareness and sober judgment to the supposed ful-filment of a host of desires in the ' hour of Germany '. Although most Catholics were eagerly engaged in proving that Catholics were good and true Germans – understandably enough in view of the trauma induced by the *Kulturkampf* – the Protestant atti-tude at the time was based on the idea of bringing to completion what was now a Protestant Reich. Here too a trauma was at work that immediately affected the church : this was the wholly un-expected cessation at the end of the First World War of the traditional sovereign government of the church in provincial ecclesiastical affairs, a government in which had been vested in principle the external order of church affairs as a ' temporal government ' within a so-called ' Christian state '. This, ostensibly a kind of successor to the Lutheran reformation, was the product of idealism and a religiously slanted romantic awakening which sought to base that state on the theory of an unrealistic Lutheran political ideology.

In Imperial times the Evangelical churches and most of their clergy and congregations saw Protestantism, Prussianism and Lesser Germany in the light of the *Kulturkampf* as the fulfilment of the Reformation. The Evangelical provincial churches were not therefore equal to the new situation brought about by the catas-

trophe of 1918. This was voiced unequivocally by the president
of the First Assembly of the German Evangelical Church to take
place after the 1919 upheaval when, speaking of the treaty of
Versailles, he mournfully declaimed : ' The splendour of the
Imperial German Empire, the dream of our fathers, the pride of
every German, is no more. The Evangelical Church of the German
Reformation is profoundly involved in this collapse . . . In our
deep grief we can do no more than solemnly testify to the intense
gratitude owed by the churches of the fatherland to their princely
protectors and to the fact that this deeply felt gratitude will
never be forgotten but will continue to activate the Evangelical
community.' Only a few apprehensive voices were raised to enquire whether the ' Evangelical Church might not in fact become
the defender of reaction '. It did.

This was the background to the resistance problems under
National Socialism within the many levels of a German Protestantism that had already become almost wholly secularised. An
analysis of the national intoxication which the ' popular revolution ' encountered from this quarter, or again of the corresponding inner defencelessness of the Evangelical churches, would present great scope and variety. Here we will only seek to clarify
the general psychological background to the Evangelical churches'
resistance problem. Nevertheless the general psychological background to this problem ought to be clear. The fact that F. Naumann's ' national-social ' dicta are not wholly unconnected with
this background increased the church's defencelessness in the
face of the new ' spirit '. Theologically, this attitude was determined on a general national basis by the idea either of divinely
ordained authority or else of the relative divinity of the state,
an idea which held, and genuinely believed, the state to be God's
representative in the field of social existence; or again it was
determined by a doctrine, erroneously attributed to Luther but
in fact neo-Lutheran, of the two realms.

According to this, church and state were much less a partnership for the common care of man's well-being and salvation than
a divinely ordained union in which the dominant partner was
the state. The doctrine of the two realms sought to prevent the
dangerous overlapping of state and ecclesiastical offices that

might result from political activity on the part of church and Christians, and by so doing inhibited criticism by the church of state measures, ' state ' here being synonymous with ' authority' in the sense of its relations with the ' subjects ', as laid down in the traditional interpretation of *Romans* 13. From here the doctrine went on to legitimate not only the extant ' authority ' but also deliberate political isolation of the ' subjects '. Concern for due respect towards the authority, for recognition of the state as a divinely ordained instrument of God, even though this might not be immediately apparent when the state took on the aspect of a ' capricious master ', always took precedence over concern for the church.

Hence the ethical problem of resistance that confronted German Protestantism belonged primarily to the realm, thought to be unpolitical, of the ' theology of the state '. This being so, Protestant (and, also, Roman Catholic) resistance to the destructive spirit of National Socialist totalitarianism, was carried on in those sectors within the church – administration, policy and proclamation – where this destructive spirit sought to exert its influence. Though the development of this resistance cannot be followed in detail, it can be seen retrospectively as belonging to many levels which may be analysed in accordance with factual criteria, yet without presenting any historical sequence. Again, it is not possible to pursue the counterplay of different motives during the course of the resistance.

In general, however, it may be said that a sober analysis of the ' church struggle' in the Third Reich, particularly in the fields of the so-called destroyed churches and the ' radical ' Confessing Church, leads to the conclusion that in some respects the latter did become a ' reluctant resistance movement ' against the National Socialist state. This means that the moral freedom to resist was only achieved by a painful struggle of conscience starting from the passive resistance enjoined by self-defence, by way of a completely unsystematic development with much attendant ' backsliding ', to new and crucial decisions, some of them concerned with the future. We must accept the fact that many German Protestant circles both before and after 1945 laid stress on their past and present disassociation from a political

Opposition hostile to the authority; furthermore we might ask whether or not the religious Opposition, at least in the beginning, ' was not just another form of " evasion " which actually helped to delay political Resistance '.[22] The Stuttgart Confession of Guilt of 1945 is a genuine acknowledgment by the Confessing Church of her belated realisation that her resistance was neither timely nor sufficiently vigorous. Nevertheless this ' reluctant Resistance ' did unquestionably have political and historical results.

The churches' resistance at various levels may be set out as follows : 1, Resistance to safeguard the traditional institution of the provincial churches; 2, Resistance in the struggle for the freedom of the Gospel; 3, As a corollary to 2, the highly complex resistance at first confined to what was necessary within the sphere of the church, but then deliberately extended to the struggle for the humanity of man and the rule of law in the state (*Rechtsstaatlichkeit des Staates*), where it joined hands with the political Resistance; 4, The attempt at resistance in those limit situations in the conflict characterised by problems arising out of the war and out of the rejection of the oath and, finally, out of tyrannicide – problems which clearly underline the seriousness of the struggle described above, with the burden of the national-Christian heritage.

1. The ethical problem inherent in the churches' policies of resistance to safeguard the Establishment largely coincides with the question of the admissibility of essentially tactical and ' lawful ' action and the legitimacy of the compromise this involved, as well as of the justification for inaction in order to ' avoid the greater evil '. Certainly there was evidence very early in the Resistance of fundamental decisions uninfluenced by tactical considerations when the question arose of the Aryan paragraph in the church. On that occasion, in the autumn of 1933, the new government of the German Evangelical Church (DEK), which was largely determined by the German Christians (*Deutsche Christen*) with National Socialist backing, tried to apply the Aryan paragraph to the church, a proposal consistent with the ' de-Semitising ' attitude of the leading ecclesio-political circles

within this group. Opposition to a church law implementing the paragraph on 6 September 1933 led to the formation of the Emergency League of Pastors under Dr Martin Niemöller. In its manifesto the league held that the 'invocation of the Aryan paragraph within the sphere of the church constituted a violation of established doctrine'.

Here was a fundamental and absolute decision that did not come lightly to those who made it, set as it was against a background of the church's customary anti-Semitism. For this anti-Semitism had not in fact yet become racial but was simply a conservative-Protestant outcry against the 'Judaisation' of German culture, custom and government from about the time of the emancipation of 1869. Again, because of anxiety about the 'Christian state' as also because, in its impotence, conservative Protestantism needed a scapegoat to propitiate the spirit of the times, anti-Semitism exerted a marked influence in many Protestant circles. And not in those circles alone. Although the Aryan paragraph does not appear ever to have been fully applied within the DEK, little progress was made towards reaching a clear-cut Christian decision on the Jewish question during the time of the Third Reich. Certainly there were many, especially within the Confessing Church, who at great risk to themselves endeavoured to help and succour baptised, and later, unbaptised Jews after the 'night of broken glass' (*Kristallnacht*) in November 1938. Much of this work was done through the Büro Gruber. On the other hand the German Evangelical Church Council and the Spiritual Consistory, on the grounds of the 'emergence of racial consciousness in our nation', requested senior ecclesiastical officials 'to take suitable measures' to ensure that baptised non-Aryans had no part in church activities in German parishes. It was a decision typical of this attitude which, out of pure expediency, sought to comply with the 'exclusion of Jews from the German community'. The position was not fundamentally clarified until 1945. But this context reveals with great clarity the extreme difficulty inherent in making a critical evaluation of the burdensome legacy of the past in order to arrive at an unequivocal position of resistance.

The decision to oppose the Aryan paragraph within the church is the first instance of resistance on principle, although it was also aimed at the preservation of the church, a feasible objective which was fostered by the existence of a clear confessional norm confirmed by Article 1 of the constitution of the DEK. Obedience to the Confession and the vows of ordination is the crucial ethical motive; behind it is the decree to obey God rather than man.

Not quite so clear-cut was the motivation behind the struggle which the non-Prussian, so-called ' intact ' Evangelical provincial churches conducted against the attempts forcibly to centralise the federal DEK and to ' integrate ', among others, the independent dioceses of Bavaria and Württemberg. The action failed since legal hearings established that Reich Bishop Müller's methods had been unlawful; the failure was also partly attributable to the resistance of the churches concerned. This resistance, which cannot here be described in detail, was a matter of general defensive expediency, even to the point of sacrificing the so-called ' destroyed ' wing of the Confessing Church, particularly in Prussia. It was not a matter of reconstructing the church *vis-à-vis* the totalitarian state, on the basis of the new theological understanding gained as a result of the church struggle and set out in the Barmen declaration, but rather of safeguarding the existence of the provincial churches. Such resistance as existed was inevitably swayed by considerations of success, and necessarily had to compromise but, as with the not insignificant ' passive ' resistance, the Confession was always the determining factor. But the ethical norm of religious commitment this invoked produced concrete results that were far less evident than was, perhaps, the case with the Reich Concordat for the Catholic Church. The limit of resistance was determined by a concern not to hazard the existing provincial churches. Moreover it was difficult for the Established Church, conscious as it still was of some obligation to the state, to impute to the latter extreme perversion of justice. Hence the church confined herself, where possible, to her domestic affairs within the meaning of the doctrine of the two realms. To evince the maximum sufferance towards the ' authority ' and towards the political and ideological conduct of the state was held to be a fundamental Lutheran attitude. Thus the resistance remained generally more or less passive and was determined by the church's own mission and interests.

2. On the plane of resistance associated with the struggle for the freedom of the Gospel against the German Christians' régime of force in the church and against the falsification of teaching in the name of the National Socialist ' fund of beliefs ', there took place in Barmen at the end of May the first Confessional Synod of the DEK. The purpose of the synod was to safeguard the established doctrine, and it succeeded, without any apparent historical precedents, in breaking free from generations of secular-religious self-delusion on the part of the church and her theology. The background to this was a theological regeneration which, from various points of departure, had been taking place since the end of the First World War, inspired more particularly by Karl Barth and other exponents of ' dialectical ' theology. The breakaway found expression in the six articles of the Barmen declaration,[23] intended formally as a valid interpretation of Article 1 of the DEK's new constitution comprising the basis of the Confession but which, materially, sought a return to the Gospel pure and simple as opposed to a secularised ' composite ' theology admitting values and truths besides those of the Gospel as a source of the church's proclamation – the German national *nomos*, for example, or German history. This emphasis on ' Jesus Christ . . . God's one Word which we hear and which in life and death we have to trust and obey ' was of immense consequence to the life of Christian obedience in ' free, thankful service ' to God's creatures; of consequence, also, to the church as a ' community of brethren ' which, by her external order, must bear witness to the Lord; of consequence to the nature of ecclesiastical office as one of service, to an understanding of the state and, finally, to the whole of the church's missionary task. It was in all a timely crystallisation of the fundamental assertions of the Evangelical Confession.

In our context Article 5 is particularly important because it speaks out more distinctly than ever before against a theological-Christian exaltation of the state and its supreme head, and goes on to describe that state in sober terms as an altogether human, restricted structure – one, that is, with limited power. Yet this state, which suffers under the delusion that it represents a ' total order ', is seen as potentially threatened by ' daemonisation '. Behind Article 5 there is plainly the painful experience of the ' legal ' remoulding into the dictatorship of a totalitarian state of the legality, understood in the purely liberal, decision-making sense, of the politically just Weimar constitution. The Article runs :

> The Scriptures tell us that the state, by divine decree, is given the task in the as yet unredeemed world, where the church also has her place, of concerning itself, to the limit of human understanding and human ability, with justice and peace when under the threat and pressure of force . . . We reject the false doctrine that the state, over and above its special charge, should become the single and totalitarian order of human life, thus fulfilling the church's mission as well.

This is no longer a theological-metaphysical discussion of the nature of the state, but of its task; and stress is laid on its humanness. This marks the beginning of the supersession of a traditional Christian concept of the state as well as of the ideal of a Christian state. The state, furthermore, as a jurist put it, is seen as an ' effective human entity which is the highest authority responsible for order and peace in a given area '.[24] It was now recognised that the church must also share responsibility for the state as a genuine *politeia*, always provided that the *politeia* was a constitutional one. But all this, of course, was only a beginning. It is no coincidence that some years later the explicit demand for a democratic constitutional state as a matter of Christian concern makes its appearance in the writings of Karl Barth.[25] When, however, on a number of occasions both before and after the end of the war, the Norwegian Primate, Bishop Berggrav, vigorously advocated a constitutional state, he met with only limited success among German Lutherans, though he himself spoke as a Lutheran. Other ecclesiastical pronouncements in Germany after 1945 on political ethics may also be viewed as a continuation of the 5th Article of Barmen. Hence this Article can indeed be considered as having ushered in a new mode of thought on basic questions of political ethics and the nature of the state, thus enabling German Protestantism to begin a tentative appraisal of the future. This appraisal displays striking parallels with the programmes and plans of the political-military Resistance movement, particularly with those of the Kreisauites, so that it is possible to speak to some extent of a common background.

The six Barmen theses then went on to urge corresponding decisions and actions, though at first only within the sphere of the church. Here it was learnt to oppose the principle of a formal legality – upon which the Reich Bishop's German Christian Church government essentially depended – with material legitimacy in questions of church order. Again, a certain analogy can be found in the field of political constitutional history, by comparing the structures of the Weimar Constitution and the Basic Law of Bonn. But the import of the six Barmen theses was greater than this and their consequences extended beyond the church herself, for the formula of Christian deliverance for thankful service to God's creatures was an inescapable reference to the responsibility of the church for the humanity of man.

3. Thus resistance within the church was extended to include the struggle for the humanness of man along the lines of the newly recognised 'watching-brief' of a church which was becoming aware of her duty of service to the world. She saw herself that is, as entrusted with the humanness of man, justice and righteousness, and constitutionalism in the state. This new attitude, which was also sharply critical of political measures, found its most powerful expression in the memorandum handed in to the Reich Chancellory by the Second Provisional Administration of the Confessing Church on 4 June 1936. An indiscretion, which resulted in the memorandum's publication by the *Basler Nachrichten* on 23 July, cost the life of the head of the Council of the Provisional Administration of the Confessing Church, the former *Landgerichtsrat*, Dr Friedrich Weissler, who died in Sachsenhausen concentration camp. It also resulted in the Confessing Church being accused of high treason by the Party, and in disciplinary proceedings being taken by both state and church

authorities against the men who had been involved.

The object of the memorandum had been to break silence, and to protest against the disguised de-Christianisation of the people and the degradation of man, and pastoral action was taken on behalf of the hard-pressed Christian conscience by the adoption of well-founded attitudes on the following questions : de-Christianisation; the deceptive Party slogan of ' positive Christianity '; the destruction of the ecclesiastical order by political measures since the compulsory church elections of July 1933; the pretext of ' deconfessionalisation ' used systematically to exclude the church from public life; the National Socialist *Weltanschauung* and racist anti-Semitism; the general destruction of ' morality and justice '. Objections were raised against the slogan ' Whatever is good for the people is right ', against the devaluation of the oath (now extended even to the Hitler Youth), against the manipulation of elections, against arbitrary justice and the perversion of justice. ' The Evangelical conscience, knowing that it must share the responsibility for the nation and the government, is sorely oppressed by the fact that in Germany – a self-styled constitutional state – there are still concentration camps, and that the activities of the secret police are not subject to any kind of judicial supervision.' The government was solemnly reminded by the Confessing Church of ' the limits that are set to all earthly power and to its ambition ', and warned against the religious personality cult which had made the Führer ' the norm, not only for political decisions, but also for morality and justice among our people '. Finally, there is the express declaration : ' Our nation threatens to break the bounds which God has set for it : it seeks to set itself up as the standard in all things. Thus human presumption is in revolt against God.'

Some 20 years earlier, at the beginning of the First World War, Evangelical sermons had proclaimed that God was compelling Germany to be the ' saviour and redeemer of many nations, and to take over the leadership of Europe '.[26] The adventitious publication of the memorandum[27] was welcomed throughout the Christian world as a breach of the church's silence that had brought blessed relief to many an oppressed conscience. It also led to a detailed restatement of the charges against ' every authority in the German nation' in a proclamation from the pulpit drafted by the Reich Council of Brethren on 23 August 1936.

This was of vital importance in that it was the first time since the Reformation that the Evangelical Church, or rather a representative section of that church, had combined an attitude of religious obedience with a direct and coherent protest as the implacable champion, in the face of authority, of man, the nation and the state. It is true that there was to be only one other official proclamation of this nature by the church, and that was the statement of the Twelfth Prussian Confessional Synod on 16/17 October 1943 in Breslau in an exegesis of the Fifth Commandment:

> It is not given to the state to wield the sword beyond killing the criminal and the enemy in war. Whoever does so notwithstanding, kills wilfully and to his own detriment. If life be taken for reasons other than those named, the mutual trust of human beings is destroyed, and with it the community of the people. Concepts such as 'extermination', 'liquidation', and 'useless life' are unknown in the divine order. The annihilation of people merely because they are related to a criminal, or because they are old or mentally sick, or because they belong to another race, is a wielding of the sword that is not given to the authority . . . Man's life belongs to God alone. It is sacred to Him, as are also the lives of the People of Israel.

At the same time, a reference to a 'state of military emergency' was rejected: 'We cannot allow our responsibility before God to be taken from us by our rulers.'

These incidents, which mark the church's decision to resist the measures of the Third Reich, resulted from views such as had been previously expressed by Martin Niemöller on 25 January 1934, during the dramatic confrontation between the leaders of the Evangelical Church and Adolf Hitler. Niemöller then declared: 'You have told us " You can leave me to look after the German people ". To this my answer is that neither you nor any other power in the world is in a position to take from us Christians and from the church the responsibility for our people that God has placed upon us.'[28] It would be difficult to explain how

Martin Niemöller had come to adopt this altogether uncompromising and exemplary attitude from an earlier position that was
very close to the German nationalist view. Hence in 1934 such
an attitude was virtually unique, but it was one that was gradually
to gain more general acceptance.

4. This situation of conflict became more acute as a result of
two circumstances, the first being the so-called oath question, the
other the threat, followed by the outbreak, of war. Both these
highlighted the tension that had arisen between the critical, forward-looking element on the one hand, and those who had retreated to traditional positions on the other. In the autumn of
1934, after Hindenburg's death, Karl Barth made his famous
gesture in refusing to take the new Officials' Oath except with the
rider: ' In so far as I can answer for it as an evangelical Christian.' The uncertainty of the oath's terms of reference seemed
to him to make that reservation necessary. On 12 December 1934,
the Provisional Administration of the Confessing Church issued
a directive on the oath materially adopting Karl Barth's reservation which it declared to be incumbent on all Christians. Later,
after Barth had been condemned in disciplinary proceedings, the
church withdrew this statement. However, in view of the church's
pronouncement, Barth himself had declared his readiness to take
the oath in the prescribed form. Whether or not this provided any
real solution to the problem of the oath need not be discussed
here; the incident merely illustrates the extreme difficulty of the
conflict. The same problem was to arise after the annexation of
Austria when by way, as it were, of a present from the DEK to
the Führer, the German Christians arranged for the pastors to
swear allegiance to Hitler under pretext of an official demand
made through the head of the Reich Church Chancellory. There
followed a discussion of the oath that went on for months, for
the Confessing Church was confronted on the one hand with the
choice between a conspicuous refusal to take the oath, thus
finally exposing itself to political defamation, and, on the other,
a public declaration of allegiance, such as even the taking of a
questionable oath involved, in the hope – and ' hope ' is the
operative word – of later being able to protest effectively against

excesses by the state. With a few exceptions, even the more radical elements in the Confessing Church now succumbed to temptation, for they were still blinded by the inherited, idealistic
concept of state and the allied conviction that the political intention of the state and National Socialist ideology were two
entirely separate entities. They refused to see the lack of moderation implicit in the oath as a symptom of a perverted state, and
Karl Barth's renewed demand, based on theological argument,
for a ' clear and unequivocal No!' met with almost universal
refusal. With this theologically inept discussion, which has still
not been elucidated even today, the ecclesiastical front showed
signs of disintegration. The tension between loyalty to the state
and confessional responsibility towards it, even if this meant
resistance, made demands on Protestantism that were too heavy,
although at the start some effort had been made to overcome this.

The conflict was further intensified by the threat and then by
the outbreak of war. The churches in Germany had always been
accustomed in time of war to bless German arms and to pray
for the victory of their own country in a just cause. We need not
here cite any of the frequently over-effusive pronouncements of
this nature. At these times the church was always particularly
close to people and state, and was concerned to perform her
' military service '. So it is understandable if regrettable that
even the radical Confessing Church should have begun to tremble
and should have felt impelled to make protests of loyalty when,
during the Czech crisis on 19 September 1938, Karl Barth wrote
the famous letter to his colleague Hromadka in Prague, contain-
ing what is still a surprisingly accurate assessment of the situation.

What is really frightening is not the spate of lies and brutality
that flows from Nazi Germany, but the danger that England,
France and America . . . may forget that upon the freedom of
your country, so far as it is humanly possible to judge, the
freedom of Europe depends, and perhaps not of Europe alone.
Will your government and your people . . . stand firm? I realise
all too clearly that in so doing you will incur infinite affliction
and hardship. Yet . . . every Czech soldier who fights and
suffers will also be doing it for us, and – I say this today with-

Q

out reservation – he will also be doing it for the Church of Jesus Christ which, in the darkness surrounding Hitler and Mussolini, is faced either with extermination or with being reduced to a laughing stock. The times must be strange indeed . . . in which it has in all soberness to be admitted that we are bidden for the sake of our faith to relegate fear of violence and love of peace firmly to second place, and to promote as firmly to first place the fear of injustice and the love of freedom! . . . But one thing is certain – such resistance as is humanly possible must be made along the borders of Czechoslovakia . . .[29]

The Second Provisional Committee of the Confessing Church, however, two days before the Munich agreement, drafted an order of prayer for 30 September in face of the immediate threat of war. In it they anticipated what moral theology has only just begun to discover in the elucidation of the problem of war. It was a single prayer of atonement which begged for peace and, if peace was not vouchsafed, placed in God's hands the soldiers and the stricken homeland. Even this prayer, from the ecclesiastical point of view wholly innocuous, aroused considerable protest. It was, *Das Schwarze Korps* declared, to be regarded as ' political incitement to betrayal, and sabotage directed at the united readiness for action of our race in the solemn hour of its fate. Enough is enough! The security of the nation makes the extermination of these criminals a duty of the state.' Again, the authors of the prayer were ' representatives of the church, tainted with Judaism . . . Enough of this treason disguised as religion!' This from German Christian newspapers. The Lutheran provincial Bishops of Bavaria, Baden, Hanover and Württemberg allowed themselves to be forced by the state into declaring that the order of prayer ' has been disavowed by us on religious and patriotic grounds, and has been rejected for use in our churches '. Here they diverged from the rest of the Confessing Church. Only one of their number, Bishop Wurm, later revoked this as a ' Judas betrayal '. Bishop Marahrens regarded the prayer as an inadmissible combination of the spiritual and political, but his own draft has a somewhat curious ring about it : ' Our prayer is for the Führer who, in his struggle against Bolshevism, must know that we are prepared to put all our strength at the service of his work.'[30]

This also foreshadows another factor which was strongly to inhibit the Resistance — anti-Bolshevism. It was to some extent to bring about the alliance of churches of all denominations with National Socialism. The Second World War was never to see the same welter of weapon-blessing and patriotic victory sermons that had marked the outbreak of the 1914 war, and even the wars of liberation, and this may have been due in part to the spirit manifested in the order of prayer; but it cannot be denied that, after Stalingrad, anti-Bolshevism led men such as Bishop Marahrens, and of course the DEK Church Chancellory, and German Christians, to intone strongly nationalist, anti-Bolshevist slogans invoking final victory. Yet there never was a unanimous crusading spirit throughout the whole church. There were signs of one final crisis with the emergence of the question, raised early on by Bonhoeffer for one, as to whether the war ought not to be outlawed by the church, ' because we cannot see war as part of the divine order of things, and hence as a command of God, and further because war cannot subsist without idealisation and idolisation '.[31] This inevitably led to the ' terrible alternative ' which, Bonhoeffer saw, confronted Christians in Germany after the outbreak of war : ' Either they must acquiesce in the defeat of their country, to ensure the survival of Christian civilisation, or in its victory, which would mean the destruction of our civilisation.'[32]

The first decision would have been in a sense negative — the final break with all thinking in terms of unconditional authority and with the ideology of the equally unconditional alliance of church and state. The action that would logically result from this must go still further, involving perhaps inevitable sabotage, oath-breaking, and ' tyrannicide ' — the exceptional necessity in which, as Bonhoeffer puts it, irrational action in free responsibility has its place :

The exceptional necessity calls for freedom of responsibility. There is no law here behind which personal responsibility can seek shelter. Hence there is no law to compel the person responsible, confronted by such necessities, to come to this or that decision. Rather, in this situation, every law must be wholly renounced in the full knowledge of the risk freely incurred by that decision, and the open admission that this means the infringement of the law and the breaking of the law : in other words, the very transgression of the law is an acknowledgment of its validity. Ultimately, then, the total renunciation of every law, and this alone, permits the surrender of the decision and the action individually arrived at to the divine guidance of history.[33]

With these words Bonhoeffer, himself a member of Resistance circles, gave permanently valid expression to the most extreme form of the questions of conscience that troubled the majority of the men of 20 July 1944. Nothing could be added and nothing taken away. Nor could the church advise more than this. There can hardly be said to have been an ethical theory of the Resistance, and only occasionally were the old questions raised of the right to resist, of an ultimate revolutionary attack on the existing government or, again, of tyrannicide. Thus, for instance, Karl Barth cited the Scottish Confession of 1560 (which includes the demand ' *tyrannidem opprimere* ' among the good works to be performed by the Christian ' for the benefit of his neighbour ' listed in the second table of the Commandments), and then proceeded to redefine the idea on the basis of religious obedience; ' the actively loving belief in Jesus Christ ' might, in certain circumstances, ' make our [political] resistance as necessary as our passive resistance or even our actual cooperation [with the state] were we not confronted by this choice '.[34]

In the same year, 1938, he also developed for Evangelical Christendom an impressive theory whose effects are only now really apparent, of the primacy of justice over power; a theory which was meant as an indication of a Christian view of the state.[35] Towards the end of the war, Bonhoeffer himself, together with other men of the 20 July, had come to the conclusion that the system as such must be eliminated, if necessary by an attempt on the Führer, and that this would be justified by religious obedience. His decision was diametrically opposed to prevalent church opinion. In July 1945 the new Brandenburg Church administration, in reference to 20 July 1944, was still able to declare : ' The Church of Jesus Christ can never condone an attack on a human life for whatever motive.'

From this it is abundantly clear how unprepared was the Evangelical Church to meet the new state of conflict and its inherent problems, such as those of the oath, the Jews, or the general question of war. For initially she had almost nothing to go by since these problems, being regarded as ' political ', had been left for centuries to the exclusive competence of the state, of the ' authority '. Here the false assumption of Christianity's basically unpolitical character proved a hindrance. It had been forgotten that the Church of Christ in the world had, from the beginning, been a political factor in that world, something of immediate import to the *Salus publica*. Nor was it really possible to disagree with a general proposition such as the following : ' It is the duty of Christians to obey the authority in so far as they are not asked to do what is contrary to God's command. It is the duty of Christians to resist, if what is asked of them is contrary to the Gospel.' This was formulated in the proclamation from the pulpit based on the Provisional Church Administration's memorandum of 23 August 1936, but no one had taught and no one had learned how to put it into practice. The problem of ' obligation ', of the duty to resist, was left open. Should this be mere sufferance of the consequences of passive disobedience? Or active resistance in obedience to religious belief, for the sake of humanity and, not least, out of concern to safeguard the state as a *politeia*? Towards the end of and after the war, the Lutheran Primate of Norway, Bishop Berggrav, advocated the principle implicit in the second alternative, declaring, with reference to a saying of Luther's on conduct towards the ' apocalyptic tyrant ': ' If the supreme authority becomes grossly despotic and tyrannical, then devilry is afoot, and the government does not stand under God. But obedience to a fiendish power can be nothing else but sin . . . Such circumstances, by definition, confer the right of revolution in one form or another.' In this, however, German confessional Lutheranism was unable to follow his lead.

Yet it could be said that German Protestantism's first decisive moves towards grappling with the problem of resistance had been achieved in the realm of the political existence and political responsibility of the Christian and the church under the pressure of unique and wholly unprecedented criteria. But these were indeed only first moves. ' Germans ', Bonhoeffer wrote, ' are only just beginning to discover what free responsibility means. It rests in God, who demands the free, religious risk of responsible action, and who promises forgiveness and consolation to anyone who becomes a sinner because of it.'[36]

It has been necessary to illustrate the moral questions of the problem of resistance from instances drawn from the sphere of Protestantism since for the Catholic Church many of the initial circumstances were wholly different; moreover, there is still much that requires unbiased research and elucidation. Yet the initial situation of involvement with nationalism, subservience to authority and an anti-democratic outlook was not entirely unlike that of Protestantism. But the Catholic Church, in accordance with her own particular nature, responded quite differently to the attacks of the state. Within the context of the church struggle there was little internal tension such as might have endangered her survival as an institution. Thus it would have been foreign to the nature of the attitude dictated by Catholicism to risk her very existence, as the Confessing Church was to in the course of her later development. Her essentially hierarchical structure meant that the Catholic Church, possessing moreover a legal instrument in the Reich Concordat, had to fight for what might be described as specifically ecclesiastical interests : the confessional school, ecclesiastical organisation, the church press and much else. Furthermore, as a partner recognised by international law, she was in a position to negotiate with the National Socialist state on ' diplomatic ' terms in the exact sense of the word.

The first clashes concerned questions of *Weltanschauung*, such as the dispute over Rosenberg's *Mythus des 20. Jahrhunderts* (' Myth of the Twentieth Century ') but these were questions of moral doctrine – sterilisation, for example, or euthanasia; as regards the latter, there was the celebrated sermon by the Bishop of Münster, Graf von Galen, in the summer of 1941, when he castigated the practice of euthanasia with unmatched and unforgettable incisiveness, describing it as ' continuous murder '. In another axiomatic sentence he declared ' At no time, however, has the church questioned the legality of the National Socialist régime, and at no time has she, either directly or indirectly, sanctioned any of the attempts to overthrow that régime ';[37] while the first half of this statement is untenable, the latter is correct in that the church never declared an official sanction of the various attempts to overthrow the régime, and indeed could not, by her nature acquired over the centuries, have declared it. Although the Episcopate representing the church was not lacking in differences of opinion in regard to National Socialism, it repeatedly and expressly condemned revolution and tyrannicide, and its condemnation was closely related to more recent Church doctrine. During the war it notably confused many of the faithful by pronouncements of nationalist tendency, although the basic tenor of its attitude was deliberately pastoral. Furthermore, the Vatican ' never desisted from the endeavour to safeguard a legal *modus vivendi* with the leaders of the Nazi régime '.[38] Nor could it really have done anything else. The many individual Catholics whose personal resistance has been built up since the war into a legend of church resistance, differed from the sections of the DEK represented by the Confessing communities and their associated church authorities in that they were in many respects left to their own devices. It would seem that determined resistance was the independent action of individuals who had to fight without any official backing from their church, although many were assured of the personal approval of their colleagues or superiors. Among the martyrs were men such as the Lichtenberg cathedral provost who intervened on behalf of the Jews; the Pallottine father F. Reinisch, a conscientious objector who refused to take the oath; Dr M. J. Metzger, a pacifist; the Jesuit father, A. Delp, a member of the Kreisau Circle, and many others. The Resistance movement also contained convinced Catholics : to name only the most famous – the Provincial of the Society of Jesus in Bavaria, A. Roesch, Jakob Kaiser, B. Letterhaus and lastly Graf von Stauffenberg in whom religious motives and the determination to resist would seem to have developed hand in hand. In addition there were Catholic writers like Reinhold Schneider, who were not afraid to make their voices heard.

It can safely be said that within the Catholic Church in Germany there is virtually no case of resistance where the motivation was analogous to that shown by one particular section of the Evangelical Church *qua* church. For in the latter instance, the motivation is often clearly in evidence, partly in the considerations underlying the politico-military Resistance, and partly as the factor that immediately determined it. Representatives of this Resistance, such as Hans Oster, came from Evangelical parsonages and, like Helmuth James Graf von Moltke and others, had reached the conviction that ' The hazards and self-sacrifice demanded of us today are such . . . as to postulate rather more than just high ethical principles '.[39] Again, there is the fact that in virtually all groups including Goerdeler's Conservatives, there was some sort of feeling that policy in the twentieth century could no longer be conducted entirely on the basis of state interest or in accordance with concepts of power, but had become preeminently a moral matter. For this reason any assessment of the Resistance that is made in terms of purely ' political ' or legal categories will of necessity be superficial and inadequate.

' Even if churches and conspirators diverged upon the crucial question of motives and aims, the revolt of 20 July is inconceivable without the spiritual support of church resistance.'[40] During proceedings in the People's Court Freisler clearly, if only superficially, apprehended this fact, though, indeed, it was quite explicitly put to to him – by Graf Yorck von Wartenburg, for instance, who declared that the conspiracy was directed against ' the totalitarian claim of the state, which excluded the moral and religious obligation of the citizen before God '.[41] The essence of the revolt was succinctly expressed by Graf Moltke in one of his last letters as the ' outrage of the Christian conscience ', and he continued : ' I stood before Freisler, not as a Protestant, nor yet as a landowner, not as an aristocrat, nor yet as a Prussian, nor yet again as a German, but as a Christian and absolutely nothing else.'[42] There can be no doubt that he and his friends in the Kreisau Circle sought a rebirth of political existence out of a Christian spirit transcending denomination, as is shown by the question, ' What can serve Christianity as a sheet-anchor in chaos?'[43] Father Delp's ' Christian Socialism' is of similar stamp. There were others, even Goerdeler himself who were seeking to establish common ground on this level. It was a religious-Christian impulse that increased in intensity among members of the conspiracy as the war proceeded. Nearly all the military conspirators were religious men. Nor was this element missing from the Social Democratic section of the conspiracy : Theo Haubach joined the church during the war, and Carlo Mierendorff was a convinced Christian. But the ' revolt of conscience' cannot be seen as belonging wholly within the Christian ambit, and any assessment of it must take into account the moral humanist motives of the Social-Democratic dissidents. Again, a decisive part was played from the beginning by political, military and nationalist elements opposed to the régime. A clear, systematic summary has yet to be made of the large number of basic and determining ideas that are to be found in the multiplicity of memoranda, speeches, diaries and so on. Yet a good deal may be gathered from the ' Declaration of Government' that was to be broadcast on 20 July :

1. The first task is to restore the Law in all its majesty . . . 4. The shattered freedom of spirit, conscience, faith and opinion will be restored. The churches will once again be given the right to work for their confessions. In future they will exist quite separately from the state . . . The working of the state is to be inspired, both in word and deed by the Christian outlook . . . 7. Ordered administration, and just division and execution of communal tasks are possible only on a constitutional basis . . . 10. . . . At this hour we must proclaim to our people that it is our highest duty courageously and patiently to purify the much defiled German name. Only we Germans can and will carry this out. Our future, whatever material form it may take, depends on our doing this unremittingly, earnestly and honestly. For God does not exist to be called upon at any and every opportunity, but He requires and ensures that His order and His commandments are not infringed . . .[44]

The extremely generalised terms in which these principles are couched betray the fact that they contain a large number of fundamentally different tendencies and viewpoints which have been reduced to a common denominator. We can be certain that, even within individual groups of the conspiracy, these differences existed. Yet they can be characterised and understood through the emphasis that predominated in each individual group. The only groups, however, with which we can concern ourselves here are those whose path led them from a general and much-stratified Opposition to the military *putsch* of 20 July, that is to say the middle-class Opposition round Goerdeler, the socialist Opposition round Leber, Mierendorff, Haubach and Leuschner, the military – from Beck, Halder and Canaris to von Tresckow, Oster and Stauffenberg – and, lastly, the Kreisau Circle. Each of these had its own different groupings, whose meetings and contacts were relatively haphazard. Very often they progressed from initial agreement with Hitler's National Socialist aims to the strongest possible repudiation of his totalitarian, brutal and unrestrained methods. In Moltke's case there can be no doubt that he actively opposed Nazism from the start.[45] For some people, commitment began with the question as to what must be done after the fall of the régime, and for others with the question of how to eliminate that régime. Their common aim was to avert a Second World War or, once war had broken out, to end it and achieve a new order of a kind that would restore the basic rights of democracy and freedom. The overthrow of Hitler was essentially only a means, reluctantly undertaken, towards that end. To this extent the description of the conspirators as a ' peace party ' is justified.[46]

Under Helmuth James Graf von Moltke, the Kreisau Circle sought, within a decentralised policy, to associate conservative and socialist values, aristocracy and workers, in a new democratic synthesis which would include the churches; towards that end they endeavoured to find guiding principles for social, cultural and economic policy as well as for the conduct of foreign affairs, principles that would be adequate to Germany's mission as mediator between East and West. They adopted a critical attitude towards Western capitalism no less than towards Weimar. This circle was chiefly concerned with overcoming the more recent past and the guilt-laden present, and more than anything, with planning a picture of what they proposed ' beyond the terrible and hopeless future . . . something to be striven for, worked for and believed in, something for which it is worth the while of the disappointed nation to make a new beginning '.[47] Hence it was only with considerable reluctance that they finally agreed that their ' *Tag X* ' must coincide with the day chosen by the ' Counts' group ' and a few of the military for the attempted assassination that now seemed inevitable. Crucial to their deliberations were the reconstruction of human community, a cure for a society corrupted by decline, and the restoration of the law and of social justice. The origins of the Kreisau members were extremely diverse; besides von Moltke, Graf Yorck von Wartenberg and Adam von Trott zu Solz, there were Prussian Conservatives such as Graf Ulrich von Schwerin-Schwanenfeld and Hans Bernd von Haeften, as also the Jesuits Delp and Roesch, Pastor Poelchau and, more peripheral perhaps, E. Gerstenmaier; further, there were among others the Social Democrats Leber, Reichwein and Haubach. Yet all, notwithstanding their diverse origins, almost entirely rejected traditional German nationalism and saw Germany's salvation, once the murderous war had been concluded, in terms of Europe. Their objectives have been described as in some degree romantic. Nevertheless, their much-deliberated conception of a close alliance between practical political considerations and Christian ethical motives were not only to prove a strong inspiration to other groups, but the work done by these ' planners ' continued to exert some influence even after the end of the war. In one of their plans dated September 1943, we read : ' The freedom-minded German workers, and with them the Christian churches, represent and lead those national forces which will enable a start to be made on reconstruction.'[48]

By contrast, the motives of the *bourgeois* Opposition round Goerdeler were multifarious and, to some extent, contradictory in their combination of moral indignation, patriotic concern, nostalgia for a strong constitutional state and reactions to the situation of the moment (for as such, perhaps, can be interpreted their occasional dalliance with the idea of a Hohenzollern restoration, or the kaleidoscope of their political proposals for the future). A characteristic feature was Goerdeler's belief in reason in politics, and his faith in his own powers of persuasion, for he held that even Hitler himself would be susceptible to argument if only he could be approached.[49] Goerdeler was one of the most dynamic elements in the formation of the conspiracy, which he hoped would increasingly assume the character of a popular movement. But, apart from the fact that he was often inadequately informed – like so many in the Resistance who consequently overrated opportunities outside Germany – he was never really able to shake off his German nationalist past, remaining reserved towards socialism, distrustful of big business and Utopian in much of his thinking and planning. Allied to this was a philosophy of history, of traditional Protestant persuasion, which finally led him – if anything written under Gestapo arrest can be considered as valid evidence – to see in the failure of the attempt on Hitler, a confirmation of ' divine judgment '; it is impossible to tell, however, whether remarks such as ' God . . . has once more entrusted this task to the Führer ' were not simply defensive, and intended to draw at least a minimum of attention to the suggestions they accompanied. Goerdeler's ally was General Beck, head of the General Staff since 1935 and thus responsible for building up the German Army. From the start Beck had been motivated by the fear that Hitler would plunge Germany into a catastrophic war, and he and Goerdeler jointly led this more or less *bourgeois* group of Conservatives, whose determined aim it was to deprive the National Socialists of power and to restore order, though they were not unanimous with regard to the form that order should take. Yet it would seem that their strength derived rather from moral candour than from political expertise for which flexibility and concerted planning must have been essential.

Goerdeler's most critical antagonist within his own Resistance circle was undoubtedly Julius Leber, himself impelled by strong moral forces, who had long been a clear-sighted and determined fighter in the cause of a viable democracy aimed above all at assuming a better future for the workers, a future based upon freedom and justice. His political programme was realistic, socially progressive, sober yet impassioned. The same is true of the other men belonging to the so-called Socialist group – Carlo

Mierendorff and Theo Haubach, who later went over to the Kreisau Circle, and Wilhelm Leuschner, who cooperated closely with Goerdeler and Beck and whose views on the future form of democracy approximated to theirs. Considered in terms of generations, Leuschner, together with Goerdeler and Beck, was one of the ' older men '. Their view of the Weimar Republic, like that of the ' younger men ' was critical both in the negative and positive sense. But whereas the political concepts of the older generation tended to turn upon earlier political events and experiences, the younger generation was less burdened by the past and its attitude to the future was therefore less preconceived, more progressive.

It was quite otherwise with Claus Graf Schenk von Stauffenberg and his circle, more especially the ' Counts' group '. At first alongside, and then in partial opposition to Goerdeler, Stauffenberg sought, during the last days before 20 July, to rally the disheartened and already disintegrating Opposition under the banner of a somewhat nebulous concept of political renewal transcending Weimar and 1933.[50] Stauffenberg's attitude to Hitler, which had at first been affirmative, underwent a change as a result of the ' night of glass ', the persecution of the Jews and the oppression of the churches, and his repudiation of the régime was confirmed by conversations with Halder and Beck. The idea that Hitler must be assassinated had already begun to germinate in his mind as early as the autumn of 1942; the idea of the social state was the result of his connection with Kreisau. All this crystallised into the comprehensive organisation of the *Walküre* plan, whose initiation necessitated Hitler's removal or elimination, since the military *putsch* was dependent on the legality of the mechanism of military command, and hence upon release from the oath of allegiance. *Walküre* also entailed the previous preparation of a multitude of orders and draft proclamations which themselves formed the outline of a future political system. In this connection, Stauffenberg was confronted with the moral and theological question of tyrannicide, and found a positive answer in early Catholic tradition (and in Luther).[51] For this reason he was comparatively unhampered by the considerations of legality that were intrinsic to the Prusso-German upbringing, based

as it was upon the predominantly Lutheran theory of state order
this in turn had its origin in the Biblical standard of 'suprem
authority' whose function was determined by a formal concep
of order. Here lay the chief source of doubt concerning the law
fulness of resistance – and of scruples concerning the means tha
should be used. But these scruples were the badge tha
distinguished the Resistance from the Nazis. Stauffenberg wa
able to accept the obligation to resist a régime branded as crimi
nal as an obligation on a higher plane to commit 'high treason'
and to justify it before his conscience as the only alternative tc
betrayal. 'It is time', he said, shortly before 20 July, 'that some
thing is done. But whoever dares to act must realise that he wil
probably go down in German history as a traitor. Yet if he fails
to act, he will be a traitor before his own conscience.'[52] Like vor
Tresckow, he was conscious of 'treachery', to which he assented
voluntarily in a voluntary assumption of guilt. This frankness,
expressive of what Bonhoeffer called 'the need [in political action
generally] for free, responsible acts even when contrary to man-
date and calling',[53] is what distinguished the 'young' from the
'old' men; the latter, restricted by the principle of legality, could
only be rebels against their will.

It was this very legality, which Hitler himself sustained by the
subtle tactic of keeping separate the Party and the state, which
was the main stumbling-block for the Opposition and afforded
the greatest protection to Hitler's person. It was only towards
the end that Goerdeler and Beck struggled to find religious
legitimation for their resistance. Hence in the early stages of
resistance there were attempts at 'legal opposition', among them
the plan in so far as it ever came within the province of professional military thought, for collective insubordination among the
generals at the outbreak of war 1939/40, at the time of Stalingrad in 1942/3, and finally at the time of the invasion in 1944.
Thus one of the early aims, amongst others, was the restoration
of the Weimar Republic. But legal opposition had to be abandoned as vain and impracticable. The risk of illegality was unavoidable, and its assumption demanded a not altogether easy
intellectual transition. The related 'process of inner development
of the Prusso-German conspirators from formal to material, from

egalistic to legitimate concepts of law and state' accompanied
the Opposition's progress towards the *coup d'état*.[54] It ranged
from express repudiation of the use of force in favour of overcoming the régime by spiritual means in the early plans for political renewal, to assent to the assassination as *ultima ratio*, as 'an
act of self-defence', as 'judgment', and at the same time as a
guilt-ridden, questionable act, and in no way an accepted form
of political procedure. No one eagerly assumed the rôle of con-
spirator; the compulsion arose from the sense of responsibility. It
demanded the decision of the individual conscience, a decision
which could not be taken by proxy, even through the churches.
If, indeed, the conspirators regarded the churches, both Confessing
and Catholic, as their 'closest and their public ally',[55] then there
is little doubt that the path taken by the Confessing Church from
legality to legitimacy played a decisive part in shaping and
elucidating that view.

The *putsch* was undertaken in the full knowledge that it stood
very small chance of success. To Stauffenberg's question as to
whether the *coup* ought still to be made in view of the invasion
of 6 June 1944, von Tresckow gave the much-quoted reply: 'The
attempt must be made whatever the cost. Even if it is not to
succeed, action must be taken in Berlin. For now it is no longer
the practical purpose that counts, but the fact that before history
and the world, the German Resistance has chanced its decisive
throw. Nothing else signifies.'[56] At all events, it was to be amply
demonstrated to the world during the short respite before the
impending military collapse that the conspirators were not concerned merely with a change of régime – though neither at the time
nor afterwards was the Allies' scepticism to acknowledge this –
but with a change of system whose democratic character would
spring from the will of the 'other Germany'. As soon as the
*putsch* had succeeded, the German people were to be asked to
state their opinion – in precise terms – of the crimes and atrocities
committed by the National Socialist régime in their name, and of
Germany's primary war-guilt. But among the conspirators there
was already some uncertainty whether the revelation of these
horrors would rouse the German people to spontaneous indignation, and inspire them with a spirit of renunciation and willing-

ness to accept liability. Their uncertainty was never resolved, since the attempt was unsuccessful, but it would seem to have been justified by the fact that such problems still remain insuperable today. And here lies the real tragedy of 20 July and the Resistance.

> The fact that this moral question demanding an individual and practical decision for or against the Hitler régime was not put to the German public on 20 July 1944, that it is, as it were, embedded in history and can never be raised again, means that the German people will be branded, as by the mark of Cain, with the symbol of a past with which they will never be able to come to terms. This, at any rate, is how it was seen by the conspirators – Beck, Goerdeler, Stauffenberg, Leber, Tresckow, Moltke, Hassell, Canaris and the rest.[57]

Nevertheless, their action did materially correct the view taken of Germany *after* the National Socialist régime, so permitting not only the belief that she was capable of eventual democratic reconstruction, but also the claim that the struggle for democratic renewal had indeed started before 1945 and was not solely the result of 're-education' imposed (if not altogether effectually) from without. Such moral rehabilitation as there is in Germany, and the laborious efforts to further it, began with the Resistance in all its aspects, its every manifestation and its total heritage of obligations; and the legitimation conferred upon it by 20 July is not merely symbolic.[58]

# References

## Resistance Thinking on Foreign Policy

1. Ritter, *Carl Goerdeler und die deutsche Widerstandsbewegung*, 3rd ed., Stuttgart 1956, p.220
2. Memorandum, *Ausgangslage, Ziele und Aufgaben*, cit. Ger van Roon's forthcoming basic work on the Kreisau Circle (referred to below as van Roon). The writer would like to express his thanks to Herr van Roon for his permission to use this exceptionally important work
3. To Lionel Curtis, *Neue Auslese*, 2nd year, No. 1, pp.9 f.
4. Memorandum, *Unsere Idee*, written in prison November 1944, p.33
5. Memorandum by Dr Etscheid, *Die innere und äussere Lage*, 1.1.1940, Bundesarchiv, Militärarchiv, Coblenz, H 08–104/2
6. Hassell, *Vom andern Deutschland*, Fischer Bücherei 1964, p.290
7. *Beck und Goerdeler, Gemeinschaftsdokumente für den Frieden* (referred to below as *Beck und Goerdeler*), ed. Wilhelm Ritter von Schramm, Munich 1965, p.45
8. Romoser, ' The Politics of Uncertainty : The German Resistance Movement ', *Social Research*, Vol. 31, 1964, No. 1, p.79
9. *Ibid.*
10. On the term ' notables ' cf. Hans Mommsen in this volume p.60
11. For instance in an essay of the summer or autumn of 1943, *Beck und Goerdeler*, p.255
12. Hassell, *Im Wandel der Aussenpolitik von der französischen Revolution biz zum Weltkrieg*, Munich 1939, p.239; Hassell, *Erinnerungen aus meinem Leben 1848-1918*, Stuttgart 1919

13. Goerdeler's memorandum, *Das Ziel, cit.*: *Beck und Goerdeler*, pp.93, 95
14. Hassell, *Im Wandel* ..., p.239
15. *Ibid.*, p.240
16. Hassell knew Schüssler personally quite well
17. Hassell, 'Untergang des Abendlandes?' *Monatshefte für Auswärtige Politik* (referred to below as *Monatsh. f. Ausw. Politik*), August 1941, pp.599 ff.
18. Foerster, *Generaloberst Ludwig Beck*, Munich 1953, pp.63 ff.
19. Goerdeler's memorandum, *Der Weg, Beck und Goerdeler*, p.195
20. A. P. Young's notes on his conversations with Goerdeler, lent to the writer by Mr Young
21. Ritter, *op. cit.*, pp.160 ff.
22. Trevor-Roper, 'Hitler's Kriegsziele', *Vierteljahrshefte für Zeitgeschichte* (referred to below as *Vjh. f. Zgesch.*), 2, 1960, p.126
23. Beck, *Studien*, Stuttgart 1955, pp.55 ff.
24. *Ibid.*, p.246 ff., 255 ff.
25. Goerdeler's memorandum, *Gesamtlage, Beck und Goerdeler*, p.268
26. Young's notes
27. Beck, *op. cit.*, p.58
28. Goerdeler's memorandum, *An den Reichskanzler*, Ritter, *op. cit.*, p.74
29. Hassell, *Vom andern Deutschland*, p.47
30. Ritter, *op. cit.*, p.161
31. Young's notes
32. *Ibid.*
33. *Ibid.*
34. *Ibid.*
35. Ritter, *op. cit.*, pp.222 f.
36. *Ibid.*, p.224
37. Hassell, *op. cit.*, pp.47 f.
38. Young's notes
39. Beck's memorandum, autumn 1939, *Die russische Frage für Deutschland*, Bundesarchiv, *op. cit.*

40. Beck's memorandum, 31.10.39, *Zwischenpause nach dem Misserfolg des deutschen Friedensangebotes*, op. cit.
41. Beck's memorandum, end September 1939, *Zur Kriegslage nach Abschluss des polnischen Feldzuges*, op. cit.
42. Hassell, op. cit., pp.77 ff.
43. Young's notes – Ritter, op. cit., p.239
44. Commander Liedig's memorandum, 7.12.39, *Die Bedeutung des russisch-finnischen Zusammenstosses für die gegenwärtige Lage Deutschlands*, Bundesarchiv, op. cit.
45. Beck's memorandum, *Zwischenpause* . . . , op. cit.
46. Private diary of Lieutenant-Colonel i. G. Grosscurth, ed. Harold Deutsch and Helmut Krausnick
47. Hassell, op. cit., p.77
48. *Der Generalquartiermeister. Briefe und Tagebuchaufzeichnungen des Generalquartiermeisters des Heeres, General der Artillerie Eduard Wagner*, Munich 1963, p.133
49. Hassell, op. cit., p.77
50. Memorandum, Etscheid, op. cit.
51. Memorandum, Liedig, op. cit.
52. Memorandum, Etzdorf/Kordt, October 1939, *Das drohende Unheil*, Bundesarchiv, op. cit.
53. Memorandum, Liedig, op. cit.
54. Etzdorf/Kordt, op. cit.
55. Hassell, op. cit., pp.114 f.
56. Memorandum, Etscheid, op. cit.
57. Hassell, op. cit., p.78; cf. Graml, ' Der Fall Oster ', *Vjh. f. Zgesch.* 1966, I, pp.26 ff.
58. Krausnick/Graml, *Der Deutsche Widerstand und die Alliierten, Vollmacht des Gewissens*, II, Frankfurt 1965, pp.493 ff.
59. Memorandum, Etscheid, op. cit.
60. Kordt, *Nicht aus den Akten*, Stuttgart 1950, p.382
61. Hassell, op. cit., pp.139 f.
62. Ritter, op. cit., p.273
63. Hassell : *Im Wandel* . . . , p.16; *Vom andern Deutschland*, p.140
64. Ritter, op. cit.
65. Record of the lecture in the Bundesarchiv, Koblenz; cf. also Herzfeld, Johannes Popitz, *Forschungen zu Staat und Ver-*

*fassung, Festgabe für Fritz Hartung*, Berlin 1958, p.349
Herzfeld's comment on Popitz's exposition (' fundamentally
a strong criticism of National Socialist Reich Utopias ') is
perhaps on the mild side

66. Hassell, *op. cit.*, p.155
67. Hassell, ' Untergang . . . ?'
68. *Ibid.*
69. Hassell, ' Dominium maris baltici ', *Jahrbuch für Auswärtige Politik* (referred to below as *Jb. f. Ausw. Politik*), March
1942, pp.195 ff.
70. *Ibid.*
71. Hassell : ' Gedanken über die Niederlande und das Reich ',
*Monatsh. f. Ausw. Politik*, March 1944, p.133; ' Untergang . . . ?'
72. Goerdeler's peace plan for the British government of
30.5.41, Ritter, p.585; elaborated in *Beck und Goerdeler*,
p.257
73. Krüger, ' Um den Reichsgedanken ', *Historische Zeitschrift*
(referred to below as *HZ*), 165, pp.457 ff.
74. Rampf, *Mitteleuropa. Zur Geschichte und Deutung eines
Begriffs, op. cit.*, pp.528 ff.
75. Popitz, *op. cit.*
76. Stubbe, ' In Memoriam Albrecht Haushofer ', *Vjh. f. Zgesch.*,
8, 1960, pp.236 ff.
77. *Das Ziel, Beck und Goerdeler*, p.93
78. Goerdeler in October 1940; Ritter, *op. cit.*, pp.278 f.
79. Hassell, *Vom andern Deutschland*, p.162
80. Krausnick/Graml, *op. cit.*, pp.502 ff.
81. This time, too, he soon reverted to scepticism – Hassell, *op.
cit.*, p.207
82. Hassell, ' Untergang . . . ?'
83. *Ibid.*
84. *Beck und Goerdeler*, pp.98, 99
85. Schramm, *op. cit.*, p.34, assumes, like Ritter, that the
memorandum was produced between the end of 1940 and
the spring of 1941. This would seem improbable, however,
since there is not a sentence in the whole document to indicate that it derived from this time. But the attack on Russia

Resistance Thinking on Foreign Policy 241

and the conquest of Russian territory is mentioned several times as a *fait accompli*. The comments on US-Japanese relations would also seem to indicate that the period concerned was the second half of 1941. Further, the memorandum does not altogether agree with the ' peace plan ' concept, a document drafted for Churchill in May 1941; Ritter, *op. cit.*, p.585

86. Hassell, 'Zwei Schwestern', *Monatsh. f. Ausw. Politik*, June 1943, pp.369 ff.

87. Hassell, ' Grosseuropa ', *Jb. f. Ausw. Politik*, November 1941, pp.895 ff.

88. *Materialsammlung* by Frau Clarita von Trott zu Solz, p.92, whom I must again thank for her kind permission to use this

89. *Ein Mann geht seinen Weg. Schriften, Reden und Briefe von Julius Leber*, Berlin 1952, p.54

90. *Ibid.*, p.41

91. Henderson, *Adolf Reichwein*, Stuttgart 1958, p.66, *Ein Mann . . .*, pp.267 ff.; van Roon

92. Van Roon

93. Brill, *Gegen den Strom*, Offenbach 1946, p.78

94. *Ein Mann . . .*, p.54

95. Fischer, 'Weltpolitik, Weltmachtstreben und deutsche Kriegsziele ', *HZ* 199, 2, pp.265 ff.

96. *HZ, op. cit.*, p.453

97. Ruedorffer (Riezler's *nom de plume*), *Die Drei Krisen*, Stuttgart 1920, pp.16 ff., 37, 60 f., 65 ff.

98. Van Roon

99. After the Second World War, Field-Marshal von Blomberg wrote that when he was a young staff officer during the First World War he felt that any doubts as to a German victory were ' sinful ' – MS of his memoirs, Archiv d. Inst. f. Zeitgesch.

100. Van Roon

101. Rothfels, ' Trott und die Aussenpolitik des Widerstandes ', *Vjh. f. Zgsch.* 1964, 3, pp.300 ff.

102. Rothfels, *Die deutsche Opposition gegen Hitler*, Fischer Bücherei 1961, p.121

103. Van Roon

104. *Ibid.*
105. *Materialsammlung*; Rothfels, Trott, *op. cit.*
106. *Materialsammlung*, pp.33 f.
107. *Ibid.*, p.149
108. *Ibid.*, p.52
109. *Ibid.*, p.118
110. Van Roon
111. Rothfels, *op. cit.*, p.302
112. *Ibid.*, p.301
113. *Materialsammlung*, p.144
114. Van Roon
115. *Ibid.*
116. *Ibid.*
117. *Ibid.*
118. Account of his conversation with a British cabinet minister, June 1939, *Materialsammlung*, pp.164 f.
119. *Ibid.*, p.180
120. *Ibid.*, pp.181 f.
121. *Ibid.*, p.103
122. *Ibid.*, p.160
123. *Ibid.*, p.152
124. *Ibid.*
125. Rothfels, Trott, *op. cit.*, p.314
126. *Ibid.*, pp.315 f.
127. Van Roon
128. Beck, *Studien*, pp.250 f.
129. Ritter, *op. cit.*, p.585
130. *Beck und Goerdeler*, p.255
131. Ritter, *op. cit.*, p.593
132. Hassell, *Vom andern Deutschland*, pp.215 f., 304
133. *Beck und Goerdeler*, p.257
134. *Unsere Idee*
135. *Ibid.*
136. *Beck und Goerdeler*, p.257
137. *Spiegelbild einer Verschwörung. Die Kaltenbrunner-Berichte an Bormann und Hitler über das Attentat vom 20 Juli 1944,* Stuttgart 1961, p.236
138. Hassell, *op. cit.*, pp.207, 257, 290, 298 f.

139. Hassell, ' Prinz Eugens europäische Sendung ', *Monatsh. f. Ausw. Politik*, June 1943, pp.369 ff.
140. *Kaltenbrunner-Berichte*, p.353
141. Hassell, *Vom andern Deutschland*, pp.300 f.; Ritter, *op. cit.*, p.593; *Beck und Goerdeler*, pp.255 ff.
142. *Beck und Goerdeler*, p.195
143. Ritter, *op. cit.*, p.593
144. *Kaltenbrunner-Berichte*, p.535
145. Ritter, *op. cit.*, p.593
146. Hassell, ' Ein neues europäisches Gleichgewicht?' *Monatsh. f. Ausw. Politik*, Nov./Dec. 1943, pp.697 ff.
147. Ritter, *op. cit.*, p.593
148. Dulles, *Germany's Underground*, New York 1947, p.133
149. *Ibid.*, p.139; Ritter, *op. cit.*, pp.393 f.
150. *Kaltenbrunner-Berichte*, pp. 101, 136, 492
151. *Ibid.*, p.189
152. Steltzer, *Von deutscher Politik*, Frankfurt 1949, p.156
153. *Kaltenbrunner-Berichte*, p.34
154. *Vjh. f. Zgesch.*, 1957, 4, pp.332 ff.
155. Gisevius, *Bis zum bitteren Ende*, II, Zürich 1946, pp.290 ff.
156. Dulles, *op. cit.*, pp.136 ff.
157. Boveri, *Der Verrat im XX Jahrhundert*, II, Hamburg 1956, p.74
158. *Kaltenbrunner-Berichte*, p.34
159. *Vjh. f. Zgesch.*, 1957, 4, pp.362 ff.
160. *Kaltenbrunner-Berichte*, p.118
161. Bell, ' Die Okumene und die innerdeutsche Opposition ', *Vjh. f. Zgesch.*, 1957, 4, pp.362 ff.
162. Van Roon
163. *Ibid.*
164. *Materialsammlung*, pp.118 f.

## Social Views and Constitutional Plans of the Resistance

1. *A German of the Resistance. The Last Letters of Count Helmuth James von Moltke*, London 1948, pp.28 f.
2. cf. H. Rothfels, *Die deutsche Opposition gegen Hitler*, Fis-

cher Bücherei 1958, p.105; Gerhard Schulz, 'Über Entscheidungen und Formen des politischen Widerstands in Deutschland', *Faktoren der politischen Entscheidung, Festgabe für Ernst Fraenkel*, Berlin 1963, p.95

3. 'The Politics of Uncertainty : The German Resistance Movement', *Social Research*, Vol. XXXI (1964), p.73; cf. Henry Pachter, 'Germany Looks in the Mirror of History', *World Politics*, Vol. XIII (1961), pp.633 ff.

4. Hannah Arendt, *Eichmann in Jerusalem*, Munich 1964, pp.134 ff.

5. cf. Hans Rothfels (ed.), 'Adam von Trott und das State Department', *Vierteljahrshefte für Zeitgeschichte* (referred to below as *Vjh. f. Zgesch.*) 7 (1959), p.524; 'Trott und die Aussenpolitik des Widerstands', *ibid.*, 12 (1964), p.314

6. cf. Emil Henk: Carlo Mierendorff, *Reden für eine Bürgerschaft*, Darmstadt 1962, p.111

7. Romoser, *op. cit.*, pp.85 f.

8. Ralf Dahrendorf, *Gesellschaft und Demokratie in Deutschland*, Munich 1965, p.441

9. Hermann Brill, 'Gegen den Strom', *Wege zum Sozialismus*, Vol. I, Offenbach 1946, pp.15 ff; Karl O. Paetel, 'Deutsche innere Emigration' (*Dokumente des anderen Deutschland*, Vol. 4), New York 1946, pp.43 ff.

10. Dahrendorf, *op. cit.*, pp.442 f.

11. Karl Mannheim, 'Das konservative Denken', *Archiv für Sozialwissenschaft und Sozialpolitik*, Vol. 57

12. cf. Klemens von Klemperer, *Konservative Bewegungen zwischen Kaiserreich und Nationalsozialismus*, Munich and Vienna 1964, p.247

13. Trott wrote an article 'Zwischengeneration' (cf. Clarita von Trott, *Adam von Trott zu Solz*, duplicated MS, 1958 (I must thank Frau von Trott for permitting me to use this); cf. also on this question Karl Epting, *Generation der Mitte*, Bonn 1953; Moltke, memorandum, *Ausgangslage, Ziele und Aufgaben* (1941) (many thanks are due to Professor G. van Roon for his kindness in allowing the author to use the proofs of his fundamental work on the Kreisau Circle [Munich 1966]), in the Appendix of van Roon's book; Dietrich Bon-

hoeffer, *Widerstand und Ergebung*, ed. W. Bethge, Munich 1956, pp.9 f.; Schlange-Schöningen, *Am Tage danach*, 1946, p.122

14. cf. Walter Lipgens, *Europapläne der europäischen Resistance*
15. Alma de l'Aigle, *Meine Briefe von Theo Haubach*, Hamburg 1947, p.59
16. Bonhoeffer, *op. cit.*, pp.24 f.
17. *Fragen der Agrarpolitik* (28.11.41) in the sources quoted in van Roon's Appendix; G. Ritter, *Carl Goerdeler und die deutsche Widerstandsbewegung*, dtv-Ausg., Munich 1964, p.299
18. Alfred Delp, *Im Angesicht des Todes*, ed. Paul Bolkovac, Frankfurt 1947, pp.103 f.; Goerdeler, memorandum, *Der Weg*, in Wilhelm Ritter von Schramm's *Gemeinschaftsdokumente für den Frieden 1941/44*, Munich 1965, p.176
19. Theodor Steltzer, *Von deutscher Politik*, Frankfurt 1949, pp.29 f.
20. *cit.* van Roon; Gerstenmaier was in close personal contact with Delp
21. Delp, *op. cit.*, pp.102 f.; the views of the Cologne circle are reflected in Eberhard Welty's book, *Die Entscheidung in die Zukunft. Grundsätze und Hinweise zur Neuordnung im deutschen Lebensraum*, Heidelberg 1946; Welty was closely connected with Father Laurentius Siemer and belonged to the Albertus-Magnus-Akademie Walberberg (I owe this information to Professor Erich Kosthorst, Münster). Welty confirms that Jakob Kaiser sometimes attended the deliberations of the Cologne circle
22. Memorandum *Ausgangslage, op. cit.*; cf. Freisler's reply to Yorck's criticism of ' the state's total claims on the citizen, to the exclusion of his religious and moral obligations towards God ', to the effect that a common feature of National Socialism and Christianity was their claim to ' the whole man ' (*20 Juli 1944*, ed. Bundeszentrale f. Heimatdienst, 1960, p.198)
23. *cit.* van Roon; Delp, *op. cit.*, pp.164 f.
24. H. Rothfels (ed.), ' Zwei aussenpolitische Memoranden der deutschen Opposition ', *Vjh. f. Zgesch.*, 5 (1957), p.394

25. Ludwig Reichhold, *Arbeiterbewegung jenseits des totalen Staates. Die Gewerkschaften und der 20 Juli 1944*, Vienna 1965, pp.9 f.; Leuschner's notes (incomplete) in Joachim G. Leithäuser's *Wilhelm Leuschner. Ein Leben für die Republik*, Cologne 1962, p.10

26. Julius Leber, *Ein Mann geht seinen Weg*, Berlin 1952, pp.213 ff., 216, 222

27. Delp, *op. cit.*, p.165

28. Clarita von Trott, *op. cit.*, p.142

29. *Das Ziel*, and Schramm's *op. cit.*, pp.86 ff.; *Goerdelers politisches Testament. Dokumente des anderen Deutschland*, ed.Friedrich Krause, New York 1945, p.49

30. *Geld spielt keine Rolle* (June 1941), pp.61 f.; (Posth. Goerdeler) BA Coblenz, No. 19; *Das Ziel, op. cit.*, p.86; *Unsere Idee* (1944), pp.5 f (*ibid.* No. 26); *Das Ziel, op cit.*, p.84

31. Clarita von Trott, *op. cit.*, p.240; *Spiegelbild einer Verschwörung. Die Kaltenbrunner-Berichte an Bormann und Hitler über das Attentat vom 20 Juli 1944*, ed. K. H. Peter, Stuttgart 1961 (henceforth referred to as *KB*), p.164; *Das Ziel, op. cit.*, pp.86, 96 ff.

32. Memorandum, *Die Bedeutung des russisch-finnischen Zusammenstosses für die gegenwärtige Lage Deutschlands* (December 1939), posth. Grosscurth, BA Coblenz H 08–104/2, cf. note 94

33. *Ibid.*

34. *Vjh. f. Zgesch.*, 7 (1959), p.324

35. Dietrich Bonhoeffer, *Gesammelte Schriften*, 1 (1958), p.371 : ' The Church and the New Order in Europe '

36. Ulrich von Hassell, *Vom andern Deutschland*, Fischer Bücherei 1964, pp.136, 158 *passim*

37. Gert Buchheit, *Ludwig Beck, ein preussischer General*, Munich 1964, pp.49 f., 165 f.

38. Hassell, *op. cit.*, p.289

39. Clarita von Trott, *op. cit.*, pp.30, 261 f.; cf. Josef Furtwängler's letter of 8.7.47 reproduced on p.240

40. *Ibid.*, pp.30, 96, 104 f., 149

41. *Ibid.*, p.149 (letter to Sheila Sokolow Grant of 20.7.38) and pp.150 f. (letter to same, 6.10.38)

42. Letter to David Astor, end of 1939, *ibid.*, pp.144 f.

43. Leber, *op. cit.*, p.203

44. ' Bemerkungen zum Friedensprogramm der amerikanischen Kirchen ', *Vjh. f. Zgesch.*, 12 (1964), pp.321 f.

45. Reproduced in van Roon, Appendix

46. Hassell, *op. cit.*, p.338; Mierendorff's programme can be found in the Appendix, van Roon; Goerdeler's memorandum on unemployment (7th sheet, undated, after 31.12.40), Goerdeler's posth. works No. 19; *Das Ziel, op. cit.*, p.119; Albert Krebs, ' Fritz-Dietlof Graf von der Schulenburg ', (*Hamburger Beiträge zur Zeitgeschichte*, II), Hamburg 1964, pp.167 f., 282 ff.; cf. Bonhoeffer *Widerstand und Ergebung*, pp.200 f.

47. Memorandum, Einsiedel, *op. cit.*; cf. A. Delp, *Zur Erde entschlossen*, ed. Paul Bolkovac, Frankfurt 1949, pp.64 ff., 71 ff.; Steltzer, *op. cit.*, pp.68 ff.; Eberhard Zeller, *Geist der Freiheit. Der Zwanzigste Juli*, Munich 1963, p.189

48. Zeller, *op. cit.*, p.254; Fahrner's report, not written until after Zeller's account had appeared (1962/3), can only be regarded as an authentic source in a limited sense, since it gives evidence of the influence of the literature on the subject and there are characteristic deviations from the few sources cited in the *KB* – Clarita von Trott, *op. cit.*, p.232

49. Leber, *op. cit.*, pp.84 f.; Goerdeler, ' Vorgesehene Rundfunkrede bei Ubernahme der Reichsregierung ', ed. Gerhard Ritter, *Die Gegenwart I* (1946), pp.11 ff., ' Das Regierungsprogramm vom 20 Juli 1944 '; dated by Ritter May/June 1944.

50. Van Roon, Chapter II

51. Moltke, *Ausgangslage, op. cit.*; Krebs, *op. cit.*, pp.82 f.

52. *Das Ziel, op. cit.*, pp.102, 120; Popitz's memorandum on questions of reconstruction, commissioned by the Ministry of the Interior 1944, copy in Goerdeler's posth. works No. 24, pp.65 f.

53. Memorandum by von Einsiedel and von Trotha, *Mission des Menschen in der Wirtschaft* (1942); Appendix, van Roon

54. Krebs, *op. cit.*, p.282; *Das Ziel, op. cit.*, p.101

55. Krebs, *op. cit.*, pp.282 ff; Goerdeler's memorandum on 39 questions relating to the reconstruction of Germany, 3.1.45, pp.33 f. (BA Coblenz R 58/57); Popitz's corresponding memorandum (posth. Goerdeler No. 24), pp.26 f.; Krebs, *op. cit.*, pp.109 ff.; *Das Ziel, op. cit.*, p.129

56. Goerdeler's secret memorandum intended for the Generals, 26.3.43, in Ritter, *op. cit.*, p.561

57. Schmölders' memorandum, *Wirtschaft und Wirtschaftsführung nach dem Kriege* (1942/3), also von Einsiedel's and von Trotha's memorandum *Mission des Menschen*, Appendix, van Roon

58. *Das Ziel, op. cit.*, p.120; cf. *Der Weg*, pp.207 *passim*

59. cf. note 46; *Das Ziel, op. cit.*, pp.120 f.

60. Hassell, *op. cit.*, pp.257 ff., 331 f.

61. *Ibid.*, p.332

62. cf. Ritter, *op. cit.*, pp.50 ff.; Memorandum for Hindenburg (April 1932) posth. Goerdeler, No. 21, cf. *Das Ziel, op. cit.*, pp.127 f.

63. *Ibid.*, p.130; cf. also memorandum *An den Herrn Reichskanzler Adolf Hitler*, August 1934, pp.8 ff., posth. Goerdeler, No. 21

64. Posth. Goerdeler No. 26 (some of it printed Ritter), pp.18 ff.; cf. Ritter, *op. cit.*, p.65

65. Memorandum for Hindenburg (April 1932), pp.12 f.

66. Ritter, *op. cit.*, pp.55 f.

67. Steltzer, *Grundsätze für die Neuordnung, op. cit.*, p.161; Goerdeler *Gedanken eines zum Tode Verurteilten, cit.* Ritter, *op. cit.*, p.544; broadcast speech 1944 (see note 49); KB, pp.316 f.

68. He demands the ' restoration of the position of the state and its machinery, as opposed to all the subversive and truly undemocratic institutions – as opposed, that is, to the omnipotence of *one party*, and equally so to the power of parties ' (*Aufzeichnung im Gefängnis*, 1944); posth. Goerdeler, No. 18, p.23; *Totalität: Das Ziel, op. cit.*, pp.83 ff.; Ludwig Beck, *Studien*, ed. Hans Speidel, Stuttgart 1955 : ' Die Lehre vom totalen Krieg ', pp.243 ff. – Schramm's thesis that parts of *Das Ziel* were written by Beck – the memorandum

a joint work (Schramm, *op. cit.*, pp.36 ff.) – has no foundation. Goerdeler's tendency to adopt the views of others would seem to make it probable enough that he had made use of Beck's draft which had already been written by the end of 1941. But Goerdeler had had similar ideas earlier. The sections attributed to Beck by Schramm are undoubtedly by Goerdeler, as can be seen from their style. Schramm's introduction contains other misleading statements. The allegation that the memorandum to which he gives the title *Der Weg* is the joint work of socialist inspiration is as improbable as the assertion that G. Leber ( ! ) sought the co-operation of Leuschner and Jakob Kaiser (p.65). All that remains of these suppositions is the fact, already noted by Ritter, that Goerdeler took up some suggestions of Beck's. Regarding the date, cf. note 109 below

69. Memorandum to Hitler, *op. cit.*, p.31; *Das Ziel, op. cit.*, p.133

70. *Praktische Massnahmen zur Umgestaltung Europas*, p.3 (Posth. Goerdeler, No. 23); Ritter, *op. cit.*, p.506, supposes the date to be 1939, but 1943 would seem more probable, as is evident from the Kreisau influence and the ‘ Europe ’ ideas. In the *Geheime Denkschrift für die Generalität Bestimmt* (Ritter, *op. cit.*, pp.557 ff.) there is still talk of independent European states – cf. Steltzer, *op. cit.*, p.25; letter from Yorck to Moltke of 9.8.1940 in van Roon; Leber, *op. cit.*, p.203; Reichhold, *op. cit.*, pp.84 f.

71. cf. Peters’ view mentioned by van Roon that ‘ the complete absorption of the individual into the community ’ such as the totalitarian state, taken to its logical conclusion, demands, is contrary to the natural order. cf. also Hermann Kaiser's memorandum, *Grundsätze der Jugenderziehung* (*KB*, pp.342 ff.). It is not possible to enter here into the Opposition's ideas on educational and academic reform

72. Yorck to Moltke, 8.8.40, *op. cit.*

73. Steltzer's memorandum of 15.7.44, *op. cit.*, p.91; C. Mierendorff, ‘ Uberwindung des Nationalsozialismus ’, *Sozialistische Monatshefte*, 73 (1931), pp.226 ff.; Haubach *cit.* van Roon, *op. cit.*, Chapter III; Leber, *op. cit.*, p.193

74. Krebs, *op. cit.*, p.79 ff.; Steltzer, *op. cit.*, pp.90 f.; *Das Ziel*, *op. cit.*, pp.93 f.; memorandum for Hindenburg (April 1932), *op. cit.*; document written end of May 1932 (no date), Posth. Goerdeler No. 9

75. *Gedanken zur Neuordnung der Selbstverwaltung*, BA 58/59, RSHA, p.9; *Aufzeichnungen in der Haft* (included with *Gedanken eines zum Tode Verurteilten*, Posth. Goerdeler No. 26), p.8

76. p.10 (Posth. Goerdeler No. 26)

77. cf. *Das Ziel*, *op. cit.*, p.125; memorandum for Hindenburg, *op. cit.*, p.21

78. Stauffenberg's formulation, *KB*, p.34 cf. pp.326 f.

79. Hildemarie Dieckmann, ' Johannes Popitz. Entwicklung und Wirksamkeit in der Zeit der Weimarer Republik ' (*Schriften zur europäischen Geschichte aus dem Friedrich-Meinecke-Institut*, Vol. IV), Berlin 1960, pp.139 f.; *KB*, p.205, cf. pp.447 f.; Krebs, *op. cit.*, p.217

80. *Cit.* van Roon, Chapter III

81. *Widerstand und Ergebung*, *op. cit.*, p.205

82. *Ausgangslage*, *op. cit.*

83. Steltzer, *op. cit.*, pp.32 f., 44; *Widerstand und Ergebung*, p.25

84. Steltzer, *op. cit.*, p.77

85. *Ibid.*, p.140; Zeller, *op. cit.*, p.254; Friedrich Hielscher, *Fünfzig Jahre unter Deutschen*, Hamburg 1954, p.393

86. *Ausgangslage* (first edition : 24.4.41, second edition : 26.6.41), enlarged edition : *Diskussion der Aufgaben*, in van Roon, Appendix; Goerdeler, *Praktische Massnahmen*, *op. cit.*, p.6

87. *KB*, p.490

88. Steltzer, *op. cit.*, p.157

89. Moltke to Yorck, 16.11.40, in Roon, *op. cit.*, Appendix; Moltke's 1939 memorandum, *Die kleinen Gemeinschaften*, *cit.* van Roon, *op. cit.* Chapter V; memorandum, Moltke *Uber die Grundlage der Staatslehre*, 20.10.40, van Roon, Appendix

90. *KB*, p.438

91. *Die Aufgaben der Zukunft* (1.–11.8.44, written while in flight), p.11 (Posth. Goerdeler No. 26)

92. Popitz's lecture to the Wednesday Club, 11.12.40 (BA Kl. Erw. 179-2); cf. Hassell, *op. cit.*, pp.155, 287; Krebs, *op. cit.*, p.205

93. cf. note 33 above

94. *Die innere und äussere Lage*, December 1939 (Posth. Grosscurth, BA H–08/104–2). The memorandum, which was probably also submitted to Halder, is typical of the thought of the *Abwehr* group, especially as regards Oster and Dohnanyi, but it also reflects the views of the then active group of conspirators and Beck's, perhaps, among them – the memorandum has been erroneously attributed to him. The memorandum, written by Etscheid, a lawyer by profession, was viewed critically by Tippelskirch, as the latter's comments show, especially in its assessment of Germany's opportunities abroad and her military prospects, which Goerdeler and Beck, both then and later, saw in a similarly pessimistic light. The volume now in preparation by Helmut Krausnick and others of Grosscurth's diary, including also material from among his surviving private papers, such as Beck's memoranda, will throw light on the individual connections existing at the time between Grosscurth and the General Staff on the one hand, and the conspirators round Beck on the other

95. cf. Hassell, *op. cit.*, p.215; also Ehlers, *op. cit.*, pp.165 f.

96. Hassell, *op. cit.*, p.114

97. Programme, reproduced by Hassell, *op. cit.*, pp.332 ff.; cf. pp.84, 115, 87

98. *Ibid.*, pp.334 f.

99. *Ibid.*, p.80

100. *Ibid.*, p.118

101. *Ibid.*, pp.336 ff.

102. Nothing survives but *Richtlinien zur Handhabung des Gesetzes über den Belagerungzustand* (also by Popitz), *ibid.*, pp.345 ff.

103. *Op. cit.*, p.329

104. Hassell, *op. cit.*, p.344; Popitz played a leading part in s

the creation of the Civil Service Law of 1937

105. Dieckmann, *op. cit.*, pp.132, 140; Popitz also drew on the Steinian tradition, *ibid.*, p.133

106. *KB*, pp.499 f.; cf. Hassell, *op. cit.*, p.305; 'Hans Herzfeld, Johannes Popitz. Ein Beitrag zur Geschichte des deutschen Beamtentums', in *Festgabe für Fritz Hartung*, Berlin 1958, pp.351, 359; cf. Schulz, *op. cit.*, p.93. The latter's opinion, that in economic matters Popitz's views differed little from those of Kreisau, overlooks Popitz's fundamentally different and very *étatiste* point of departure

107. cf. Goerdeler's unfinished memorandum, *Kritik am Verwaltungsaufbau und Gedanken zur Neuordnung der Selbstverwaltung* (end of 1944), p.39 (R 58/59 BA Coblenz); *KB*, p.449; lecture before the Wednesday Club of 11.12.40, *op. cit.*

108. Rothfels, *op. cit.*, pp.98 ff.; Herzfeld's (*op. cit.*, pp.351 f.) cautious view of Popitz as 'not just a man of the political right' is only acceptable – and that in direct opposition to his arguments – in so far as Popitz gave his assent to a very considerable measure of fascist methods of control. Popitz's personal integrity is not here in question

109. Ritter, *op. cit.*, p.506, puts the memorandum at the beginning of 1941, especially since it contains parts of the *Gesamtlage* (November 1940) and a memorandum of 1.7.40 (excerpts of both in Schramm, *op. cit.*, pp.265 ff.). However, it also quotes early accounts of travels. This does not really help in estimating its date, as parts of earlier writings are incorporated in later ones. Even if some parts of the memorandum were written earlier, *Das Ziel* as a whole – if it is compared with the other memoranda enumerated by Ritter – could not have been written before the Russian campaign. Ritter's assumption that the Opposition knew about it beforehand is not supported by the text, where the campaign appears as a fait accompli. Schramm, *op. cit.*, p.34, wrongly relates the memorandum to the plans for revolution of the spring of 1940. This is not at all the case, for the tenor of *Das Ziel* is entirely different from that of those particular programmes (cf. above pp.108 ff.). In January

1942 Hassell noted that Goerdeler had written a 'document' in anticipation of a revolution (which they then hoped was going to take place), and that this had been the subject of deliberations in the group of conspirators round Hassell. That document was *Das Ziel*, and this explains both the title and the structure of the memorandum. He must have been writing the memorandum after December 1941, and have put it before the circle in January 1942. At this time Beck's Ludendorff study, given as a lecture before the Wednesday Club in June, 1942 – as well as others of his lectures – must have been available to Goerdeler, hence the copious quotations from those sources, as also the degree of compliance shown towards the generals. Schramm's assertion (*op. cit.*, p.31) that Point 11 of the memorandum which contains a programme of dissimilation in the Jewish question was 'dropped' at the latest in 1942, is wrong. Goerdeler continued to hold to this programme after that time, as is evident from the memorandum *Gedanken eines zum Tode Verurteilten* of September 1944, and from *Unsere Idee*.

Our dating is confirmed by the fact that he passed on the first part of *Das Ziel*, either verbally or in writing, to Leuschner either after or just before the beginning of 1942, as is apparent from the latter's undated notes written on a leaf torn from a calendar (fifty-third week, 28-31 December 1941) (original in the possession of Herr Wilhelm Leuschner Jr, reproduced in Lipgens, *op. cit.*). Leuschner has noted points of verbal agreement: 'Revolution of '33 artificially induced and technically organised, not organic continuation, too much tension, but also reaction to long-past epochs of our history', and *Das Ziel*, p.87: 'The revolution of 1933 was artificially induced and technically organised; it is not an organic continuation, but its concomitant is hypertension, as was the reaction in various long-past epochs of our history . . .' There are other literal excerpts from *Das Ziel*, pp.88, 89 and 90. Thus, as opposed to Ritter and Schramm, we would date *Das Ziel* late 1941/early 1942

110. Schramm thinks differently *op. cit.*, p.274, note 7. But this is not a literal transcription!

111. cf. Hassell, *op. cit.*, pp.218, 303

112. cf. van Roon, Appendix; principles in Steltzer, *op. cit.* pp.156 ff.

113. In various, chronologically distinct, pieces, Goerdeler gives alternative proposals in brackets

114. Krebs, *op. cit.*, p.267

115. cf. Steltzer, *op. cit.*, pp.91 ff.; Delp advised W. Cornides to study Stein's works (see van Roon, short biography of Delp); cf. Hans Peters: ' Verfassungs– und Verwaltungsreformbestrebungen innerhalb der Widerstandsbewegung gegen Hitler', (*Schriften der Freiherr-von-Stein-Gesellschaft*, No. H.3), Münster 1961, p.12

116. Leber, *op. cit.*, pp.222, 104 f.; cf. Goerdeler, *Aufzeichnungen in der Haft*, *op. cit.*, p.11; the second ballot system of the time of the imperial Reich was, he believed, responsible for party fragmentation

117. Leithäuser, *op. cit.*, pp.223 f.; Steltzer, *op. cit.*, p.50; *Der Weg*, *op. cit.*, pp.170 f.; whence Bergstraesser's censorious remark about ' jobbery between the Parties ', which also reveals the fact that Bergstraesser's memorandum arose out of a controversy with Goerdeler; *Das Ziel*, pp.147 f.

118. Memorandum of September 1933, part of which is reproduced in Theodor Steltzer, *60 Jahre Zeitgenosse*, Munich 1966, pp.270 ff., esp. p.275

119. cf. Ritter, *op. cit.*, pp.31 ff.; *Das Ziel*, *op. cit.*, p.153; cf. on Leber's view, Margret Boveri, *Der Verrat im 20. Jahrhundert, II. Für und gegen die Nation*, Hamburg 1956, p.77: the Parties, he thought, were the ' weights on the living scales of government '

120. Memorandum for Hindenburg (April 1932), *op. cit.*, p.18

121. *Das Ziel*, *op. cit.*, pp.152, 164; by a typical contradiction, which testifies to Goerdeler's lack of insight into the functioning of public political policy-making, he sought at the same time to ' keep the head of state above the muddy tidemark of the assembly ' (*Aufzeichnungen aus dem Gefängnis, op. cit.*, p.11)

22. Steltzer, *Von deutscher Politik*, p.140; cf. Eugen Gerstenmaier, ' Der Kreisauer Kreis ', *20 Juli 1944*, p.34

23. Rothfels differs, *op. cit.*, p.130; also Marion Gräfin Dönhoff's version in Pechel, *op. cit.*, p.187; her use of the term ' parliamentarism ' shows her misunderstanding of the nature of the system of government which was the aim of Kreisau

124. *Gedanken eines zum Tode Verurteilten*, in Ritter, *op. cit.*, p.543; *KB*, pp.350, 415, 479, 212

125. *KB*, p.257; cf. Ritter, *op. cit.*, p.521; cf. also M. Boveri, ' Goerdeler und der deutsche Widerstand ', *Aussenpolitik*, IV (1955), p.79

126. Writings (Posth. 26), p.15. Goerdeler talks of a ' terrible omission when, invited by Hindenburg, Schleicher and Papen, and with the support of almost the whole people – popular in the best sense of the word – I failed to follow the pressing call . . .'

127. Goerdeler's prepared broadcast, *op. cit.*, p.12; that this point is expressly mentioned (the declaration was obviously not written by Goerdeler alone) is proof of the extent to which the Resistance was conscious of spiritual isolation, and this was also the case with their ' foreign-affairs men '. See also Hermann Graml's contribution to this volume on this problem

128. ' The Christ and the New Order ', *Collected Works*, I, p.366

129. Information given by Dr van Roijen in Clarita von Trott, *op. cit.*, p.255

130. *Ibid.*, p.173; Leithäuser, *op. cit.*, pp.133, 212, 219; the fact that Steinian political ideas were not out of harmony with socialist thinking, is apparent from the programme of the oppositional ' Freiherr-von-Stein-Kreis ' uncovered by the Gestapo in 1937, which was attempting to link Strasser's socialist ideas with the tradition of self-government (BA Coblenz, KI. Erw., Chief Public Prosecutor in the People's Court, indictment of Elizabeth von Gustedt, 7.9.36)

131. Steltzer, *op. cit.*, pp.118, 120 f.

132. *Das Ziel, op. cit.*, p.148; R 58/59 BA, pp.10 f.; *Der Weg, op. cit.*, pp.171, 186; for the anti-democratic nature of the self-

government ideology, see E. Holtzmann: 'Der Weg zur deutschen Gemeindeordnung vom 30.1.1935', in *Zschr. f. Politik* 12 (1965) p.362. In this, Holtzmann quotes a letter from Oberbürgermeister Strölin, a member of the conspiracy round Goerdeler, of 8.6.34, in which he points out the dangers introduced into communal government by a parliamentary-democratic system. Goerdeler did not go as far as Strölin in repudiating communal electoral bodies; at the time the latter welcomed National Socialism as having overcome the democratic parliamentary system

133. *Gedanken zur Neuordnung der Selbstverwaltung, op. cit.*, pp.5 f.; *Aufgaben der deutschen Zukunft* (Posth. Goerdeler No. 26), pp.9 f.

134. Whereas Goerdeler wanted to split up the associations into groups, 'employers', 'employees', 'workers', Kreisau held that every elector should have the right to elect an employers' and a works' representative (cf. second Kreisau meeting, in van Roon, Appendix). It is characteristic of this view that it envisaged a general prohibition of strikes and lock-outs, and that this, too, was a development of Wichards von Moellendorff's train of thought

135. cf. Krebs, *op. cit.*, p.266; in this context it is not possible to enter into the Opposition's aspirations for administrative reforms

136. cf. Werner Münchheimer, 'Verfassungs– und Verwaltungsreformbestrebungen der deutschen Opposition gegen Hitler zum 20 Juli 1944', *Europa Archiv* 5 (1950), p.3188 ff. Van Roon produces new evidence against Münchheimer's account. It is also erroneous in other respects, for instance the assumption that the *Land* 'Lord-Lieutenant' and the *Land* Administrator were one and the same (*Grundsätze*), which has been adopted in minor literature from this source

137. Leithäuser, *op. cit.*, pp.221 ff.

138. Steltzer, *op. cit.*, pp.112, 130

139. *KB*, p.412

140. Ritter, *op. cit.*, p.543; Goerdeler's accounts of his journey to Bulgaria (Posth. No. 14), p.2; Goerdeler would seem to

have borrowed his suggestion that the age of eligibility be
30 from the Bulgarian model

141. Peters, *op. cit.*, p.14

142. *KB*, pp.235, 393

143. Steltzer, *op. cit.*, p.161; van Roon, Chapter III

144. Clarita von Trott, *op. cit.*, pp.288 f.

145. *KB*, pp.315 ff., 468; Goerdeler, notes on Wallenberg for London (19.–21.5.43) (Posth. Goerdeler No. 23), Pkt. 23

146. *KB*, pp.315 f., 499 f. Helldorf, Gisevius and Strünck were also the opponents of trade unions – Leithäuser, *op. cit.*, p.208; cf. Reichhold, *op. cit.*, pp.23 ff.

147. Krebs, *op. cit.*, pp.278 f.; letter from Eberhard Welty to Professor Kosthorst, Münster, 11.6.64

148. *KB*, p.205; Maass had similar ideas, as Frau Elfriede Kaiser-Nebgen recalls, for he spoke of them in her circle

149. Leithäuser, *op. cit.*, pp.221 f.

150. Manoïlescu, Bln. 1941 – Information from Frau Kaiser-Nebgen

151. Krebs, *op. cit.*, p.117

152. Joachim Kramarz, *Claus Graf Stauffenberg*, Frankfurt 1965, p.200; Zeller, *op. cit.*, p.489, speaks of ' information handed down, that is well-attested but not generally known ' (it derives from information given by Professor Rudolf Fahrner, which elsewhere is expressly quoted by Zeller); this would seem suspect, the more so since it is also stated that Stauffenberg continued up to the very last to work on the formulation of the oath, so that at the very most this was never definitive

153. Mierendorff's programme in van Roon, Appendix; *KB*, p.257

154. Van Roon, overwritten: ' Readiness of a German group to cooperate militarily with the Allies '

155. Dulles, *op. cit.*, pp.171 ff.; Hassell, *op. cit.*, p.214; *KB*, p.118, 205 f.; cf. also Ehlers, *op. cit.*, p.162, Pechel, *op. cit.*, p.46

156. *Ibid.*, pp.165 f.

157. Ritter, *op. cit.*, p.543; Leber, *op. cit.*, pp.283 f.; *KB*, pp.234 f., 505

158. Dulles, *op. cit.*, pp.170 ff.; Hassell, *op. cit.*, p.214; *KB*, pp.118, 205 f.; cf. also Ehlers, *op. cit.*, p.162; Pechel, *op. cit.*, p.46

159. *KB*, pp.19, 206, 373

160. cf. van Roon, Chapter III; *KB*, p.34; this does not necessarily contradict Ehlers' opinion that it was questionable whether Stauffenberg had his own concept of political renewal (*op. cit.*, pp.117, 237)

161. *KB*, pp.465, 500; Zeller, *op. cit.*, p.241

162. cf. van Roon, Appendix

163. Bodo Scheurig, *Freies Deutschland. Das Nationalkomitee und der Bund deutscher Offiziere in der Sovjetunion 1943-1945*, Munich 1960, pp.143 ff., stresses the Resistance's intense aversion for the *Nationalkomitee* but only touches on the psychological reactions to the latter's activities. If it is correct, Meinecke's report, quoted p.147, of Beck's statement about the national reliability of the German Communists, shows that Beck was prepared to fall in with Stauffenberg's plans for an anti-National Socialist coalition cabinet with Communist participation: cf. *KB*, pp.507 f., also Ehlers, *op. cit.*, p.161

164. cf. Kramarz, *op. cit.*, pp.172 f.; *KB*, pp.234, 538

165. *Unsere Idee* (posth. No. 26), p.25; Dulles, *op. cit.*, p.218; Gisevius' romantic account of these events (*Bis zum bitteren Ende*, Vol. 2, Hamburg 1947), although plainly indicative of anti-National Socialist emotions, reveals a faulty assessment of the collective political attitude of the protagonists; the account is nevertheless symptomatic of the misunderstandings that arose in the Opposition camp before the attempt and is partially confirmed by Goerdeler's writings (probably based on information from Gisevius) in prison. Marxist-Leninist research follows Gisevius' lead – thus, recently, Daniil Melnikow: *Der 20 Juli 1944. Legende und Wirklichkeit*, German translation, East Berlin 1964, pp.185 ff. A discussion of this work is precluded for reasons of space

166. Zeller, *op. cit.*, pp.245 f.

167. *KB*, pp.101 f.

168. Leber, *op. cit.*, pp.280 f.; Clarita von Trott, op. cit., pp.259 f. (Leber dated 23 February 1944)

169. *Ibid.*, p.120

170. P. Bolkovac in: Delp, *Zur Erde entschlossen*, pp.5 f.

171. cf. Clarita von Trott, *op. cit.*, pp.241 f.

172. For Oster cf. *KB*, p.529; a typical manifestation of the German officer's unpolitical mentality is Eduard Wagner's diary (*Der 'Generalquartiermeister. Briefe und Tagebuchaufzeichnungen des Generalquartiermeisters des Heeres, Eduard Wagner*, ed. Elisabeth Wagner, Munich/Vienna 1963, pp.93, 195 or thereabouts). For Halder the forthcoming *Grosscurth-Tagebuch*. It appears doubtful whether the statements made by Halder in his letters may be used as a source for Stauffenberg's political attitude, as is done by Kramarz, *op. cit.*, pp.88 f.; cf. further F. L. Carsten, ' Nationalrevolutionäre Offiziere gegen Hitler' in *Gewissen gegen Gewalt, Schriften der Bundeszentrale für politische Bildung*, pp.46 ff.

173. Goerdeler, subtitle of the economic primer (top carbon, Posth. No. 13, of the fair copy with copious corrections by C. v. Dietze and critical commentaries by Gerhard Albrecht) in the possession of Frau Dr Marianne Meyer-Krahmer, Heidelberg, originating from 1942; Krebs, *op. cit.*, pp.219, 277; Leithaüser, *op. cit.*, p.210; Gerstenmaier in: Eric H. Boehm, *We Survived. The Stories of Fourteen of the Hidden and Hunted in Nazi Germany*, New Haven 1946, p.182

174. Dahrendorf, *op. cit.*, pp.54 ff.; H. Plessner, *Die verspätete Nation*, Stuttgart 1959; E. Fraenkel, *Deutschland und die westlichen Demokratien*, Stuttgart 1964

175. Brill, *op. cit.*, pp.19 ff.; cf. Karl O. Paetel, ' Revolutionäre und restaurative Tendenzen in der deutschen Widerstandsbewegung' in *Die Neue Gesellschaft*, 2 (1955), pp.82 ff.

176. Henderson, *op. cit.*, pp.70 f.

## Resistance in the Labour Movement

1. Erich Matthias, 'Die Sozialdemokratische Partei Deutschlands' in *Das Ende der Parteien 1933*, ed. Erich Matthias and Rudolf Morsey, Düsseldorf 1960, pp.195 f.
2. For further literature on this subject cf. Matthias, *ibid.*, pp.101 ff.; Karl-Dietrich Bracher; Wolfgang Sauer; Gerhard Schulz, 'Die Nationalsozialistische Machtergreifung. Studien zur Errichtung des totalitären Herrschaftssystems in Deutschland 1933/4', *Schriften des Instituts für Politische Wissenschaft*, Vol. 14, Cologne and Oppladen 1960, pp.62 ff.
3. Julius Leber, *Ein Mann geht seinen Weg – Schriften, Reden und Briefe*, ed. by his friends, Berlin and Frankfurt-am-Main 1952, p.243
4. cf. Karl-Dietrich Bracher, *Die Auflösung der Weimarer Republik. Eine Studie zum Problem des Machtzerfalls in der Demokratie*, 2nd ed., Stuttgart and Düsseldorf 1957, pp.582 ff.; Matthias, *op. cit.*, pp.127 ff.
5. Matthias, *op. cit.*, pp.139 ff.
6. More than a dozen former *Reichsbanner* members in Berlin confirmed this when questioned by the author
7. Matthias, *op. cit.*, pp.151 ff.
8. Gerhard Ritter, *Carl Goerdeler und die deutsche Widerstandsbewegung*, 3rd ed., Stuttgart 1956, p.101
9. Bracher, Sauer, Schulz, *op. cit.*, p.64; Matthias, *op. cit.*, pp.164 ff.
10. With regard to the Free Trade Unions during this phase cf. Wolfgang Abendroth, *Die deutschen Gewerkschaften*, Heidelberg 1954, p.34; Hans Gerd Schumann, *Nationalsozialismus und Gewerkschaftsbewegung* (series by the Institut für wissenschaftliche Politik, Marburg/Lahn, 6), Hanover and Frankfurt-am-Main 1958, pp.53 ff.; Ursula Hüllbüsch, *Gewerkschaften und Staat. Ein Beitrag zur Geschichte der Gewerkschaften zu Anfang und zu Ende der Weimarer Republik*, diss. phil. Heidelberg 1958, typewritten; Matthias, *op. cit.*, p.174; Hans J. Reichhardt, *Die deutsche Arbeits-*

*front. Ein Beitrag zur Geschichte des nationalsozialistischen Deutschlands und zur Struktur des totalitären Herrschafts-systems*, diss. phil. Berlin 1956 (dup.), pp.25 ff.; Bracher; Sauer; Schulz, *op. cit.*, pp.175 ff.

11. Paul Hertz, ' Unsere Aufgaben und ihre Erfüllung ' in *Zeitschrift für Sozialismus*, Nos. 12/13, Sept./Oct. 1934, p.422; Bracher; Sauer; Schulz, *op. cit.*, pp.194 ff.; Matthias, *op. cit.*, pp.185 ff.

12. Matthias, *op. cit.*, pp.187 ff.

13. cf. ' Der Berliner Jugendkonflikt vom April 1933 ' (extract from a typed manuscript by Erich Schmidt) in Matthias, *op. cit.*, pp.242 ff.

14. cf. Erich Matthias, ' Der Untergang der alten Sozialdemo-kratie 1933 ' in the *Vierteljahrshefte für Zeitgeschichte*, 4th year, No. 2, pp.198 ff.

15. Verbal information by Erich Ollenhauer, Alfred Nau, and Fritz Heine. As one of the Prague Executive's couriers, Heine attended several of this group's meetings in Berlin

16. Otto Bauer, *Die illegale Partie*, Paris 1939, p.15

17. Where no sources have been quoted, the ensuing comments are based on the author's interviews with members of illegal Berlin groups

18. Bauer, *op. cit.*, pp.47 ff.

19. Another good example is the *Sozialistische Front* in Han-over. cf. the account, *Erfahrungen in der illegalen Arbeit*, written by its leader, Werner Blumenberg, which he sent to the Party headquarters in Hanover immediately after his flight in 1936. Extracts from this are in Matthias, ' Der Untergang...' pp.201 ff. Also Matthias, ' Die Sozialdemokra-tische Partei ', pp.269 ff. Also the detailed extracts from the group's illegal *Sozialistische Blätter* quoted in the record (15 J 1/37 of 23 September 1937) of the findings at the trial of six members of the Socialist Front in the People's Court

20. Now the Senator for Economics in Berlin

21. This quotation, like those that follow, is drawn from the Berlin Supreme Court Public Prosecutor's indictment (O.J. 133.34)

22. cf. also Günther Weisenborn, *Der lautlose Aufstand. Bericht über die Widerstandsbewegung des deutschen Volkes 1933-45*, Hamburg 1953, pp.162 f. Also *Neuer Vorwärts*, No. 64, 2 September 1934

23. cf. Bracher; Sauer; Schulz, *op. cit.*, pp.348 ff.

24. Verbal account by Walter Löffler

25. Verbal accounts by Erich Ollenhauer and Fritz Heine

26. *Deutschland-Berichte des* SPD *Vorstands* (*Sopade-Berichte*), 1st year, No. 3, August/September 1934

27. Erich Matthias, *Sozialdemokratie und Nation. Zur Ideengeschichte der sozialdemokratischen Emigration 1933-1938*, Stuttgart 1952, pp.25 ff.

28. Record of findings 17 J 336/35

29. Verbal accounts by Erich Ollenhauer and Fritz Heine

30. cf. p.174

31. *Deutschland-Berichte des* SPD-*Vorstandes* (*Sopade-Berichte*), 4th year, No. 5, May 1937

32. Gestapo situation report, 1937, quoted by Weisenborn in *Der lautlose Aufstand*, pp.153 f.

33. Verbal account by Fritz Heine

34. For the part played by the Social Democrats in the 20 July conspiracy see particularly : Eberhard Zeller, *Geist der Freiheit – Der zwanzigste Juli 1944*, Munich 1957, pp.51 ff.; Ritter, *op. cit.*, pp.292 ff.; Emil Henk, *Die Tragödie des 20 Juli 1944. Ein Beitrag zur Politischen Vorgeschichte*, Heidelberg 1946; Annedore Leber, *Das Gewissen entscheidet*, Berlin/Frankfurt 1962, pp.38 f.; Annedore Lebel and Freya Gräfin Moltke, *Entscheidungen in Deutschland*, Berlin 1962, pp.93 ff.; Joachim G. Leithäuser, *Wilhelm Leuschner. Ein Leben für die Republik*, Frankfurt-am-Main, Zürich, Vienna 1962, pp.175 ff., 199 ff.; Hans Rothfels, *Die deutsche Opposition gegen Hitler*, Frankfurt 1962, pp.101 ff.; *Spiegelbild einer Verschwörung. Die Kaltenbrunner-Berichte an Bormann und Hitler über das Attentat vom 20 Juli 1944. Geheime Dokumente aus dem ehemaligen Reichssicherheitshauptamt*, Archiv Peter für historische und politische Dokumentation, Stuttgart 1961

35. Franz Borkenau, *Der europäische Kommunismus. Seine Ge-*

*schichte von 1917 bis zur Gegenwart*, Munich 1952, pp.66 f.;
Bracher; Sauer; Schultz, *op. cit.*, pp.62, 64 f.

36. Siegfried Bahne, 'Die Kommunistische Partei Deutschlands' in *Das Ende der Parteien*, pp.683 ff.; Babette L.
Gross, 'Volksfrontpolitik in den dreissiger Jahren', supple-
ment to the weekly *Das Parlament*, 24 October 1962

37. Matthias, *Die Sozialdemokratische Partei*, pp.261 ff.

38. Bracher; Sauer; Schulz, *op. cit.*, p.63

39. Herbert Wehner, *Erinnerungen* (hectographed) 1946, p.33

40. Otto Winzer, *Zwölf Jahre Kampf gegen Faschismus und
Krieg. Ein Beitrag zur Geschichte der* KPD *vom 1933 bis 1945*,
East Berlin 1955, p.36; Bahne, *op. cit.*, pp.691, 700

41. Bahne, *op. cit.*, p.691

42. This is derived from a series of circulars issued by the Hesse
police in Darmstadt in the last half of 1932 based on information from Berlin (Document Centre, Berlin)

43. Rudolf Diels, *Lucifer ante portas*, Stuttgart 1950, pp.192
ff., 402 ff.; Margarete Buber-Neumann, *Von Potsdam nach
Moskau*, Stuttgart 1957, pp.261 f.; Bahne, *op. cit.*, p.692;
Wehner, *op. cit.*, pp.37 f.

44. Bahne, *op. cit.*, p.694; Wehner, *op. cit.*, pp.38 ff.; Carola
Stern, *Ulbricht. Eine politische Biographie*. Cologne, Berlin
1964, pp.74 ff.

45. After his release from arrest in the autumn of 1933 Kattner
gave valuable help to the Gestapo in their search for leading
Communists. As a consequence Rudolf Schwarz, one of the
leading members of the KPD's counter-intelligence organisation, entrusted Kurt Granzow with the task of removing
Kattner from the scene. On 1 February 1934 the latter was
shot in his home by one Hans Schwarz on Granzow's instructions. The Gestapo looked in vain for the perpetrators, Granzow and Hans Schwarz having contrived to flee the country,
but on 2 February in what was clearly an act of reprisal,
John Schehr, Erich Steinfurth, Eugen Schönhaer, and Rudolf Schwarz were shot 'while attempting to escape'. All
four were allegedly being taken from Berlin to the offices
of the *Staatspolizei* in Potsdam for questioning in connection with Kattner's murder. 'While negotiating the so-called

Kilometer Hill in Wannsee the police car had to slow down because of the slippery surface; as it did so the Communists freed themselves and jumped out' (*Vossische Zeitung*, 3 February 1934). Granzow was handed over to the Gestapo from a French internment camp and sentenced to death by the People's Court on 19 August 1942 (Record of findings 10 J 520/43); cf. also Wehner, *op. cit.*, p.88

46. Wehner, *op. cit.*, pp.52 ff.
47. Bahne, *op. cit.*, p.700
48. *Rundschau über Politik, Wirtschaft und Arbeiterbewegung*, Basle, No. 2/1933, p.231; cf. also Wehner, *op. cit.*, p.42
49. Bahne, *op. cit.*, p.701
50. Stern, *op. cit.*, pp.72 f.; Wehner, *op. cit.*, pp.46 f., 57 f., 86 ff.; Hermann Weber, *Ulbricht fälscht Geschichte. Ein Kommentar mit Dokumenten zum ' Grundriss der Geschichte der deutschen Arbeiterbewegung'*, Cologne 1964, pp.87 ff.; Hermann Weber, *Der deutsche Kommunismus – Dokumente*, Cologne 1963, p.319
51. Quotation from the July 1933 number of the weekly *Die Kommunistische Internationale* in the Public Prosecutor's indictment (O.J. 684.33) in the Berlin Supreme Court
52. Bahne, *op. cit.*, p.709
53. This account is based on the report of the findings (17 J 582/33 and 17 J 627/33) of the Reich Supreme Court in Leipzig, as well as those at the People's Court, 17 J 170/34 (1H 42/34) and 17 J 175 (2H 135/41). See also Wehner, *op. cit.*, pp.43 f. and 55 f.
54. *Rundschau über Politik, Wirtschaft und Arbeiterbewegung*, Basle No. 16/1933, pp.501 f.
55. See descriptions of the fate of these groups in Walter A. Schmidt, *Damit Deutschland lebe. Ein Quellenwerk über den deutschen antifaschistischen Widerstandskampf 1933-1934*, East Berlin 1958, pp.468 ff.
56. Winzer, *op. cit.*, pp.40 f.; Bahne, *op. cit.*, pp. 703 ff.
57. Record of findings 8 J 796/30 (1H 31/34) against Hans Fladung
58. Wehner, *op. cit.*, pp.54 f.; 67 ff.

59. Gustav Regler, *Das Ohr des Malchus*, Cologne, Berlin 1958, p.231

60. The former *Reichstag* deputy, Philipp Daub (North Westphalia), had already approached Wehner and Kox at the beginning of 1934. On instructions from Paris, the former *Reichleiter* of the *Rote Junge Front*, Otto Wahls, was made head of the National Committee in Berlin in April 1934, an appointment against which Wehner, Kox, and Daub protested in vain. All three were sent to the Saar in the summer of 1934 in order to take part in preparations for the coming plebiscite. Their places were taken by Adolf Rembte, Paul Merker, who had returned to Germany for a brief period, and Werner Eggerath who was made responsible for RGO activities but was arrested at the end of 1934. Later Wahls and Merker were replaced by the former *Reichstag* deputies, Robert Stamm (Weser-Ems) and Max Maddalena (Breslau). Record of findings 17 J 171/35 (2H 17/37) against Rembte, Stamm, and Maddalena; cf. also Wehner, *op. cit.*, p.65

61. cf. the April 1935 report of the Berlin-Charlottenburg Police Institute on the underground development of the KPD quoted in Bahne, *op. cit.*, pp.737 ff.

62. Wehner, *op. cit.*, pp.64 f.

63. *Ibid.*, pp.30 f., 42, 50

64. *Rundschau über Politik, Wirtschaft und Arbeiterbewegung*, Basle, No. 10/1935, p.551; Weber, *Der deutsche Kommunismus*, pp.348 ff.; cf. also Wehner, *op. cit.*, pp.82 f.; record of findings 17 J 171/35 (2H 17/37) against Rembte, Stamm and Maddalena

65. *Dokumente zur Geschichte der Kommunistischen Partei Deutschlands aus den Jahren 1935 bis 1939*, Berlin, no date (1946), pp.22 ff.; cf. also Gross, *op. cit.*, pp.534 ff.

66. Matthias, *Sozialdemokratie und Nation*, pp.37 f.

67. Altogether there were six sector committees : Zentrum in Prague, later in Copenhagen and Stockholm, responsible for Berlin and Central Germany; Nord in Copenhagen for Northern Germany; Süd in Switzerland for Southern Germany; Südwest in Brussels for the Middle Rhine; Saar in France for the former Saar territories; West in Amsterdam

for the Lower Rhine, the Ruhr, and Bremen (indictment 9 J 51/44). As regards the reshaping of the organisation cf. also Wehner, *op. cit.*, pp.106 f.

68. Record of findings 17 J 377/37 (1H 36/38)

69. There is insufficient space here to list all the trials. All court records connected with this complex may be found in the Berlin Document Centre; cf. also the 1937 Gestapo situation report of the KPD quoted in Weisenborn, *op. cit.*, pp.151, 153

70. Record of findings 17 J 377/37 (1H 36/38)

71. *Zur Geschichte der Kommunistischen Partei Deutschlands. Eine Auswahl von Materialien und Dokumenten aus den Jahren 1914 bis 1946*, East Berlin 1954, pp. 383 ff.

72. Winzer, *op. cit.*, p.129

73. At any rate according to the record of findings 7. o. Js.218.40

74. Gestapo report of 16.2.40 on completion of the case in connection with the Adlerhow Sub-District. Indictments and records of findings 17 J 42/40, 17 J 44/40, 17 J 66/40, 17 J 68/40, 17 J 70/40 as well as 7. o. Js.241.40 A–J

75. cf. also the KPD Central Committee's declaration of 25 August 1939 in *Rundschau über Politik, Wirtschaft und Arbeiterbewegung*, Basle, No. 46/1939, pp.1323 ff.; Walter Ulbricht's article 'Hilferding über den Sinn des Krieges', *Die Welt*, No. 6, 9 February 1940, pp.135 ff., reproduced in Weber, *Der deutsche Kommunismus*, pp.364 ff.; Walter Bartel, *Deutschland in der Zeit der faschistischen Diktatur 1933-45*, 2nd ed., East Berlin 1956, pp.181 f.

76. Wehner, *op. cit.*, p.186

77. Indictment and record of findings 9 J 51/44 g, Indictment 10 J 548/43

78. Indictments 9 J 777/43 g A–D. cf. Weisenborn, *op. cit.*, pp.172 ff.; Winzer, *op. cit.*, pp.196 f.; Harald Poelchau, *Die letzten Stunden. Erinnerungen eines Gefängnispfarrers*, issued by Graf Alexander Stenbock-Fermor, Berlin 1949, pp.96 f.

79. cf. Gertrud Glodajewski and Heinz Schumann, *Die Neubauer-Poser-Gruppe. Dokumente und Materialien des illegalen antifaschistischen Kampfes* (Thuringia 1935-1945), East Berlin 1957; Ilse Krause, *Die Schumann-Engert-Kresse-*

*Gruppe. Dokumente des illegalen antifaschistischen Kampfes* (Leipzig 1943/45), East Berlin 1960

80. From the grounds for conviction in the trial of Saefkow, Jacob, and Bästlein quoted in Gerhard Nitzsche, *Die Saefkow-Jacob-Bästlein-Gruppe. Dokumente und Materialien des illegalen antifaschistischen Kampfes* (1942-45), East Berlin 1957, p.91

81. From a facsimile of the first two pages of the indictment quoted in Nitzsche, *op. cit.*, p.133

82. *Ibid.*, p.92

83. The latest indictment (no reference number) held by the Berlin Document Centre is dated 16 April 1945 and concerns a group which is alleged to have started up a Communist organisation in Spandau at the beginning of 1945 and to have planned propaganda activities. Its members were arrested in the middle of February

84. cf. Kurt Kliem, *Der sozialistische Widerstand. Dargestellt an der 'Gruppe 'Neu Beginnen'*, diss. phil. (typewritten), Marburg 1957, p.13

85. The booklet's full title was *Neu Beginnen! Faschismus oder Sozialismus. Diskussionsgrundlage zu den Streitfragen unserer Epoche*, Miles ('Probleme des Sozialismus' *Sozialdemokratische Schriftenreihe* No. 2), Carlsbad, undated (1933). After the appearance of the booklet the organisation was often termed the Miles Group

86. For the cause of the arrests cf. the statements made by various members of *Neu Beginnen* quoted in Kliem, *op. cit.*, pp.126 ff., 141 ff., 169

87. *Indictments* 7a 0. Js. 207, 35 and 7a. 0. Js. 127. 36; cf. also the report on the later trial in *Nachrichten des Auslandsbüros 'Neu Beginnen'*, Nos. 4-5, April 1936

88. Wehner, *op. cit.*, pp.116 ff.

89. Hermann L. Brill, *Gegen den Strom*, Offenbach 1946, pp.18 ff.

90. Originally 100 copies were produced with the help of Dr Ernst Fraenkel, a lawyer and former legal adviser to the Free Trade Unions

91. Indictment 9 J 138/39 g, record of findings 10 J 453/38 g

T

## Political and Moral Motives Behind the Resistance

1. *Die im Braunschweiger Remer-Prozess erstattenen moral-theologischen und historischen Gutachten nebst Urteil*, ed. Herbert Kraus, Hamburg 1953, p.128
2. Hans Rothfels, *Die deutsche Opposition gegen Hitler. Eine Würdigung* (Fischer Bücherei 198), Frankfurt 1958, p.25; the American edition appeared in 1948, the first German version in 1949
3. Fabian van Schlabrendorff, *Offiziere gegen Hitler* (Fischer Bücherei 305), Frankfurt 1959, pp.77 ff.; in this form since the revision in 1951 of the book, which was first published by the Europa Verlag, Zürich, in 1946
4. Terence Prittie, *Germans against Hitler*, London 1964, p.264
5. *Ibid.*, p.265
6. *Remer-Prozess*, p.18
7. Harald Poelchau, ' Die Rolle der Kirche innerhalb der Opposition in Deutschland ', *Denken-Glauben-Handeln*, Almanac for the fiftieth anniversary of the Furche-Verlag, Hamburg 1966, p.84
8. *Op. cit.*, p.83
9. Paul Graf Yorck von Wartenburg, ' Das christliche Gewissen und die Verschwörung des 20 Juli 1944 ', *Denken-Glauben-Handeln*, pp.53 ff.
10. *Ibid.*, p.63
11. *Ibid.*, pp.60 f.
12. *Ibid.*, p. 58
13. Prittie, *op. cit.*, p.20
14. *Ibid.*, p.20
15. Rothfels, *op. cit.*, p.48
16. *Ibid.*, p.50
17. Symptomatic of the revival: A. Evertz, *Der Abfall der evangelischen Kirche vom Vaterland*, Velbert 1964
18. Reinhold Seeberg in *Die Religionswissenschaft in Selbstdarstellungen*, ed. Erich Stange, 1, Leipzig 1925, p.192
19. Paul Althaus, *Das Erlebnis der Kirche*, Leipzig 1919, p.3
20. In the omnibus volumes edited by Leopold Klotz : *Die Kirche*

*und das Dritte Reich. Fragen und Forderungen deutscher Theologen*, Gotha 1932, II, pp.38 ff.

21. For the whole section cf. a) Ernst Wolf, *Kirche im Widerstand?*, Munich 1965, and *Die evangelischen Kirchen und der Staat im Dritten Reich* (Theol. Studien 74), Zürich 1963 and the bibliography; in both these booklets, the sources of quotations; b) for the overall position of Protestantism in the twentieth century: Karl Kupisch, *Zwischen Idealismus und Massendemokratie*, Berlin 1955, and, *Quellen zur Geschichte des deutschen Protestantismus 1871-1945*, Göttingen 1960; Karl-Wilhelm Dahm, *Pfarrer und Politik, Soziale Position und politische Mentalität des deutschen evangelischen Pfarrerstandes zwischen 1918 und 1933*, Cologne 1965; Gottfried Mehnert, *Evangelische Kirche und Politik 1917-1919*, Düsseldorf 1959; for the theological problems of the Resistance cf. my article ' Widerstandsrecht ', in *Religion in Geschichte und Gegenwart*, Tübingen 3rd ed. 1962. Vol. VI, p.1681, also the extensive bibliography

22. Rothfels, *op. cit.*, p.47

23. Cf. Ernst Wolf, *Barmen, Kirche zwischen Versuchung und Gnade*, Munich 1957

24. U. Scheuner in *Staatsverfassung und Kirchenordnung. Festgabe für Rudolf Smend*, Tübingen 1962, p.258

25. See also E. Wolf, *Der Rechtsstaat. Angebot und Aufgabe*, Theol. Existenz heute NF 119, Munich 1964

26. Mehnert, *op. cit.*, p.66

27. Wilhelm Niemöller, *Die Bekennende Kirche sagt Hitler die Wahrheit*, Bielefeld 1954

28. Wilhelm Niemöller, *Hitler und die evangelischen Kirchenführer*, Bielefeld 1958, p.40

29. Karl Barth, *Eine Schweizer Stimme*, Zollikon 1948, pp.58 ff.

30. W. Niemöller, ' Ein Gebet für den Frieden ', in *Evangel. Theologie* 10, 1950/1, pp. 175-189

31. Dietrich Bonhoeffer, *Gesammelte Schriften*, ed. Eberhard Bethge, I, Munich 1958, p.155

32. *Ibid.*, p.320

33. Dietrich Bonhoeffer, *Ethik*, compiled and edited by Eberhard Bethge, Munich 1949, p.186

34. Karl Barth, *Gotteserkenntnis und Gottesdienst nach reformatorischer Lehre*, Zollikon 1938, pp.212 ff.

35. Karl Barth, *Rechtfertigung und Recht* (1938), now in *Eine Schweizer Stimme*, pp.13 ff.

36. Dietrich Bonhoeffer, *Widerstand und Ergebung – Briefe und Aufzeichnungen aus der Haft*, edited by Eberhard Bethge, Munich 1951, 10th ed. 1961, p.14

37. Guenter Lewy, *Die katholische Kirche und das Dritte Reich*, Munich 1964, p.348; *Katholische Kirche und Nationalsozialismus*, ed. E. Müller, dtv-dokumente, Munich 1965

38. Dieter Ehlers, *Technik und Moral einer Verschwörung. 20 Juli 1944*, Frankfurt 1964, p.142

39. V. Moltke, *Letzte Briefe aus dem Gefängnis Tegel*, Berlin 1963, p.20

40. Ehlers, *op. cit.*, p.87

41. *Op. cit.*, p.87

42. *Letzte Briefe*, p.56

43. *Ibid.*, p.41

44. Ehlers, *op. cit.*, p.85

45. *Letzte Briefe*, p.20

46. Ehlers, *op. cit.*, p.15

47. *Letzte Briefe*, p.20

48. Joachim Kramarz, *Claus Graf Stauffenberg, 15 November 1907 bis 20 Juli 1944. Das Leben eines Offiziers*, Frankfurt 1965, p.140

49. G. Ritter, *Carl Goerdeler und die deutsche Widerstandsbewegung*, Stuttgart 1954, p.424; for the *bourgeois*-national Utopia cf. now *Beck und Goerdeler, Gemeinschaftsdokumente für den Frieden 1941-1944*, ed. W. Ritter von Schramm, Munich 1966

50. Shortly before the attempt Stauffenberg formulated the aim: 'We want a new order which makes every German an upholder of the state and which guarantees him law and justice' – *Das Gewissen steht auf*, Berlin 1954, p.231

51. Ehlers, *op. cit.*, p.141; Kramarz, *op. cit.*, p.156

52. Kramarz, *op. cit.*, p.201

53. D. Bonhoeffer, *Ethik*, pp.185 f.
54. Ehlers, *op. cit.*, p.144
55. *Ibid.*, p.142
56. Kramarz, *op. cit.*, p.186
57. Ehlers, *op. cit.*, p.173
58. It is not possible to do more than allude to the works quoted and to the other fairly comprehensive literature on the German Resistance: the well-known works of Gisevius (1946), Pechel (1947), Zeller (1952), Weisenborn (1953), Krausnick (1954), M. Boveri (1956), the biographies of L. Beck (1952 and 1965), C. Goerdeler (1954), Canaris (1954), W. Leuschner (1962), von der Schulenburg (1964), the compilations of the writings, letters, speeches and so on of von Hassell (1946), A. Delp (1947), J. Leber (1952), the memoirs of E. Von Weizsäcker (1950) and A. Heusinger (1950) among others. Also R. Manvell and H. Fraenkel, *The July Plot*, London 1966

# Index

Abs, H. J., 89
ADGB, *see* General Trades Union Federation
Adler, Friedrich, 185
Ahlmann, Wilhelm, 80
Alsace-Lorraine, 23
Althaus, P., 204
Amsterdam, 178
Anlauf, 166
Ansbach Advice, 206
anti-Semitism, 203, 205, 210-11, 216; *see also* Jews
*Arbeitsdienst, see* Labour Service
Arendt, Hannah, 58
Aryan paragraph, 210-11
Ashton Gwatkin, F., 10
Austria, 2, 7, 18, 39, 51, 218
*Auswärtige Politik*, 46-7

Baden, 220
Balkans, 6, 12, 15, 22, 26, 43
Baltic, 6, 15, 22, 26
Barmen Theological Declaration, 206, 212-15
Barth, Karl, 213-14, 218-19, 222
*Basler Nachrichten*, 215
Bästlein, Bernhard, 179-80
Bavaria, 212, 220, 224
Beck, Colonel-General Ludwig, 2, 4-5, 7-8, 14-16, 19, 24, 41, 48, 136, 140; and Bolshevist threat, 73-5; and leadership, 93, 95; and authoritarian state, 104-5, 108, 110; and constitutional proposals, 115, 123; and party system, 134;

and military failure, 138; moral motives of, 228, 230-2, 234
Belgian Congo, 9
Belgium, 7, 9, 22, 46
Berber, Friedrich, 47
Berggrav, Bishop, 214, 223
Bergstraesser, 85, 116, 124, 128, 133, 144
Berlin, resistance activities in, 161-2, 169-71, 174-80, 182, 185-6
Berlin transport service (BVG), 153
Berlin University, 159
*Berliner Volkszeitung* (BVZ), 177
'Berne Conference', 176
Bethmann Hollweg, Th. von, 31-3
Beveridge Plan, 90
Birkenauer, Erich, 166
Bismarck, Bismarckian Empire, 2-3, 5, 24-5, 31, 42-3, 54, 63, 71, 91, 95, 114, 120, 123, 159, 203
Blessing, K., 89
Boehm, Max Hildebert, 80
Bohemia, 18-19
Bolshevism, 16-17, 19, 21, 26-7, 40, 44-5, 48, 50, 68, 72-8, 93, 107, 123, 134-5, 137-40, 142, 145, 221
Bonhoeffer, Dietrich, 52, 65-7, 74, 99, 101, 124, 145, 221-2, 224, 232
Bonn, Basic Law of, 215
Bosch, 88
Boveri, Margret, 76
Brandenburg Church administration, 223